IT'S LIFE AS I SEE IT

Black Cartoonists in Chicago, 1940–1980

TOM FLOYD • GRASS GREEN • SEITU HAYDEN
JAY JACKSON • CHARLES JOHNSON • YAOUNDÉ OLU
TURTEL ONLI • JACKIE ORMES • MORRIE TURNER

ESSAY BY
CHARLES JOHNSON

AFTERWORD BY
RONALD WIMBERLY

COMPILED AND EDITED BY
DAN NADEL

COVER DESIGNED BY
KERRY JAMES MARSHALL

NEW YORK REVIEW COMICS
MUSEUM OF CONTEMPORARY ART CHICAGO

Published in conjunction with the Museum of
Contemporary Art Chicago, on the occasion
of *Chicago Comics: 1960s to Now,* June 19–
October 3, 2021. Curated by Dan Nadel.

Dedicated to Tim Jackson, with gratitude, for
his generosity and his essential book,
Pioneering Cartoonists of Color.

Library of Congress Cataloging-in-Publication Data

Names: Nadel, Dan, editor. | Museum of Contemporary Art Chicago (Chicago, Ill.),
   host institution.
Title: It's life as I see it : black cartoonists in Chicago 1940-1980 /
   edited by Dan Nadel.
Description: New York : New York Review Books, 2021. | Series: New York
   Review comics | "Work by Tom Floyd, Grass Green, Seitu Hayden, Jay
   Jackson, Charles Johnson, Yaoundé Olu, Turtel Onli, Jackie Ormes, Morrie
   Turner ; essays by Charles Johnson, Dan Nadel, Ronald Wimberly" |
   Identifiers: LCCN 2020050717 | ISBN 9781681375618 (paperback)
Subjects: LCSH: African-American cartoonists—Exhibitions. | Caricatures
   and cartoons—Illinois—Chicago—Exhibitions. | African American
   newspapers—Illinois—Chicago. | Comic books, strips, etc.—Social
   aspects—United States. | African Americans in popular culture. |
   African-Americans and mass media.
Classification: LCC NC1427.C5 I87 2021 | DDC 741.5/6977311—dc23
LC record available at https://lccn.loc.gov/2020050717

ISBN 978-1-68137-561-8

Printed in the United States of America on acid-free paper.
10 9 8 7 6 5 4 3 2 1

TABLE OF CONTENTS

INTRODUCTION
Dan Nadel

Jay Jackson's *Home Folks*, March 12, 1954. Courtesy of Tim Samuelson.

It's 2024 in America, and taxis won't stop for a white man. White people wear pointy caps labeled "WHITE" and are second-class citizens. People of color, especially those of the green race, rule North America. "On a continent of prejudiced green people . . . the green folks have ideas much the same as present-day Americans but they vent their hatred against whites!" So goes the story of Jay Jackson's *Bungleton Green and the Mystic Commandos*, published in the 1940s pages of the great Black newspaper of the twentieth century, *The Chicago Defender*.

Chicago, like few other cities in the world, has a rich and diverse history of cartooning. I knew this before the Museum of Contemporary Art Chicago's James W. Alsdorf Chief Curator Michael Darling asked me to organize an exhibition on the subject, but then I lived it as I engaged with digital archives, print folios, and longtime cartoonists. The great tradition of Chicago comics as it's most often been taught—that of Frank King, Chester Gould, and Harold Gray—is brilliant, but it was never the full story. More than any other city in the country, Chicago had a vibrant yet utterly separate Black publishing industry that encompassed multiple comic strip genres in the *Defender* newspaper and a raft of panel cartoons about Black life in the locally published magazines, including *Jet* and *Negro Digest*. Stumbling across Jay Jackson's brilliant comics and graphics is what led me to that history. His work on *Bungleton Green* is among the most politically radical comics of the first half of the twentieth century, and yet it's unaccounted for in all but a single survey of the medium—Tim Jackson's landmark 2016 book, *Pioneering Cartoonists of Color*.

It's Life As I See It (which takes its name from the Charles Johnson cartoon on page 107) accompanies my exhibition at the Museum of Contemporary Art Chicago, *Chicago Comics: 1960s to Now,* but is instead focused on Black cartoonists from 1940 to 1980. It maintains the same thematic criteria as the show, focusing on cartoonists using the medium for independent and personal expression who worked or primarily published in Chicago. This meant excluding political cartooning and superheroes, though both are important and parallel forms of cartooning with different constraints and goals. The selection of work in this book reflects the flowering and decline of the Black press in the United States in the middle part of the twentieth century. These cartoonists have had to tell their own history, as they have been roundly ignored by most major cartoon historians. Before working on the exhibition, I was largely unaware of the artists and work included in this book, but learned of their work through a combination of Tim Jackson's research, chance discoveries in online archives, and a lot of advice from the surviving artists.

Their relative obscurity is due in part to the racism baked into the art and business of cartooning. Comic drawing came from caricature, a reduction of humans into recognizable but often exaggerated stereotypes. Cartoons and caricature thrived in turn-of-the-century newspapers that catered to a variety of different ethnicities and classes, who could experience their own lives and cultures in a group of shapes and lines. As they slowly became accepted as full-fledged "Americans" in the late 1930s and 1940s, the Italian, Irish, Chinese, and Jewish stereotypes receded from the funny pages, but the Black stereotypes, also rooted in the visuals of minstrel performance, persisted across the medium.

It's impossible to imagine that these images didn't impact the generation of readers who grew up and became the first historians of cartooning. Newspaper comics were rarely anthologized, reprinted, or otherwise historicized until decades after their unwieldy birth in the late nineteenth-century American press. As with jazz, it was often white enthusiasts (like me) who had the cultural clout to establish a canon. Fans and aficionados—also, for comics, a primarily white category—collected and documented newspapers and comic books destined for landfills. We have them to thank for most of our primary sources, but they could save only what they were aware of or valued, which, intentionally or not, left the Black press without any kind of advocate or spokesperson. Likewise, libraries across the country subscribed to numerous local and national newspapers, but neglected many of the Black newspapers. Those that did subscribe to Black newspapers usually transferred them to microfiche and then, as was standard for most libraries, disposed of the originals. This meant that for decades nearly all records of the great Black newspapers of the twentieth century existed only as microfiche collections in just a handful of libraries, and were mostly inaccessible until very recent digitization efforts.

Comics history for Black cartoonists in Chicago begins with *The Chicago Defender*, founded in 1905 by Robert Sengstacke Abbott to serve the growing Black population migrating from the American South to the South Side. The *Defender*, like other Black newspapers, among them the *California Eagle* and the *Pittsburgh Courier*, sought not just to inform but to elevate its readership by producing stories and images of Black uplift and editorializing against political and cultural racism. The two earliest cartoonists in this collection, Jay Jackson and Jackie Ormes, aimed to challenge the common depiction of Black people in popular media through their strips. In *Bungleton Green*, Jackson, who was well-versed in early science fiction, upended the racial dynamics of fellow Chicagoan Edgar Rice Burroughs's John Carter of Mars stories (in which a white Confederate soldier battles green and red races on Mars). Jackie Ormes, one of the great subversives in the medium's history, combined political commentary and the social signifiers of high fashion to give vivid life to Black women characters in multiple comic strips beginning in 1937. The radical nature of these strips can't be overstated: Black people producing humanized images of themselves in newspapers.

But for Jackson, Ormes, and their cartoonist contemporaries, the medium could never be a full-time occupation. Commercially successful cartoonists sold their strips to multiple newspapers through syndicates, and neither Black cartoonists nor the *Defender* had a reach comparable to Chester Gould and the *Chicago Tribune*. Moreover, the *Tribune* and other primarily white outlets were notoriously uninterested in either Black cartoonists or Black subject matter. While Robert Abbott understood the value of cartooning to his papers, he couldn't provide steady, sustainable income. Black cartoonists before 1960 simply didn't have the financial support that affords the corresponding time and focus it takes to establish the long-lasting characters that help sustain a public presence and a base of collectors and historians.

The other major outlet for Black cartooning, Johnson Publishing, launched in 1942 with *Negro Digest* (later called *Black World*), followed by *Jet*, *Ebony*, and others. For years, these magazines were a collective hub for Black culture and politics. *Negro Digest/Black World* and *Ebony Jr.* were especially supportive of emerging Black cartoonists, including Morrie Turner, Charles Johnson, Yaoundé Olu, Turtel Onli, and Seitu Hayden.

Aside from the Johnson Publishing magazines, homegrown communities supported young cartoonists. The fanzine and underground cartoonist Richard "Grass" Green, of Fort Wayne, Indiana, with a teenage Seitu Hayden, produced the adventure comic strip *Lost Family* for the Black newsweekly *Frost Illustrated* in 1969. In the early 1970s Tom Floyd attempted to bring together these and other Black artists for a series of Black superhero comic books, but yielded only a single issue due to a lack of interest from comic book distributors. The *Defender*, which might have given these artists a voice, was on the wane.

By the end of the 1960s, Black newspapers still publishing cartoons ran packages by one of the national syndicates. This meant a steady diet of *Mickey Mouse*, *Mandrake the Magician*, and *Popeye*. As Tim Jackson notes, there were exceptions, but only by freelancers such as Hayden and Onli, and their strips were sometimes run out of order or dropped altogether: "By the dawning of the 1970s, the Black press's most gifted writers and editors drifted to better and more consistently paying mainstream publications that were in need of Black journalists . . . explaining relevant Black issues to White readers." This left only older staff members, whose work often seemed out of touch to the younger readers of the 1970s.

Far more relevant to this audience was the Black Arts Movement of the late 1960s and 1970s, which emphasized independent cultural activities rooted in self-sustaining communities and collectives. It was in this environment that Yaoundé Olu and Turtel Onli, inspired by the underground and alternative comics of the time but seeking their own means of publishing, found their voices in comics. Like the musicians Sun Ra and George Clinton, Olu and Onli rooted their work in what are now called Afrofuturist ideas.

They published in the mainstream but also on their own, creating their own networks of art and influence. The 1980s and 1990s offer more material to discover, as literary comics slowly, haltingly integrated. There is, of course, much more to be read, not least our cover artist Kerry James Marshall's graphic novel, *Rythm Mastr*. Marshall's work is a reimagining, as are the stories in this book, of once-traditionally white comic genres through the Black experience. The work in *It's Life as I See It* expands our understanding of science fiction, fashion, autobiography, and identity in comics. It is another example of the richness of twentieth-century Black Chicago culture, and perhaps most importantly a signpost pointing to the need for a larger recovery of the Black contribution to comics history in the Windy City and in America at large.

Dan Nadel is curator at large for the Manetti Shrem Museum of Art at the University of California, Davis. His previous books include *Peter Saul: Professional Artist Correspondence, 1945–1976*; *Art Out of Time: Unknown Comics Visionaries 1900–1969*; and, with Frank Santoro, *Return to Romance: The Strange Love Stories of Ogden Whitney* (New York Review Comics).

MY LIFE AS A CARTOONIST
Charles Johnson

Charles Johnson's *Black Humor* in *Chicago Tribune Magazine*, 1970.

Humor is the only test of gravity, and gravity of humor; for a subject which will not bear raillery is suspicious, and a jest which will not bear serious examination is false wit.

—Aristotle

When I was fifteen years old in the early 1960s, I studied with the cartoonist and writer Lawrence Lariar in his two-year correspondence course. He was prolific (something I admired), the author of more than a hundred books, some of which were murder mysteries he wrote under pseudonyms. He was the cartoon editor of *Parade* magazine, and the editor of the *Best Cartoons of the Year* series; at one time he was an idea man at Disney. He was liberal, Jewish, and lived on Long Island, where he delighted in infuriating his neighbors by having black artists over to his house for drawing lessons. I found Lariar when I was reading *Writer's Digest* profiles of famous cartoonists—my heroes—and came across an ad for his course.

The only serious disagreement I ever had with my father was when I announced to him that I planned on a career as an artist.

My dad was quiet for a few seconds, and then said, "Chuck, they don't let black people do that. You need to think of something else." His words shocked me, and I could not accept them, but they have haunted me all my life, for they were the product of what he had experienced as a black man living through America's grim era of racial segregation.

If I couldn't draw or create, I didn't want to live. I didn't want to think of something else. I wrote Lariar a letter, explaining what my father had said, and asked him if he agreed. I never expected to receive a reply, but Lariar fired back a letter to me within a week in which he said, "Your father is wrong! You can do whatever you want with your life. All you need is a good teacher."

My father backed down when I read him that letter, admitting that when it came to the arts in the 1960s, he didn't know what the hell he was talking about. He paid for my lessons with Lariar from 1963 until 1965, the year I became a professional, *paid* artist when I published my first illustrations in a Chicago magic company catalog. (I framed one of those first dollars and still have it in my study.) I began publishing short stories in the literary section of my high school newspaper, the *Evanstonian*, as well as drawing sports cartoons and a satirical comic strip titled *Wonder Wildkit*, a spoof on *Wonder Wart-Hog* that I made with a friend (he wrote, I drew). In 1966, that comic strip and one of my many sports cartoons both received second-place awards in a national contest for high school cartoonists sponsored by Columbia University's School of Journalism. Some of that high school work is anthologized in *First Words: Earliest Writing from Favorite Contemporary Authors*, edited by Paul Mandelbaum (1993).

During those two years of study with Lariar, I twice took a Greyhound bus from Illinois to New York; each time I stayed with my relatives in Brooklyn for a week and, after calling editors at different places to set up visits, I pounded the pavement in Manhattan with my "swatch" of cartoons (samples), going from one publishing house to another, looking for work. It was during one of those meetings that I met a young editor and cartoonist, Charles Barsotti, whose simple but endearing cartoons appeared regularly in *The New Yorker*, which at the time had a notorious history of not using the work of black cartoonists. In 1996, *The New Yorker* published a special "Black in America" double issue, which featured the work of thirteen "gag artists," only one of whom was black; eight black people who submitted work were rejected, and the magazine's cartoon editor, Lee Lorenz, admitted that *The New Yorker*'s stable of cartoonists at the time was still entirely white. Sometimes I've wondered if my father's original warning to me contained an element of truth.

Barsotti was undoubtedly aware of the whiteness of cartoonists whose work appeared in that publication. (Lariar once complained to me how *his* work was always turned down by *The New Yorker*, a publication where I never submitted my own work.) After one of my trips to New York, Barsotti wrote to tell me that as a young black cartoonist I could work with racial material that "an old white guy" like him and his friends wouldn't be able to touch. It would be a few years, however, before his suggestion fully took hold of me.

I always visited Lariar during my trips to New York. He fixed me lunch when I was in my teens and dinner when my wife, newborn son, and I visited him during my time in the philosophy PhD program at Stony Brook University (as an undergraduate at Southern Illinois University I was a journalism major who took loads of philosophy courses, then after graduation immediately began the long journey to a master's degree and doctorate in that field). He loaded me up with original art from the days when he had a syndicated strip (he wrote, someone else drew it), and regaled me with stories about the comic artists I so admired. During my undergraduate college years, I sent him copies of editorial, panel cartoons, comic strips, and illustrations I published. Between 1965 and 1972, hundreds of these drawings ran in Midwest periodicals like the *Chicago Tribune*, black magazines such as *Jet*, *Ebony*, *Black World*, *Players*, and a St. Louis magazine called *Proud*, and he always wrote back something encouraging.

I drew furiously from 1965 to 1969—cartoons, illustrations, and comic strips (*The God Squad*, *Trip*) for my college newspaper, the *Daily Egyptian*; editorial cartoons for the *Southern Illinoisan* in Carbondale, Illinois; one-page scripts for Charlton Comics; and a design for a Southern Illinois commemorative stamp. I was obsessed in my teens with being published. The art supply store was my second home. I was always ready to draw *any*thing for *any*one who would put my work into print. The challenge for me was always, "What can I draw next?" because when I figured out how to draw something, it almost felt as if I owned it.

In January 1969, I went to a poetry reading by Amiri Baraka, one of the principal architects of the Black Arts Movement, which was the cultural wing of the Black Power movement until the mid-1970s. During the Q&A he refused to take questions from white members of the audience. I thought that was unnecessarily rude, but something he said to the black students struck me thunderously, as if he was talking directly to me. He said, "Bring your talents back home to the black community." I began to wonder: What if I directed my drawing and everything I knew about comic art to exploring the history and culture of black America? I suddenly returned to what Barsotti had suggested to me four years earlier—to focus my work on black humor.

I remember walking back to my dormitory in the rain from Baraka's reading, dazed by what he'd said. I sat down before my drawing board, my inkwell, my pens. I started to sketch. I worked furiously for a solid week, cutting my classes. The more I drew and took notes for gag lines, the faster the ideas came. After seven intense days of creative outpouring, I had a book, *Black Humor*. My only problem was I didn't know where to send it. But the school of journalism offered me an internship for the coming summer at the *Chicago Tribune*. There, I worked on the newspaper's *Action Express* public service column and occasionally did a drawing for it. One day I had an eventful discussion with the book editor, Bob Cromie, and told him about *Black Humor*. He suggested I show the book to publisher John H. Johnson down the street at *Ebony* magazine, which I did. Before the summer of 1969 was over, he accepted it for publication in 1970.

That same year I hosted the PBS how-to-draw show *Charlie's Pad*, with fifty-two fifteen-minute lessons based on Lariar's two-year course, and inspired by a TV spot he did in the 1950s or 1960s when at the end of a news program he drew something funny about that day's headlines. There was no causal connection between *Black Humor* and *Charlie's Pad*. The television program was a separate project. In 1967 Congress created the Corporation for Public Broadcasting. That led to "educational television" stations around the country needing content for programming. I didn't know that in 1969, but one day when I was in my dormitory room feeling bored, I wrote to the local station, WSIU-TV, and asked if they'd be interested in my doing a cartooning show for them. They were, because it was cheap and easy to do—all they needed were two cameras and me at a drawing table. That show was broadcast around the country for about ten years.

I produced a few other books of cartoons after that. The second, *Half-Past Nation Time* (1972), was done by a fly-by-night California publisher called Aware Press, which disappeared as soon as they sent me my author's copies—I have only one copy now, and it can otherwise only be found these days in library rare-book rooms. I did an entire book of cartoons on slavery, *I Can Get Her for You Wholesale*, which the publisher of Aware Press disappeared with, and another devoted entirely to Eastern philosophy, *It's Lonely at the Top*. Although never published as a book, these drawings have appeared here and there in different magazines; seven appear in *Buddha Laughing: A Tricycle Book of Cartoons* (1999).

My work as a cartoonist eventually gave way in the early 1970s to the time required to earn my doctorate in philosophy—and to the years I spent writing novels and short stories, essays, screenplays, literary criticism, and Buddhist-oriented books and articles, as well as teaching English and creative writing for thirty-three years at the University of Washington. What I taught can be found in *The Way of the Writer: Reflections on the Art and Craft of Storytelling* (2016). When Lariar read my debut novel, *Faith and the Good Thing* (1974), he wrote me a letter, saying, "You have 'the touch.'" But I could never stop drawing.

For a period in 1971, while I was working on my master's degree, I finished five single-panel cartoons a day (I'd usually sell five of the twenty-five I did during the week, which was enough to pay for groceries), I did draw birthday cards for my kids as they were growing up, and these days work on illustrations requested by friends and former students. After my third novel, *Middle Passage* (1990), received the National Book Award for fiction, I again leaped at every opportunity to draw something—even for free, which I know distressed my literary agents. For a time I drew cartoons for the *Quarterly Black Review of Books*, and for a free New York literary journal called *Literal Latte*. When my daughter Elisheba suggested that we do a children's book together, I seized the chance to cowrite with her what are now three books in the *Adventures of Emery Jones, Boy Science Wonder* YA series simply because each book gave me a chance to draw around twenty illustrations.

After fifty-five years of steadily publishing stories and drawings, I still need to externalize on the page images and ideas that exist only in my head where no one can see them. As a writer, I think visually, and no creative pleasure is greater for me than the physical (as well as mental) process of comic art. Other writer/artists have felt this way—for example, John Updike once confessed that none of his literary work brought him the deep satisfaction he experienced as a cartoonist during his college years. I think I know why he felt that way. I love the fibrous texture and feel of drawing paper beneath my fingers. I love, too, the odor of India ink; working with a T-square and triangle; playing with push pens and masking tape, with hard and soft erasers (remember: all real art involves, to some degree, play); the messiness of white correcting fluid, different pens and brushes, the concentration necessary for doing sketches or early drafts to arrive at a bal-anced composition, one deliberately and deceptively simple with strong, bold outlines yet occasionally detailed in respect to costuming, props, hairstyles, shading, etc. I especially relish the inking phase in the wee hours of morning as I'm listening to soft jazz.

One might ask, what causes this lifelong addiction to drawing comic art? The answer, I believe, is a time-honored reply: We think in pictures. Like music, the content of a drawing can be universally recognized; it cuts across language barriers, and can be "worth a thousand words."

TOM FLOYD
1929–2011

Photographer unknown. *Integration Is a Bitch!*, 1969.

Tom Floyd was born and raised in Gary, Indiana, a center of postwar Black culture. The town nurtured Floyd and Grass Green, among other artists. Floyd was a Big Ten track-and-field champion at the University of Illinois, where he majored in advertising and commercial art. Warned that cartooning was extremely difficult to enter for a Black person, he studied mechanical illustration, graphic design, and caricature. He freelanced for *The Chicago Defender*, but found both a stable gig and good subject matter working for a leading Chicago industrial company, Inland Steel. Floyd eventually joined the staff in 1957, producing all of its visual materials, from posters to instructional manuals to cartoons. The 116-page book *Integration Is a Bitch!*, published in 1969, is his record of entering and exiting the white-collar workforce. Aside from Charles Johnson's *Black Humor*, Floyd's work was the only book-length cartoon critique of racism of its time. Its mere existence in 1969 was revolutionary. Floyd's unique take on that moment in race relations made the book a crossover success. In the 1970s and 1980s, Floyd was staff illustrator and cartoonist for the *Gary Post-Tribune*.

In 1972 he self-published, under the imprint Leader Comics Group, *Blackman*, a comic about a "Proud, Strong, and Black!" superhero who was the "soul wonder of the world." Costumed in the colors of the Pan-African flag, with manacles on his wrists and chains around his waist and neck, Blackman flew by pulling on his boot-straps. A younger collaborator, Ira Harmon, recalls that "when [Floyd] went to New York with the drawings of Blackman under his arm to meet with Stan Lee, he was turned away without a deal. Shortly thereafter *Luke Cage, Hero for Hire* appeared. The character design was lifted from Floyd's portfolio, but the comic was a minstrel show. A far cry from what we had planned." Floyd had hoped to start up a whole superhero universe, with Harmon and Seitu Hayden working on *Black Woman* and *Big Dunkin* and Richard "Grass" Green working on *Joe Chitlin*, but the combination of what he viewed as a theft and an apathetic reaction to his comic book left him disillusioned. In 1973 Floyd self-published *The Hook Book: The ABC's of Drug Abuse*, a cautionary comic book about the perils of narcotics. Floyd never quite recovered his footing as a cartoonist, but nearly every artist featured in this anthology owned a copy of *Integration Is a Bitch!*. In the 1980s and 1990s, Floyd designed church windows depicting only Black figures and constructed from acrylic plastic tiles, which were displayed throughout Gary. In a survey of Black cartoonists in the July 16, 1995, issue of the *Chicago Tribune*, Floyd, then working in advertising, said he was still hoping to find a home for Blackman and friends.

Integration Is a Bitch!, Opinion News Syndicate, Inc., 1969.

Hire some Negroes .. Quick !

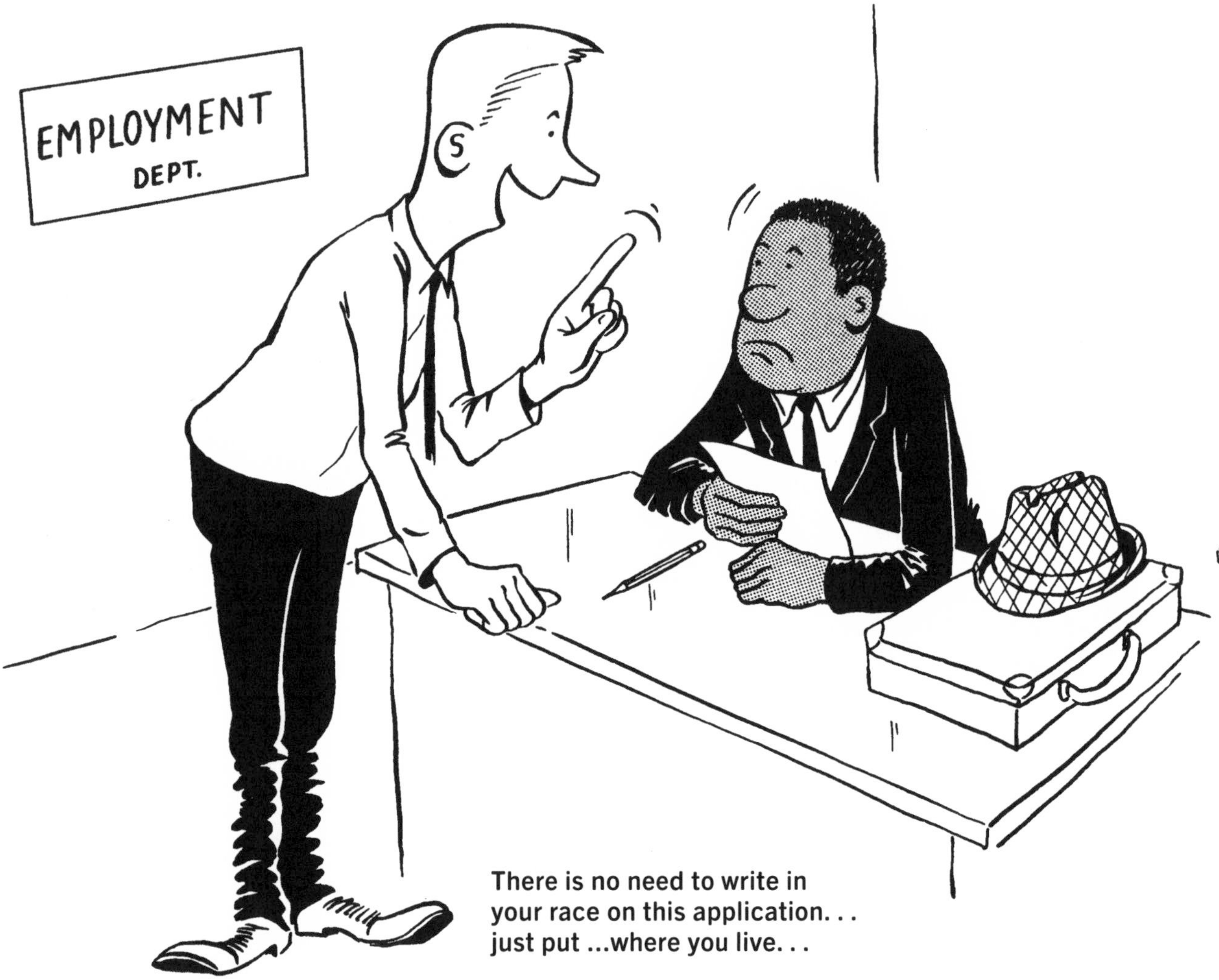
EMPLOYMENT
DEPT.
FLOYD

There is no need to write in
your race on this application. . .
just put ...where you live. . .

We do everything to make our employees happy here!

Well-we won't be needing this
anymore......

We felt that you would like
a window with a view.......

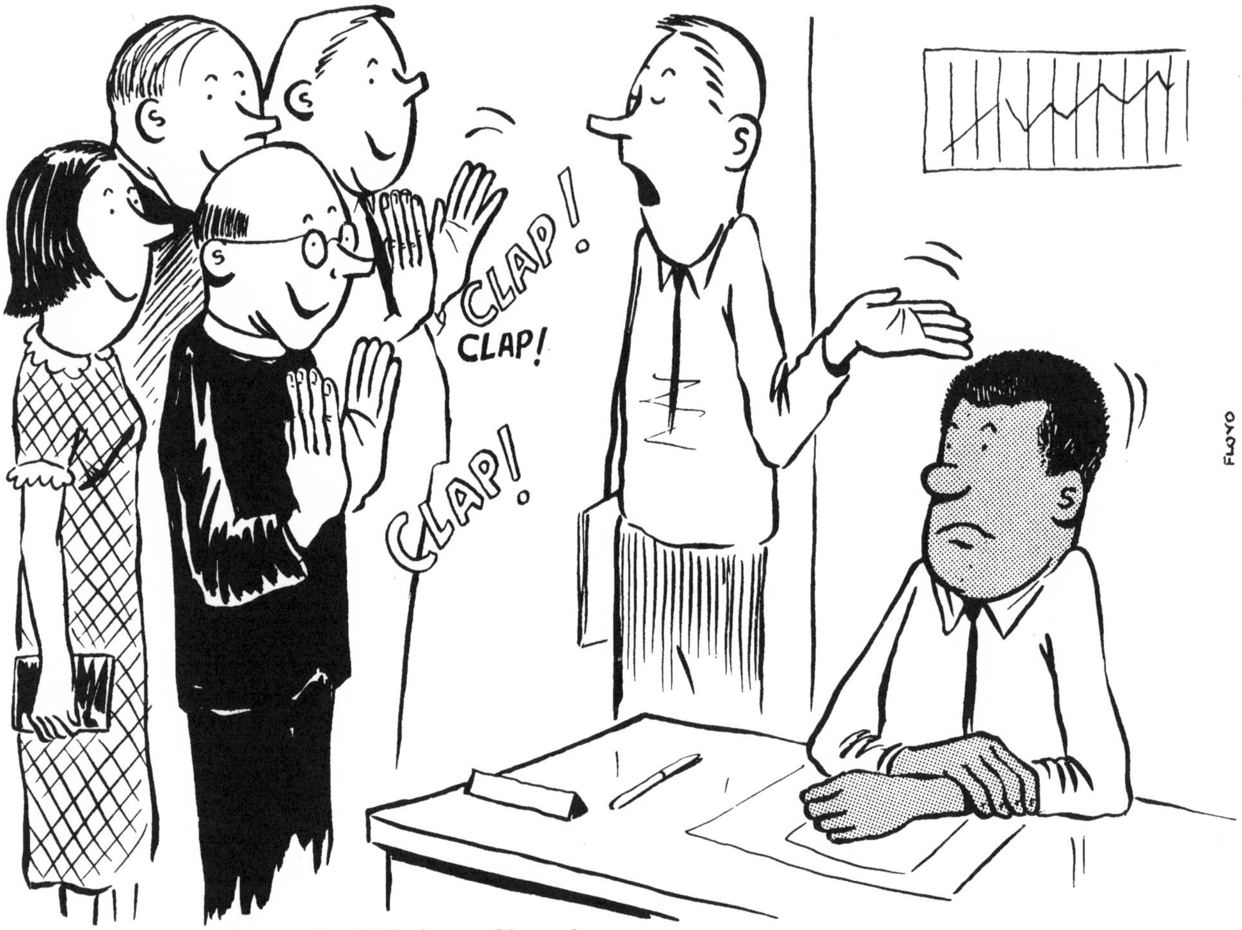
CLAP!
CLAP!
CLAP!
. . .And this is our Negro!

You will be our second attempt at integration.

Make sure that these pictures
are sent to the black dispatch
. . . . . .Afro American news, etc.

We had a nice colored man cutting
our grass yesterday . . .and you know. .
he didn't steal a thing. . . .

It will take a while before the neighbors get used to you!

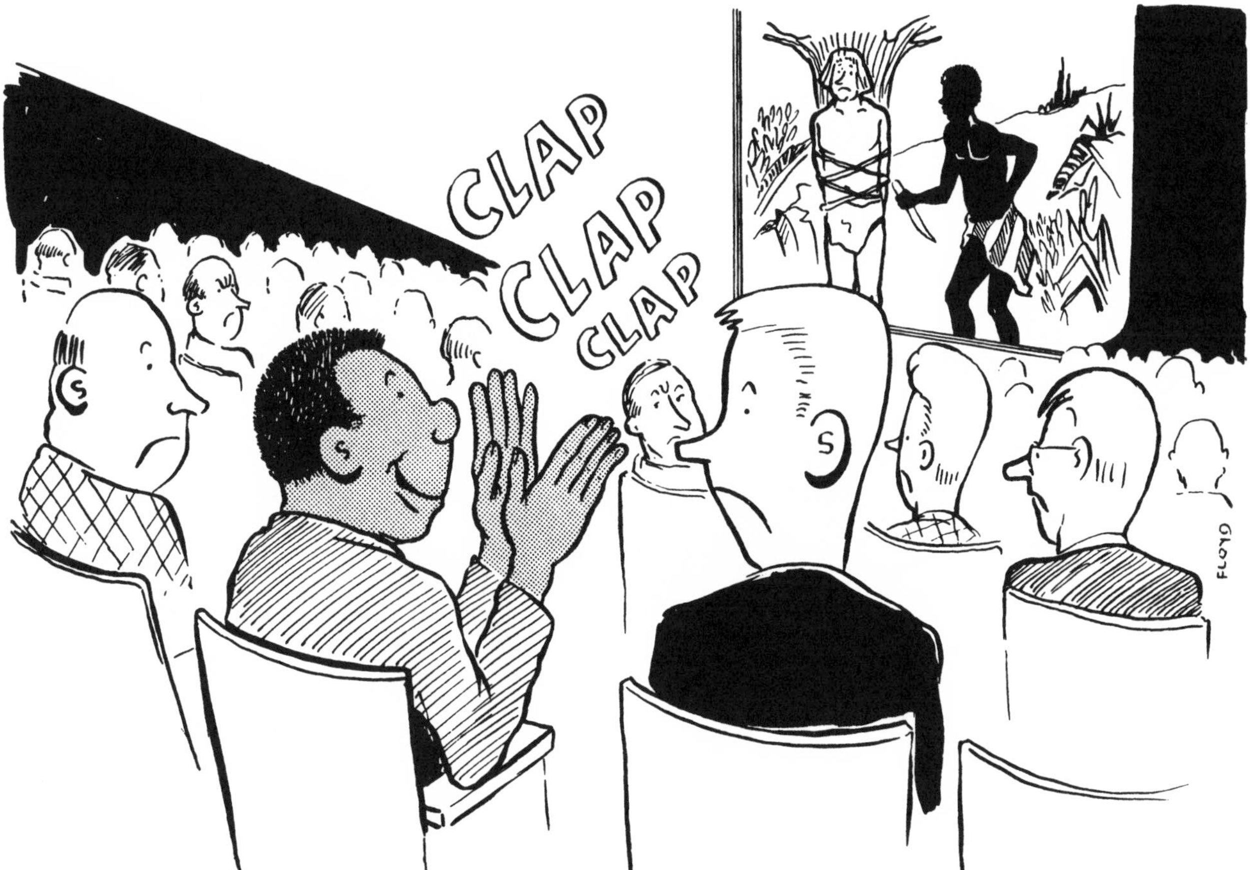
CLAP
CLAP
CLAP
FLOYD

Here are some of my kids old clothes. . .I thought that your kids could use them. . . .

7 more minutes of
integration!

RICHARD "GRASS" GREEN

1939–2002

Photographer unknown, c. 1980s. Courtesy of William H. Foster.

The cartoonist, performer, and entrepreneur Richard "Grass" Green was another cartooning native of Gary, Indiana. He first became known through superhero fandom, contributing to *Xal-Kor the Human Cat*, to *The Adventures of Wildman and Rubberboy*, and to mimeographed fanzines throughout the 1960s. Green aspired to work for Marvel Comics, but never got past the letters columns. Instead, he drew comics for the smaller outfit Charlton and eventually found more receptive audiences in the underground press, where he published in anthologies including *Teen-Age Horizons of Shangrila*, *Snarf*, and *Bizarre Sex*, as well as his own title, *Super Soul Comix*. He often focused on superhero parodies, but in smaller minicomics and the occasional longer story he would turn to autobiography, race, and sex. Alongside his cartooning, Green ran REGCo (the Richard Eugene Green Company), which produced ready-to-use layout art boards, with panels printed in non-repro blue ink to allow cartoonists a ready-made panel grid. He also played guitar and sang in clubs in the northern Indiana region. *Smoke Power* was commissioned by Seitu Hayden for an unpublished prototype of a "Black *Mad*" called *Ain't That a Blip.* Though long past our 1980 cutoff, this strip is representative of Green's work; by 1990 he had been making comics for thirty years. Green remained popular in fandom circles throughout his life, and kept his hand in comics until his death in Fort Wayne, Indiana.

Smoke Power, unpublished, 1990.

'EY, FOLKS! HOWZIT HANGIN', AH?

ME? I AIN' BEEN DOIN' BADLY AT ALL! ALTHO I HAVE PROBLEMS JUST LIKE ANY OTHER AVERAGE GUY, I THINK LIFE, OVER ALL, HAS BEEN PRET-TEE DAM' GOOD!

I FIGURE IT LIKE THIS: EITHER LIFE'S NEGATIVES HAVE EASED UP A BIT, OR I, IN MY OLD AGE — I'M 51 — MAYBE I'VE JUST.. UH.. KINDA MORE-LESS MELLOWED OUT.

I MEAN, LIKE, WHEN I WAS IN MY 20'S AND 30'S, I'D GET UPSET ABOUT ANYTHING AND EVERYTHING, Y'KNOW?
~PUF, POF.~

—YOU NAME IT, I PROBABLY WORRIED ABOUT IT! INSECURE, ANXIOUS, DOUBTFUL, RESTLESS, LONELY, SCARED OF THE FUTURE, ETC., ETC.

AND BROKE! DON'T FORGET BROKE.. LAWDY!

THEN SOMEHOW, I GOT INTO THE BIBLE. JUST READING IT NOT ONLY HELPED ME TO FIND ME, BUT I FOUND THAT THE MORE I READ THE BIBLE, THE LESS LONELY I FELT! IN FACT, I BEGAN T'FEEL BETTER ABOUT ER'RYTHING!

AND, YA KNOW WHAT ELSE?

NEXT THING I KNOW, I'M GOIN' T'CHURCH AGAIN AND STARTIN' TO FEEL PRET-TEE GOOD ABOUT MYSELF. I STOPPED DRINKIN' AND PARTYIN', CUT OUT THE CAROUSIN' AND ONE-NIGHT STANDS..

WHICH CUT OUT MY WORRY ABOUT GETTING AIDS, TOO!

TOOK A WHILE, BUT FOLLOWING BIBLICAL ADVICE, I PRAYED FOR GOD TO SEND ME A WOMAN TO LOVE, THEN I JUST WAITED. YOU'VE GOTTA TRUST GOD, Y'KNOW, AND BE PATIENT. IT WAS DIFFICULT, BUT I WAS DETERMINED TO HANG IN THERE.

AND, FINALLY!, THIS SHAPELY, CUTE LIL' DREAMBOAT CAME INTO MY LIFE! — IT WAS KINDA UNUSUAL HOW IT (PUFF PUFF) HAPPENED! (PUFF) I—

HEY, PAL—GIMME A BREAK, AH?

MASH MASH MASH MASH

THUMP THUMP

35

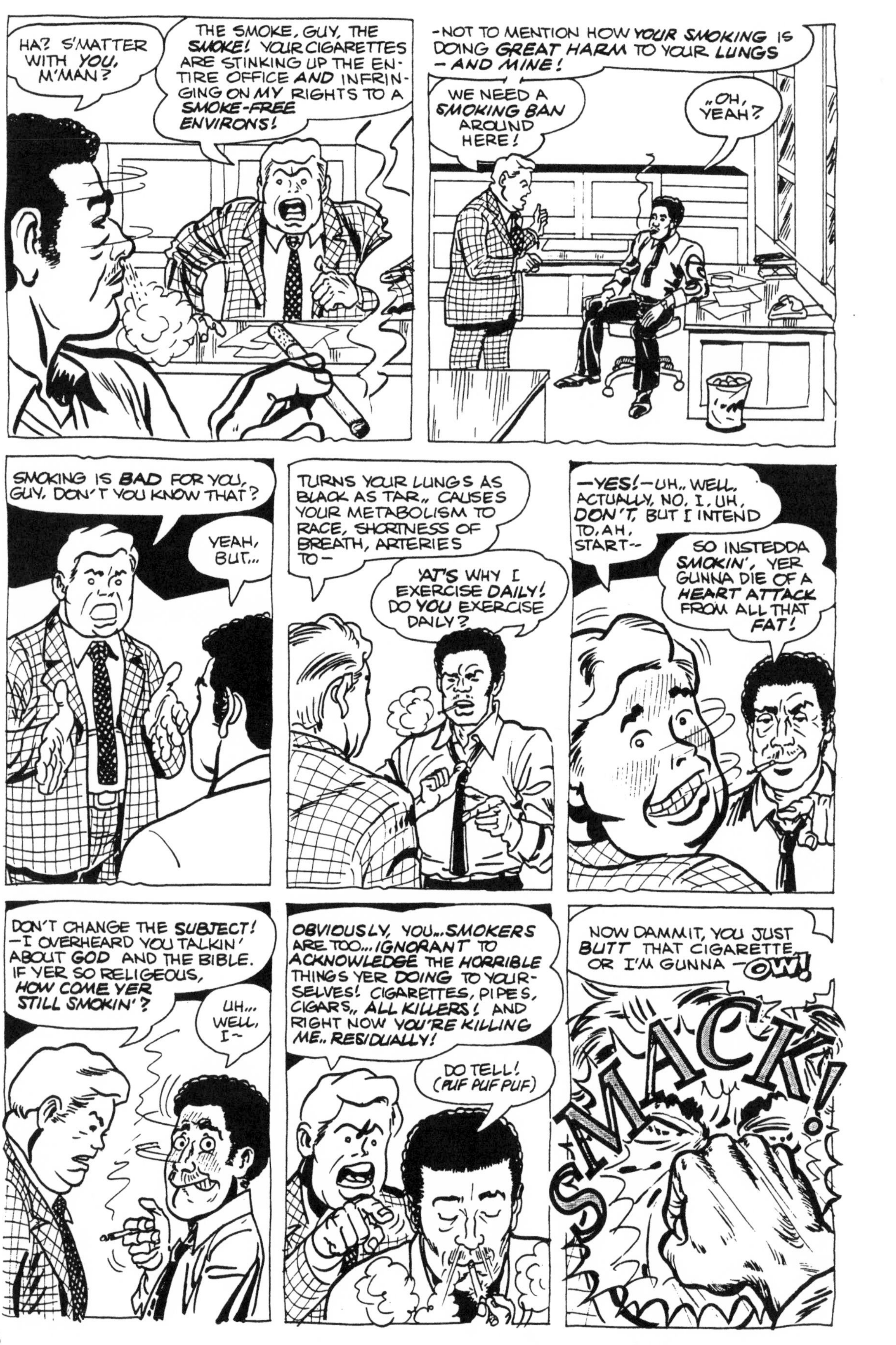
HA? S'MATTER WITH YOU, M'MAN?
THE SMOKE, GUY, THE SMOKE! YOUR CIGARETTES ARE STINKING UP THE ENTIRE OFFICE AND INFRINGING ON MY RIGHTS TO A SMOKE-FREE ENVIRONS!
-NOT TO MENTION HOW YOUR SMOKING IS DOING GREAT HARM TO YOUR LUNGS - AND MINE!
WE NEED A SMOKING BAN AROUND HERE!
..OH, YEAH?
SMOKING IS BAD FOR YOU, GUY, DON'T YOU KNOW THAT?
YEAH, BUT...
TURNS YOUR LUNGS AS BLACK AS TAR.. CAUSES YOUR METABOLISM TO RACE, SHORTNESS OF BREATH, ARTERIES TO-
'AT'S WHY I EXERCISE DAILY! DO YOU EXERCISE DAILY?
—YES!—UH.. WELL, ACTUALLY, NO, I, UH, DON'T, BUT I INTEND TO, AH, START--
SO INSTEDDA SMOKIN', YER GUNNA DIE OF A HEART ATTACK FROM ALL THAT FAT!
DON'T CHANGE THE SUBJECT! -I OVERHEARD YOU TALKIN' ABOUT GOD AND THE BIBLE. IF YER SO RELIGEOUS, HOW COME YER STILL SMOKIN'?
UH... WELL, I-
OBVIOUSLY, YOU... SMOKERS ARE TOO... IGNORANT TO ACKNOWLEDGE THE HORRIBLE THINGS YER DOING TO YOURSELVES! CIGARETTES, PIPES, CIGARS.. ALL KILLERS! AND RIGHT NOW YOU'RE KILLING ME.. RESIDUALLY!
DO TELL! (PUF PUF PUF)
NOW DAMMIT, YOU JUST BUTT THAT CIGARETTE OR I'M GUNNA -OW!
SMACK!

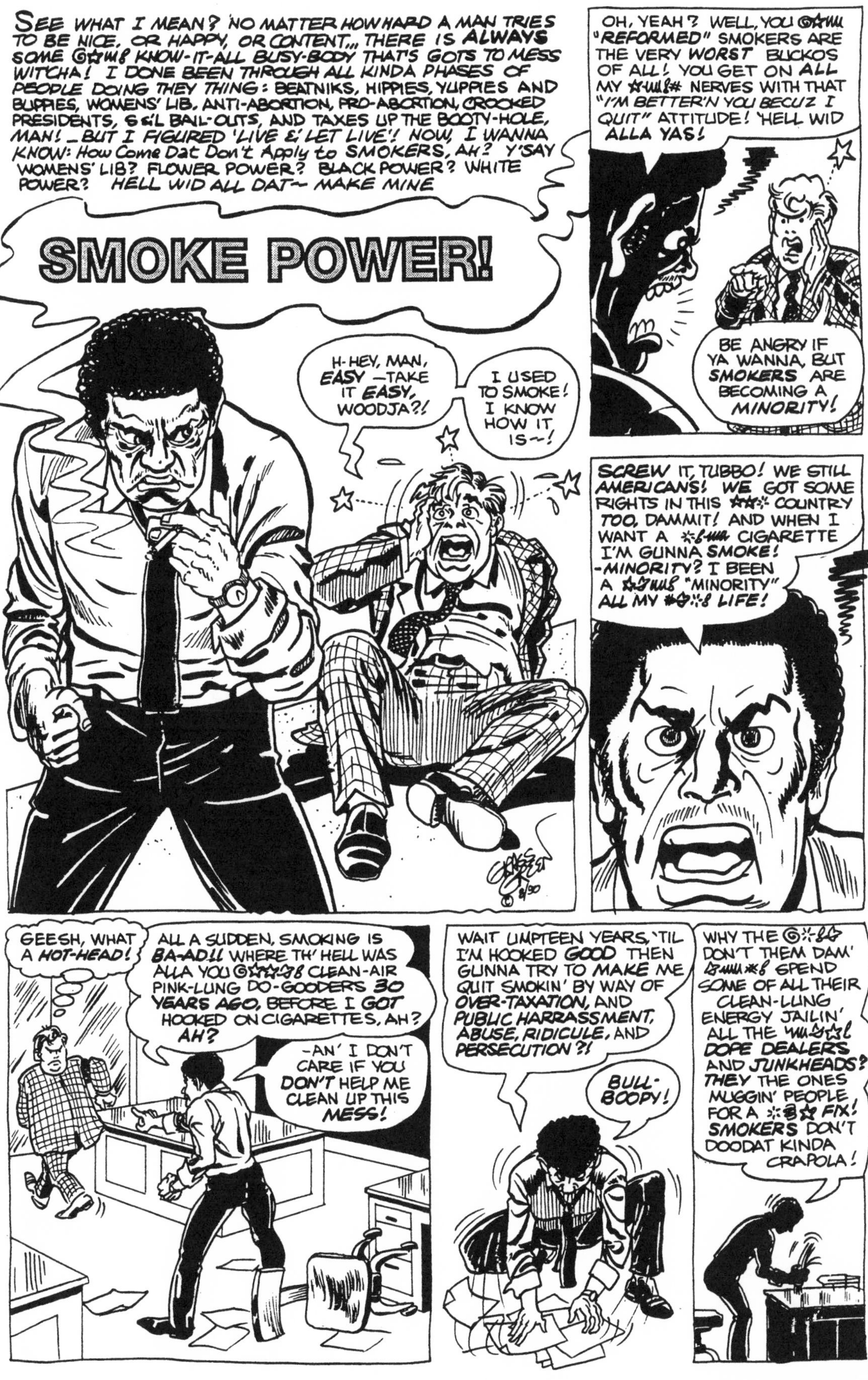

SEE WHAT I MEAN? NO MATTER HOW HARD A MAN TRIES TO BE NICE, OR HAPPY, OR CONTENT... THERE IS ALWAYS SOME @☆#! KNOW-IT-ALL BUSY-BODY THAT'S GOTS TO MESS WITCHA! I DONE BEEN THROUGH ALL KINDA PHASES OF PEOPLE DOING THEY THING: BEATNIKS, HIPPIES, YUPPIES AND BUPPIES, WOMENS' LIB, ANTI-ABORTION, PRO-ABORTION, CROOKED PRESIDENTS, S&L BAIL-OUTS, AND TAXES UP THE BOOTY-HOLE, MAN! — BUT I FIGURED 'LIVE & LET LIVE'! NOW, I WANNA KNOW: How Come Dat Don't Apply to SMOKERS, AH? Y'SAY WOMENS' LIB? FLOWER POWER? BLACK POWER? WHITE POWER? HELL WID ALL DAT— MAKE MINE
SMOKE POWER!
H-HEY, MAN, EASY —TAKE IT EASY, WOODJA?!
I USED TO SMOKE! I KNOW HOW IT IS—!
OH, YEAH? WELL, YOU @☆#! "REFORMED" SMOKERS ARE THE VERY WORST BUCKOS OF ALL! YOU GET ON ALL MY ☆#!# NERVES WITH THAT "I'M BETTER'N YOU BECUZ I QUIT" ATTITUDE! HELL WID ALLA YAS!
BE ANGRY IF YA WANNA, BUT SMOKERS ARE BECOMING A MINORITY!
SCREW IT, TUBBO! WE STILL AMERICANS! WE GOT SOME RIGHTS IN THIS ☆#! COUNTRY TOO, DAMMIT! AND WHEN I WANT A ☆#! CIGARETTE I'M GUNNA SMOKE! —MINORITY? I BEEN A ☆#! "MINORITY" ALL MY #@! LIFE!
GEESH, WHAT A HOT-HEAD!
ALL A SUDDEN, SMOKING IS BA-AD!! WHERE TH' HELL WAS ALLA YOU @☆#! CLEAN-AIR PINK-LUNG DO-GOODERS 30 YEARS AGO, BEFORE I GOT HOOKED ON CIGARETTES, AH? AH?
—AN' I DON'T CARE IF YOU DON'T HELP ME CLEAN UP THIS MESS!
WAIT UMPTEEN YEARS, 'TIL I'M HOOKED GOOD THEN GUNNA TRY TO MAKE ME QUIT SMOKIN' BY WAY OF OVER-TAXATION, AND PUBLIC HARRASSMENT, ABUSE, RIDICULE, AND PERSECUTION?!
BULL-BOOPY!
WHY THE @☆#! DON'T THEM DAM' @☆#! SPEND SOME OF ALL THEIR CLEAN-LUNG ENERGY JAILIN' ALL THE @☆#! DOPE DEALERS AND JUNKHEADS? THEY THE ONES MUGGIN' PEOPLE FOR A ☆#! FIX! SMOKERS DON'T DOODAT KINDA CRAPOLA!

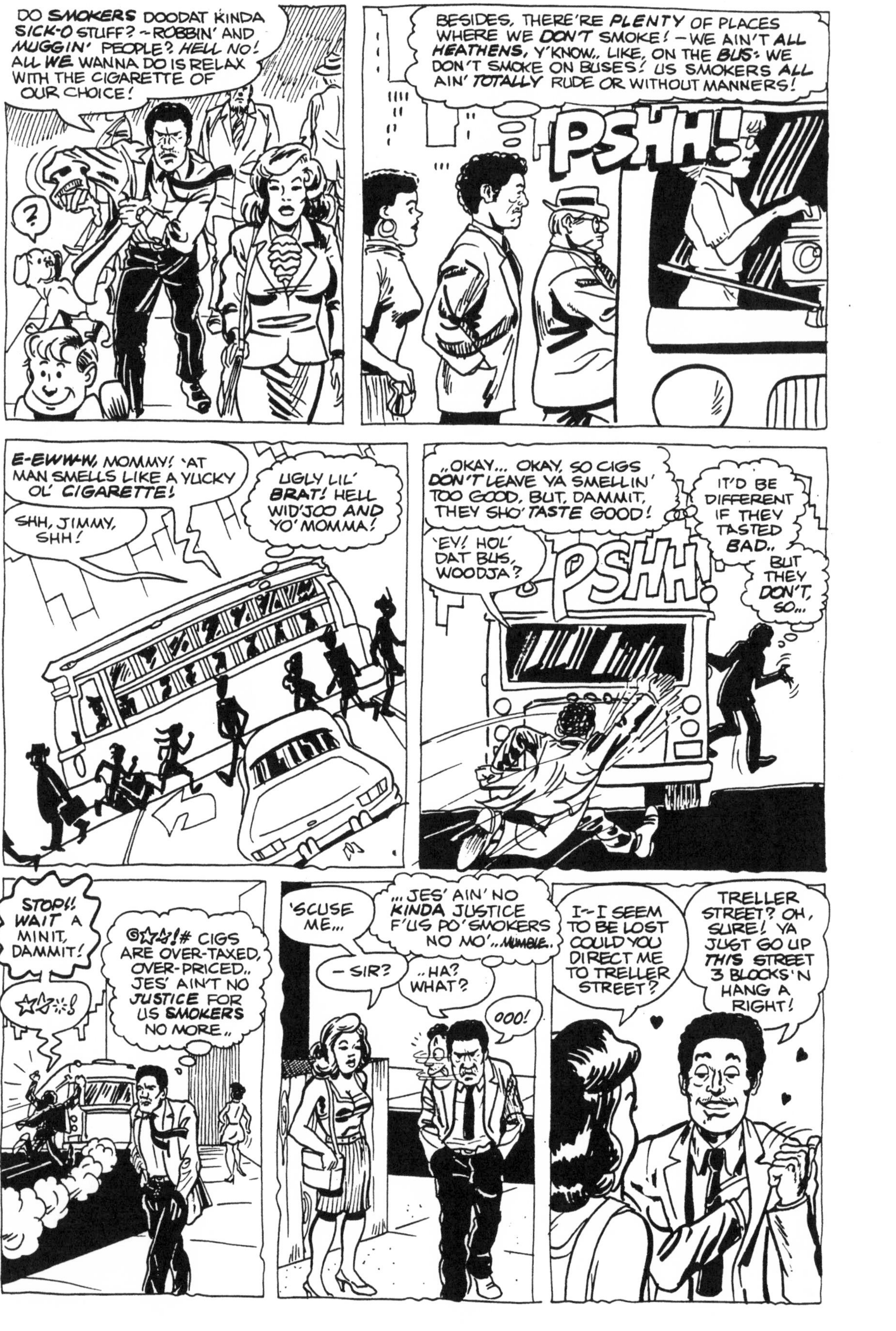
DO SMOKERS DOODAT KINDA SICK-O STUFF? – ROBBIN' AND MUGGIN' PEOPLE? HELL NO! ALL WE WANNA DO IS RELAX WITH THE CIGARETTE OF OUR CHOICE!
?
BESIDES, THERE'RE PLENTY OF PLACES WHERE WE DON'T SMOKE! – WE AIN'T ALL HEATHENS, Y'KNOW,, LIKE, ON THE BUS: WE DON'T SMOKE ON BUSES! US SMOKERS ALL AIN' TOTALLY RUDE OR WITHOUT MANNERS!
PSHH!
E-EWW-W, MOMMY! 'AT MAN SMELLS LIKE A YUCKY OL' CIGARETTE!
SHH, JIMMY, SHH!
UGLY LIL' BRAT! HELL WID'JOO AND YO' MOMMA!
..OKAY... OKAY, SO CIGS DON'T LEAVE YA SMELLIN' TOO GOOD, BUT, DAMMIT, THEY SHO' TASTE GOOD!
IT'D BE DIFFERENT IF THEY TASTED BAD..
'EY! HOL' DAT BUS, WOODJA?
PSHH!
BUT THEY DON'T, SO...
STOP!! WAIT A MINIT, DAMMIT!
@☆☆!# CIGS ARE OVER-TAXED, OVER-PRICED,, JES' AIN'T NO JUSTICE FOR US SMOKERS NO MORE..
'SCUSE ME...
...JES' AIN' NO KINDA JUSTICE F'US PO' SMOKERS NO MO'.. MUMBLE..
– SIR?
..HA? WHAT?
OOO!
I--I SEEM TO BE LOST COULD YOU DIRECT ME TO TRELLER STREET?
TRELLER STREET? OH, SURE! YA JUST GO UP THIS STREET 3 BLOCKS 'N HANG A RIGHT!

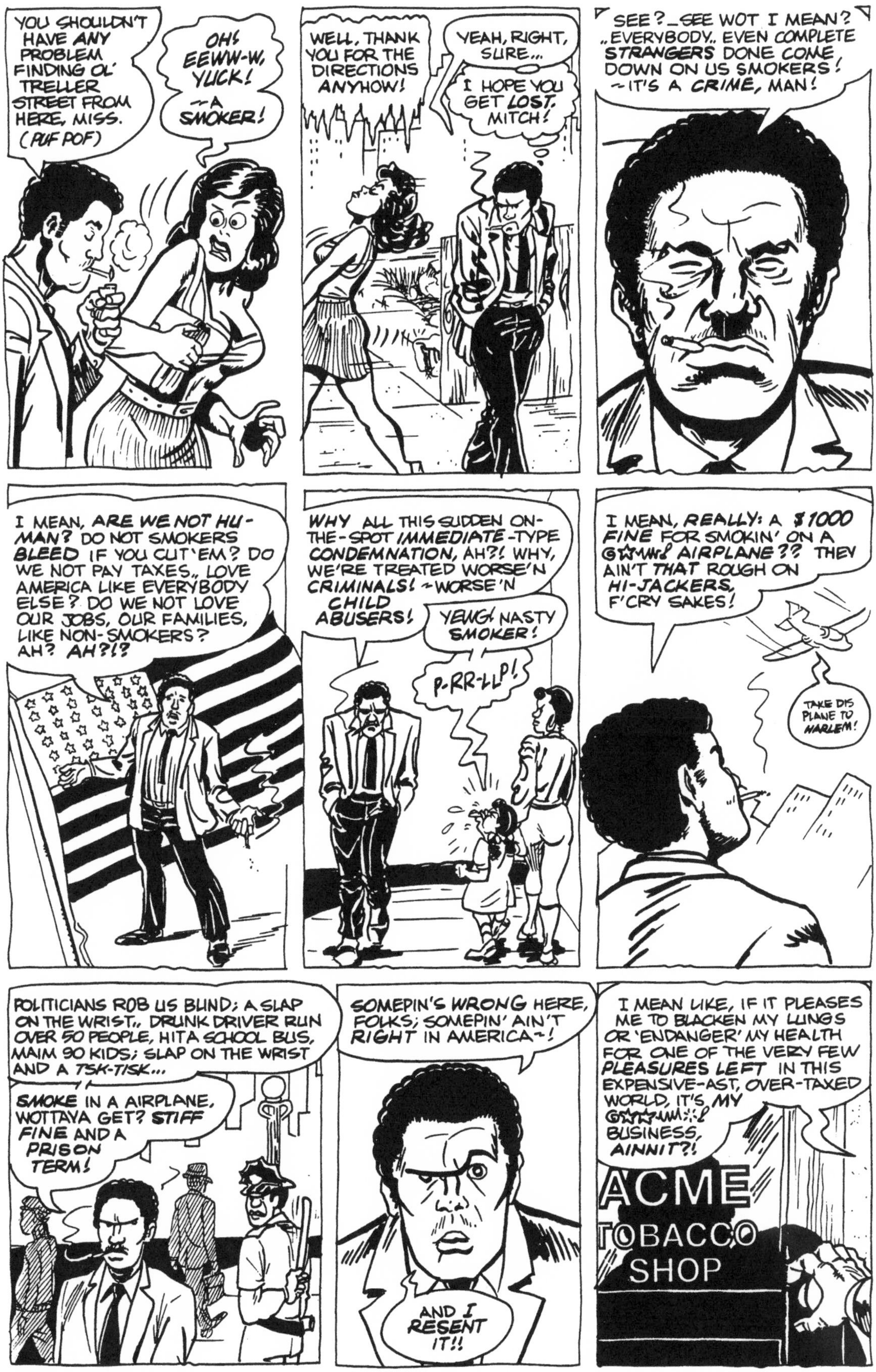

YOU SHOULDN'T HAVE ANY PROBLEM FINDING OL' TRELLER STREET FROM HERE, MISS. (PUF POF)
OH! EEWW-W, YUCK! ~A SMOKER!
WELL, THANK YOU FOR THE DIRECTIONS ANYHOW!
YEAH, RIGHT, SURE...
I HOPE YOU GET LOST, MITCH!
SEE?_SEE WOT I MEAN? ..EVERYBODY.. EVEN COMPLETE STRANGERS DONE COME DOWN ON US SMOKERS! ~IT'S A CRIME, MAN!
I MEAN, ARE WE NOT HUMAN? DO NOT SMOKERS BLEED IF YOU CUT 'EM? DO WE NOT PAY TAXES.. LOVE AMERICA LIKE EVERYBODY ELSE? DO WE NOT LOVE OUR JOBS, OUR FAMILIES, LIKE NON-SMOKERS? AH? AH?!?
WHY ALL THIS SUDDEN ON-THE-SPOT IMMEDIATE-TYPE CONDEMNATION, AH?! WHY, WE'RE TREATED WORSE'N CRIMINALS! ~WORSE'N CHILD ABUSERS!
YEUG! NASTY SMOKER!
P-RR-LLP!
I MEAN, REALLY: A $1000 FINE FOR SMOKIN' ON A G☆%#&! AIRPLANE?? THEY AIN'T THAT ROUGH ON HI-JACKERS, F'CRY SAKES!
TAKE DIS PLANE TO HARLEM!
POLITICIANS ROB US BLIND; A SLAP ON THE WRIST.. DRUNK DRIVER RUN OVER 50 PEOPLE, HIT A SCHOOL BUS, MAIM 90 KIDS; SLAP ON THE WRIST AND A TSK-TSK...
SMOKE IN A AIRPLANE, WOTTAYA GET? STIFF FINE AND A PRISON TERM!
SOMEPIN'S WRONG HERE, FOLKS; SOMEPIN' AIN'T RIGHT IN AMERICA~!
AND I RESENT IT!!
I MEAN LIKE, IF IT PLEASES ME TO BLACKEN MY LUNGS OR 'ENDANGER' MY HEALTH FOR ONE OF THE VERY FEW PLEASURES LEFT IN THIS EXPENSIVE-AST, OVER-TAXED WORLD, IT'S MY G☆%#&! BUSINESS, AINNIT?!
ACME TOBACCO SHOP

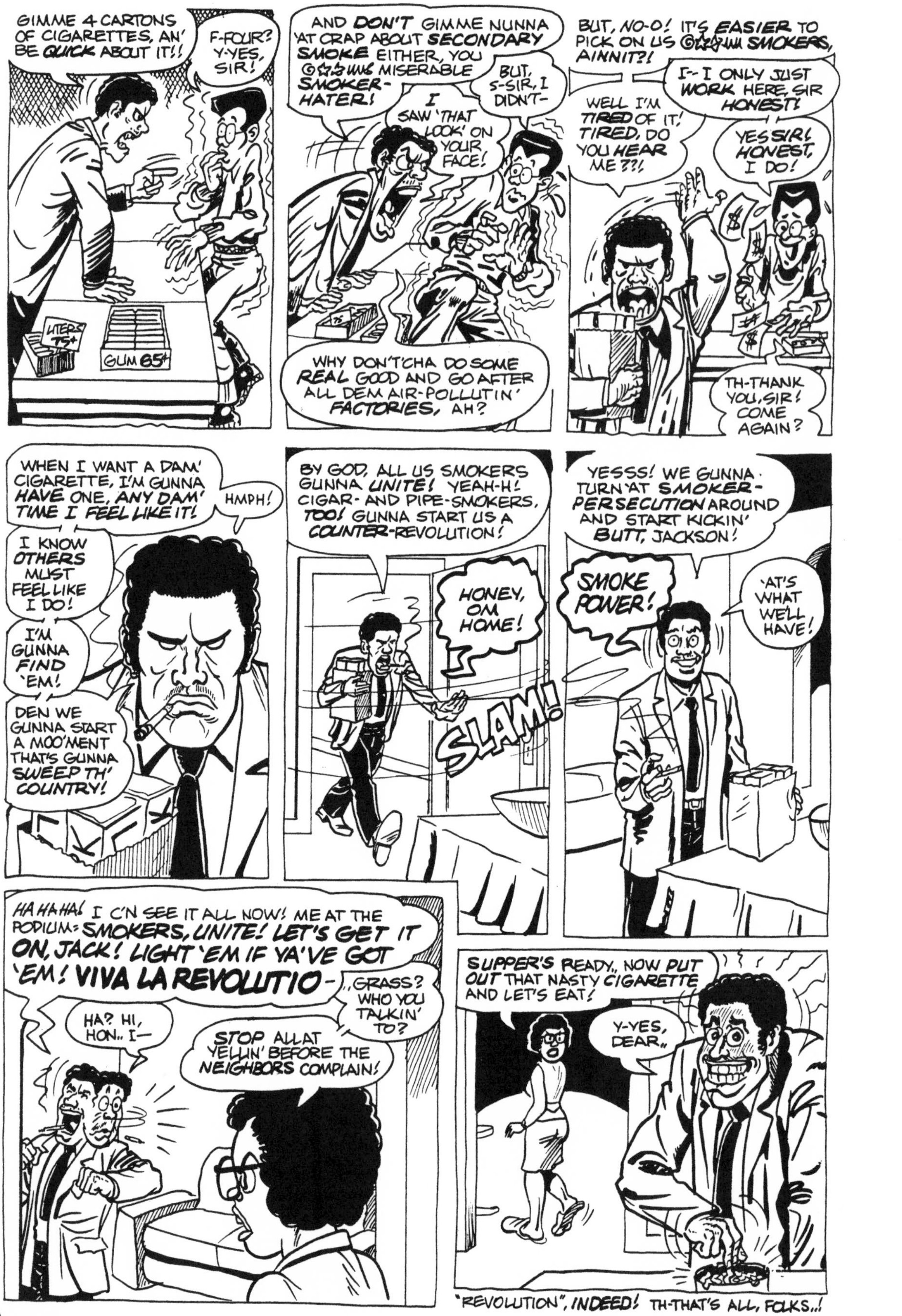
GIMME 4 CARTONS OF CIGARETTES, AN' BE QUICK ABOUT IT!!
F-FOUR? Y-YES, SIR!
LITERS 75¢
GUM 65¢
AND DON'T GIMME NUNNA 'AT CRAP ABOUT SECONDARY SMOKE EITHER, YOU MISERABLE SMOKER-HATER!
BUT, S-SIR, I DIDN'T-
I SAW 'THAT LOOK' ON YOUR FACE!
WHY DON'T'CHA DO SOME REAL GOOD AND GO AFTER ALL DEM AIR-POLLUTIN' FACTORIES, AH?
BUT, NO-O! IT'S EASIER TO PICK ON US SMOKERS, AINNIT?!
I-- I ONLY JUST WORK HERE, SIR HONEST!
WELL I'M TIRED OF IT! TIRED, DO YOU HEAR ME??!
YES SIR! HONEST, I DO!
TH-THANK YOU, SIR! COME AGAIN?
WHEN I WANT A DAM' CIGARETTE, I'M GUNNA HAVE ONE, ANY DAM' TIME I FEEL LIKE IT!
HMPH!
I KNOW OTHERS MUST FEEL LIKE I DO!
I'M GUNNA FIND 'EM!
DEN WE GUNNA START A MOO'MENT THAT'S GUNNA SWEEP TH' COUNTRY!
BY GOD, ALL US SMOKERS GUNNA UNITE! YEAH-H! CIGAR- AND PIPE-SMOKERS, TOO! GUNNA START US A COUNTER-REVOLUTION!
HONEY, OM HOME!
SLAM!
YESSS! WE GUNNA TURN 'AT SMOKER-PERSECUTION AROUND AND START KICKIN' BUTT, JACKSON!
SMOKE POWER!
'AT'S WHAT WE'LL HAVE!
HA HA HA! I C'N SEE IT ALL NOW! ME AT THE PODIUM: SMOKERS, UNITE! LET'S GET IT ON, JACK! LIGHT 'EM IF YA'VE GOT 'EM! VIVA LA REVOLUTIO-
GRASS? WHO YOU TALKIN' TO?
HA? HI, HON.. I—
STOP ALLAT YELLIN' BEFORE THE NEIGHBORS COMPLAIN!
SUPPER'S READY. NOW PUT OUT THAT NASTY CIGARETTE AND LET'S EAT!
Y-YES, DEAR..
"REVOLUTION", INDEED! TH-THAT'S ALL, FOLKS..!

SEITU HAYDEN
b. 1953

Photographer unknown. *The Chicago Defender*, April 28, 1973.

Seitu Hayden's stories of family life are rooted in the large Black community in which he grew up in Fort Wayne, Indiana. Grass Green was an important mentor to Hayden beginning in junior high. Green encouraged Hayden to pursue cartooning and gave him his first job assisting him at *Frost Illustrated*. In the fall of 1971, Hayden moved to downtown Chicago to attend art school. Ensconced in a dorm building amongst other young artists, he sold his comic strip *Waliku* to *The Chicago Defender* just two months into his first semester.

With characters and urban legends based on Hayden's life, he conceived of *Waliku* as a more realistic and serious portrayal of Black life than what he regarded as the soft-focus version in Morrie Turner's *Wee Pals*. Hayden's drawings are closer to the cartoon realism of Spider-Man artist John Romita Sr. (a significant influence) than Turner. His figures have weight, and lived-in presence, and the spaces they inhabit are well observed. *Waliku* also reflected Hayden's growing interest in the Black cultural nationalism then popular among young people looking for a way forward after the civil rights movement. In the early 1970s Hayden also contributed to the underground comic books *Yellow Dog* and *Slow Death*, and briefly worked alongside Tom Floyd on the Blackman universe. *Waliku*, while startlingly prescient in subject matter and approach, was sometimes published out of order or with an incorrect title. It was also criticized within the *Defender* for its urban language and sometimes somber tone. The strip didn't find a larger following, and ended in 1975. In the ensuing years Hayden worked in advertising, collaborated on various projects with P-Funk artist Pedro Bell, and continued making comics, including the artwork for Marvel/Epic's *Tales from the Heart*. He continues to live and work in Chicago.

Waliku, The Chicago Defender, 1972–1975.

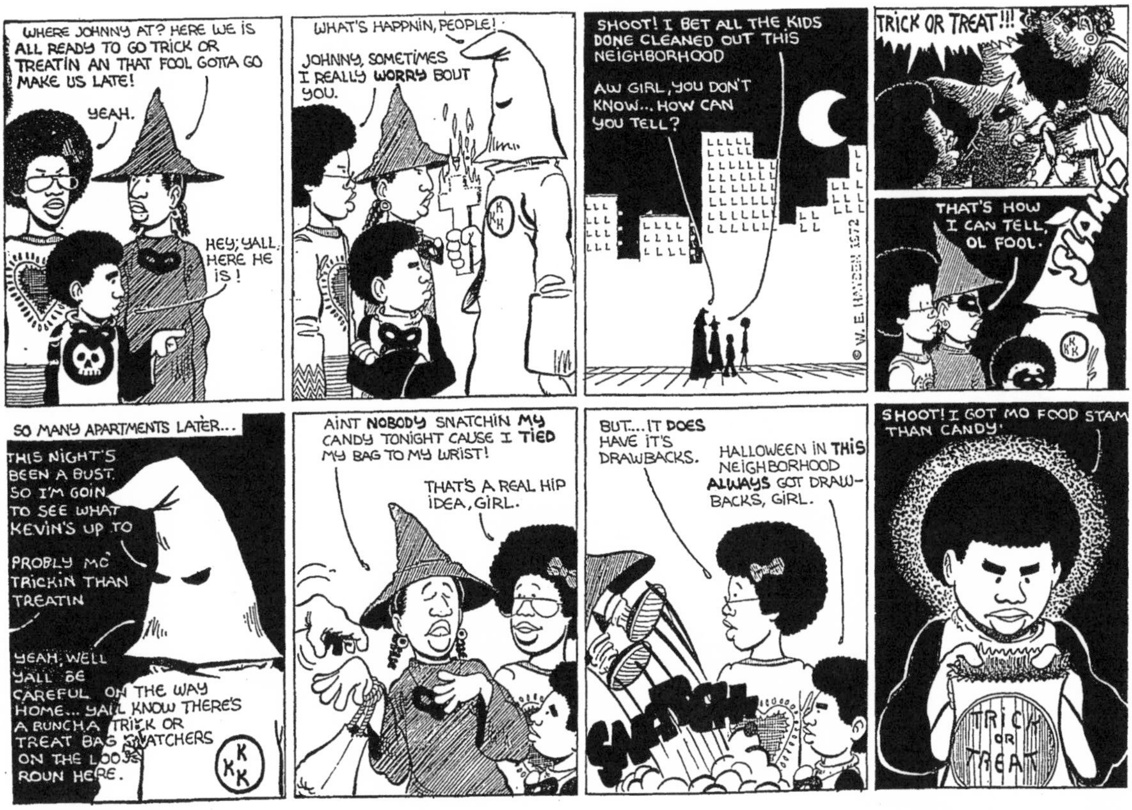
WHERE JOHNNY AT? HERE WE IS ALL READY TO GO TRICK OR TREATIN AN THAT FOOL GOTTA GO MAKE US LATE!
YEAH.
HEY; YALL, HERE HE IS!
WHAT'S HAPPNIN, PEOPLE!
JOHNNY, SOMETIMES I REALLY WORRY BOUT YOU.
SHOOT! I BET ALL THE KIDS DONE CLEANED OUT THIS NEIGHBORHOOD
AW GIRL, YOU DON'T KNOW... HOW CAN YOU TELL?
© W. E. HAYDEN 1972
TRICK OR TREAT!!!
SLAM
THAT'S HOW I CAN TELL, OL FOOL.
SO MANY APARTMENTS LATER...
THIS NIGHT'S BEEN A BUST. SO I'M GOIN TO SEE WHAT KEVIN'S UP TO
PROBLY MO TRICKIN THAN TREATIN
YEAH, WELL YALL BE CAREFUL ON THE WAY HOME... YALL KNOW THERE'S A BUNCHA TRICK OR TREAT BAG SNATCHERS ON THE LOOSE ROUN HERE.
AINT NOBODY SNATCHIN MY CANDY TONIGHT CAUSE I TIED MY BAG TO MY WRIST!
THAT'S A REAL HIP IDEA, GIRL.
BUT.... IT DOES HAVE IT'S DRAWBACKS.
HALLOWEEN IN THIS NEIGHBORHOOD ALWAYS GOT DRAW-BACKS, GIRL.
SHOOT! I GOT MO FOOD STAM THAN CANDY.
TRICK OR TREAT

November 11, 1972

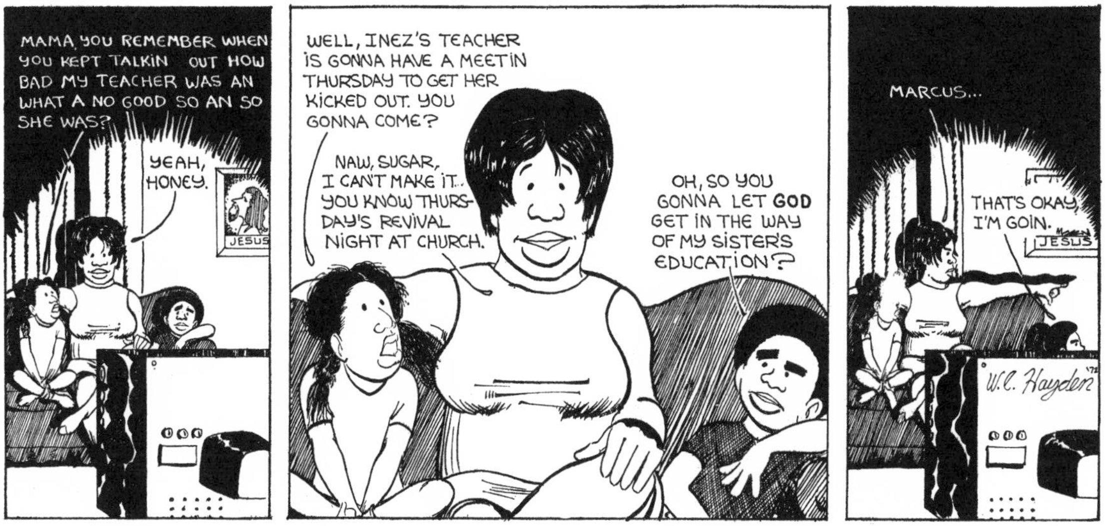
MAMA, YOU REMEMBER WHEN YOU KEPT TALKIN OUT HOW BAD MY TEACHER WAS AN WHAT A NO GOOD SO AN SO SHE WAS?
YEAH, HONEY.
JESUS
WELL, INEZ'S TEACHER IS GONNA HAVE A MEETIN THURSDAY TO GET HER KICKED OUT. YOU GONNA COME?
NAW, SUGAR, I CAN'T MAKE IT. YOU KNOW THURS-DAY'S REVIVAL NIGHT AT CHURCH.
OH, SO YOU GONNA LET GOD GET IN THE WAY OF MY SISTER'S EDUCATION?
MARCUS...
THAT'S OKAY, I'M GOIN.
JESUS
W.E. Hayden '72

1972

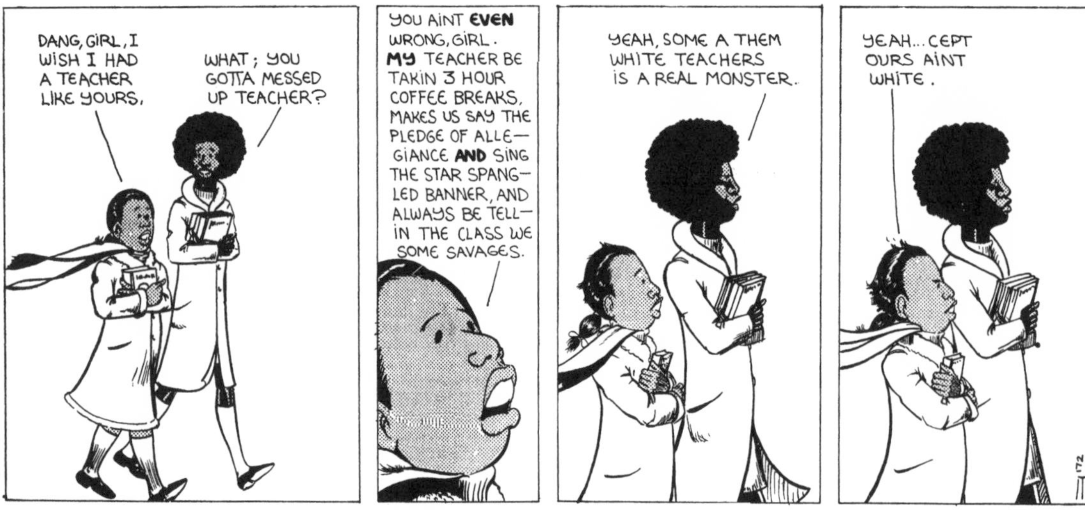
DANG, GIRL, I WISH I HAD A TEACHER LIKE YOURS,
WHAT; YOU GOTTA MESSED UP TEACHER?
YOU AINT **EVEN** WRONG, GIRL. **MY** TEACHER BE TAKIN 3 HOUR COFFEE BREAKS, MAKES US SAY THE PLEDGE OF ALLE— GIANCE **AND** SING THE STAR SPANG— LED BANNER, AND ALWAYS BE TELL— IN THE CLASS WE SOME SAVAGES.
YEAH, SOME A THEM WHITE TEACHERS IS A REAL MONSTER.
YEAH...CEPT OURS AINT WHITE.

1972

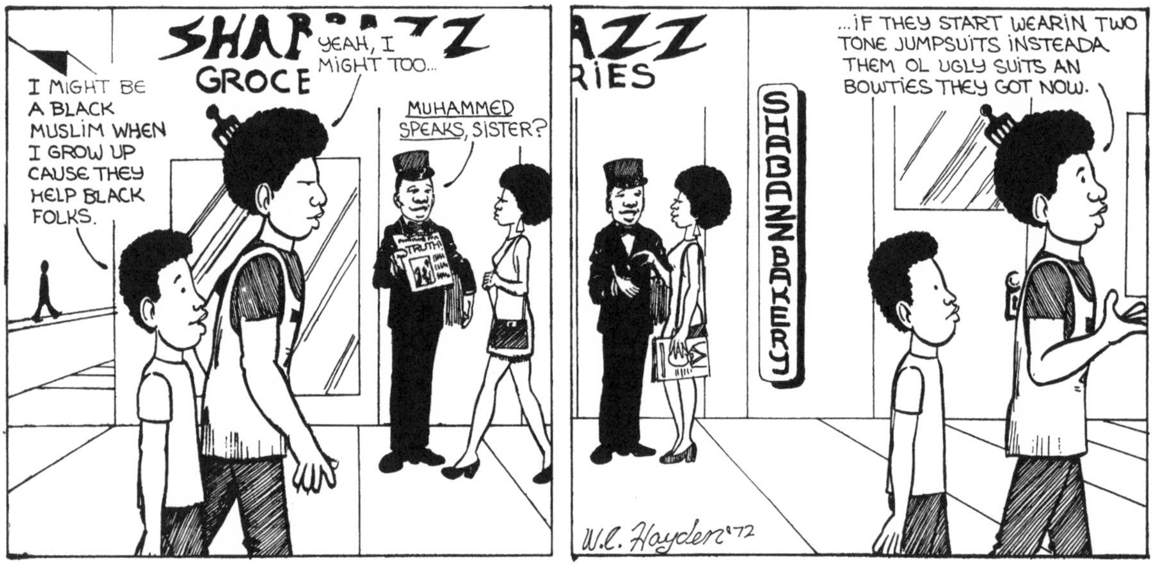
I MIGHT BE A BLACK MUSLIM WHEN I GROW UP CAUSE THEY HELP BLACK FOLKS.
YEAH, I MIGHT TOO...
MUHAMMED SPEAKS, SISTER?
TRUTH
...IF THEY START WEARIN TWO TONE JUMPSUITS INSTEADA THEM OL UGLY SUITS AN BOWTIES THEY GOT NOW.
SHABAZZ BAKERY
W.C. Hayden '72

1972

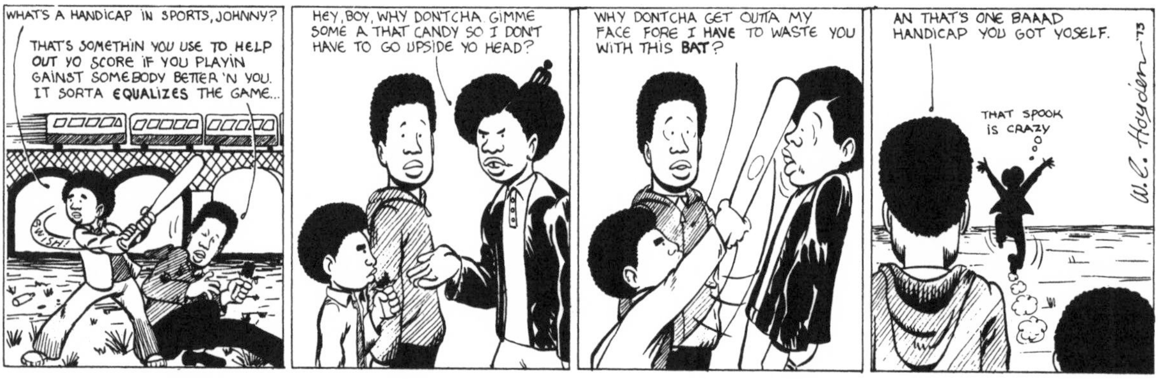
WHAT'S A HANDICAP IN SPORTS, JOHNNY?
THAT'S SOMETHIN YOU USE TO HELP OUT YO SCORE IF YOU PLAYIN GAINST SOMEBODY BETTER 'N YOU. IT SORTA **EQUALIZES** THE GAME...
SWISH!
HEY, BOY, WHY DONTCHA GIMME SOME A THAT CANDY SO I DON'T HAVE TO GO UPSIDE YO HEAD?
WHY DONTCHA GET OUTTA MY FACE FORE I HAVE TO WASTE YOU WITH THIS **BAT**?
AN THAT'S ONE BAAAD HANDICAP YOU GOT YOSELF.
THAT SPOOK IS CRAZY
W.C. Hayden '73

April 7, 1973

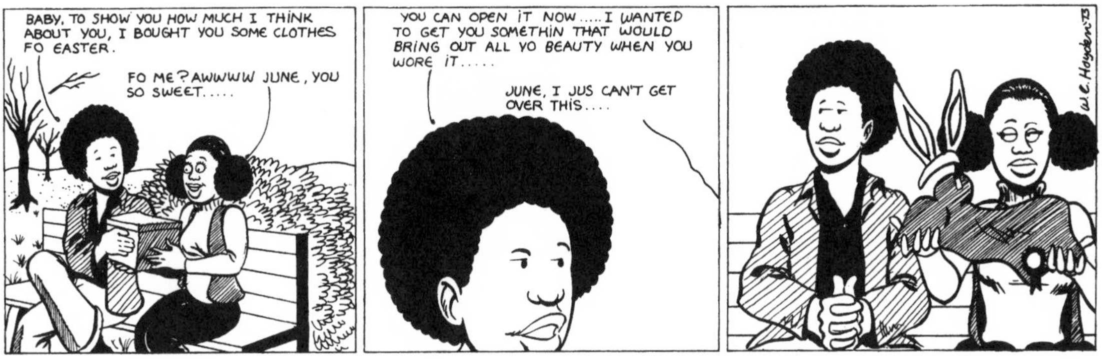
BABY, TO SHOW YOU HOW MUCH I THINK ABOUT YOU, I BOUGHT YOU SOME CLOTHES FO EASTER.
FO ME? AWWWW JUNE, YOU SO SWEET.....
YOU CAN OPEN IT NOW.....I WANTED TO GET YOU SOMETHIN THAT WOULD BRING OUT ALL YO BEAUTY WHEN YOU WORE IT.....
JUNE, I JUS CAN'T GET OVER THIS....
W.C. Hayden '73

April 14, 1973

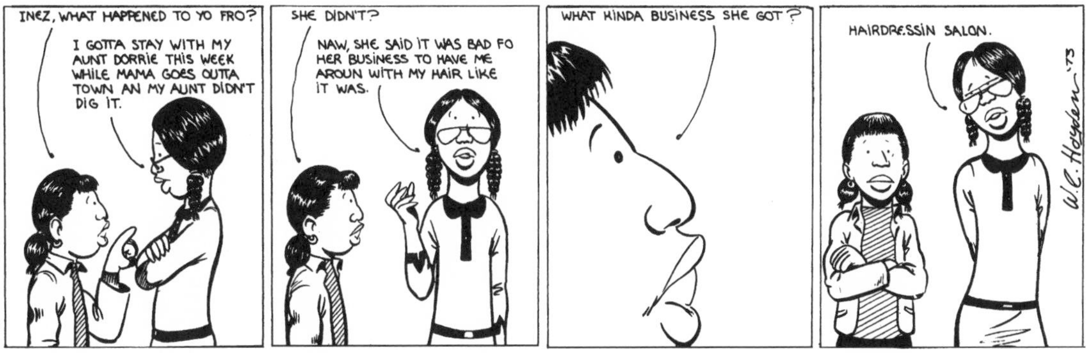
INEZ, WHAT HAPPENED TO YO FRO?
I GOTTA STAY WITH MY AUNT DORRIE THIS WEEK WHILE MAMA GOES OUTTA TOWN AN MY AUNT DIDN'T DIG IT.
SHE DIDN'T?
NAW, SHE SAID IT WAS BAD FO HER BUSINESS TO HAVE ME AROUN WITH MY HAIR LIKE IT WAS.
WHAT KINDA BUSINESS SHE GOT?
HAIRDRESSIN SALON.
W.C. Hayden '73

May 5, 1973

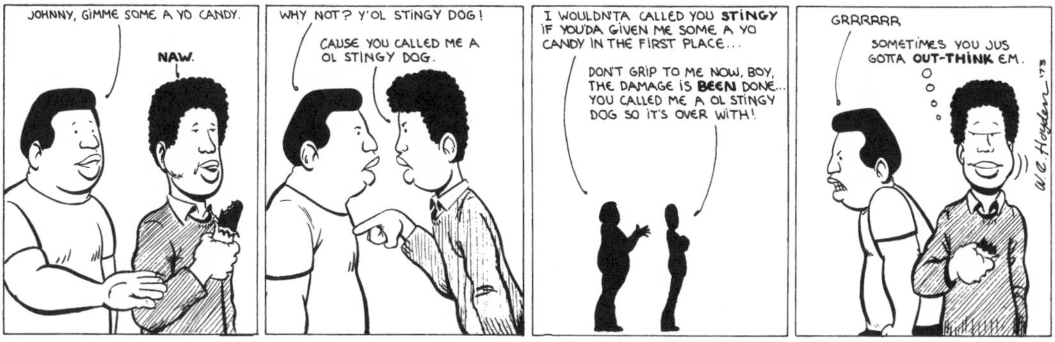
JOHNNY, GIMME SOME A YO CANDY.
NAW.
WHY NOT? Y'OL STINGY DOG!
CAUSE YOU CALLED ME A OL STINGY DOG.
I WOULDN'TA CALLED YOU STINGY IF YOU'DA GIVEN ME SOME A YO CANDY IN THE FIRST PLACE...
DON'T GRIP TO ME NOW, BOY, THE DAMAGE IS BEEN DONE... YOU CALLED ME A OL STINGY DOG SO IT'S OVER WITH!
GRRRRRR
SOMETIMES YOU JUS GOTTA OUT-THINK EM.
W.C. Hayden '73

May 12, 1973

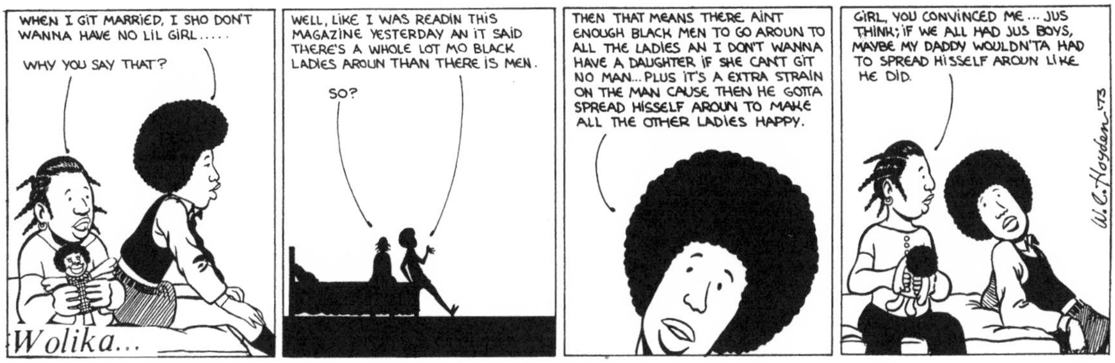
WHEN I GIT MARRIED, I SHO DON'T WANNA HAVE NO LIL GIRL.....
WHY YOU SAY THAT?
Wolika...
WELL, LIKE I WAS READIN THIS MAGAZINE YESTERDAY AN IT SAID THERE'S A WHOLE LOT MO BLACK LADIES AROUN THAN THERE IS MEN.
SO?
THEN THAT MEANS THERE AINT ENOUGH BLACK MEN TO GO AROUN TO ALL THE LADIES AN I DON'T WANNA HAVE A DAUGHTER IF SHE CAN'T GIT NO MAN... PLUS IT'S A EXTRA STRAIN ON THE MAN CAUSE THEN HE GOTTA SPREAD HISSELF AROUN TO MAKE ALL THE OTHER LADIES HAPPY.
GIRL, YOU CONVINCED ME... JUS THINK; IF WE ALL HAD JUS BOYS, MAYBE MY DADDY WOULDN'TA HAD TO SPREAD HISSELF AROUN LIKE HE DID.
W.C. Hayden '73

1973

October 6, 1973

October 13, 1973

October 27, 1973

November 17, 1973

November 12, 1973

November 24, 1973

1973

December 8, 1973

December 22, 1973

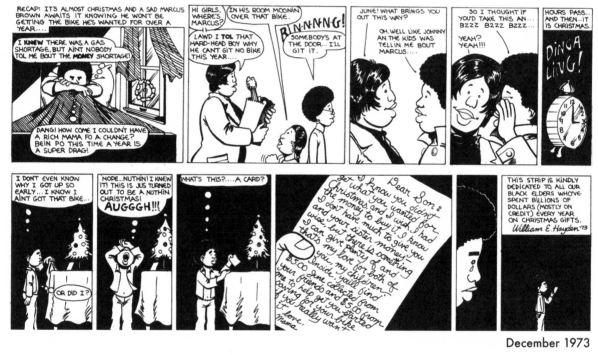

December 1973

January 19, 1974

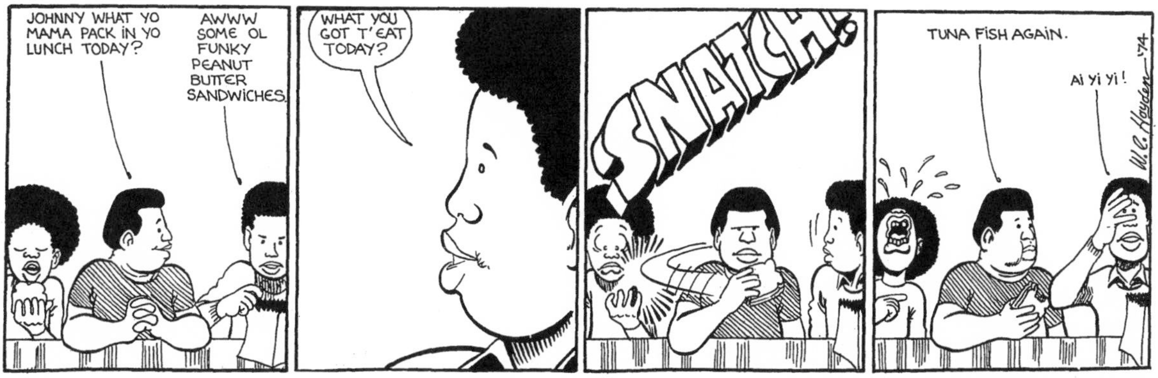
JOHNNY WHAT YO MAMA PACK IN YO LUNCH TODAY?
AWWW SOME OL FUNKY PEANUT BUTTER SANDWICHES.
WHAT YOU GOT T'EAT TODAY?
SNATCH!
TUNA FISH AGAIN.
Ai Yi Yi!
W.C. Hayden '74

January 26, 1974

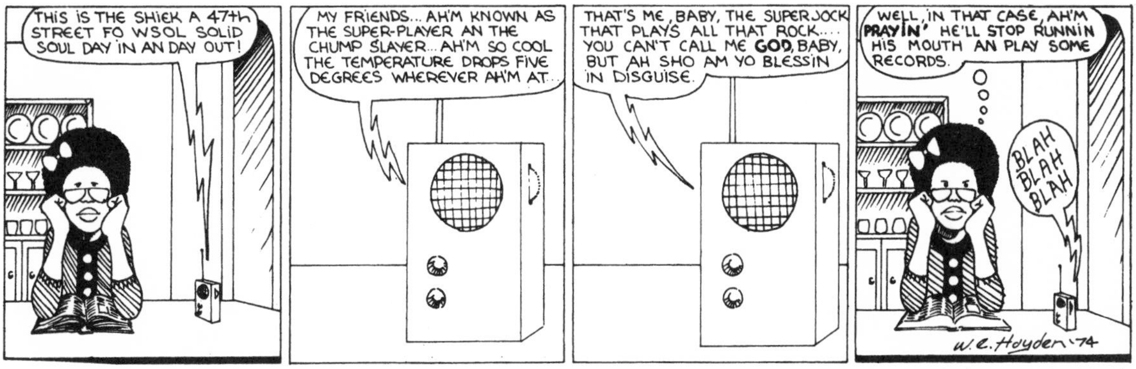
THIS IS THE SHIEK A 47th STREET FO WSOL SOLID SOUL DAY IN AN DAY OUT!
MY FRIENDS... AH'M KNOWN AS THE SUPER-PLAYER AN THE CHUMP SLAYER... AH'M SO COOL THE TEMPERATURE DROPS FIVE DEGREES WHEREVER AH'M AT...
THAT'S ME, BABY, THE SUPERJOCK THAT PLAYS ALL THAT ROCK.... YOU CAN'T CALL ME GOD, BABY, BUT AH SHO AM YO BLESSIN IN DISGUISE.
WELL, IN THAT CASE, AH'M PRAYIN' HE'LL STOP RUNNIN HIS MOUTH AN PLAY SOME RECORDS.
BLAH BLAH BLAH
W.C. Hayden '74

February 2, 1974

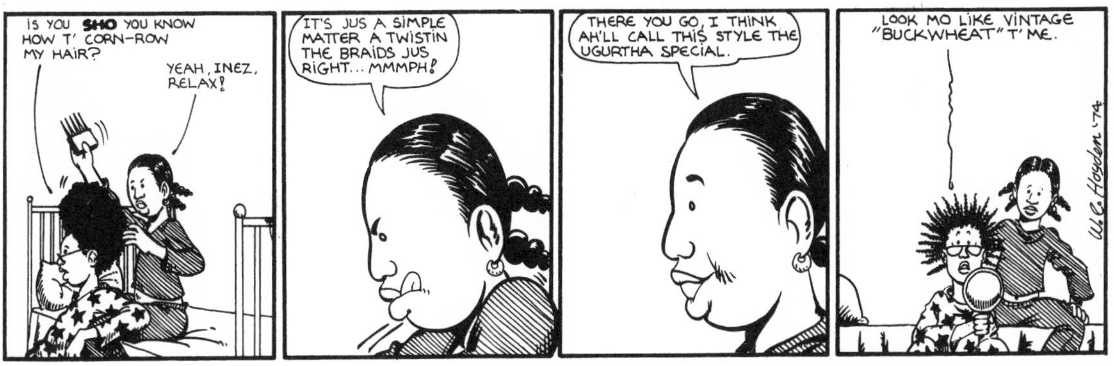
IS YOU SHO YOU KNOW HOW T' CORN-ROW MY HAIR?
YEAH, INEZ, RELAX!
IT'S JUS A SIMPLE MATTER A TWISTIN THE BRAIDS JUS RIGHT... MMMPH!
THERE YOU GO, I THINK AH'LL CALL THIS STYLE THE UGURTHA SPECIAL.
LOOK MO LIKE VINTAGE "BUCKWHEAT" T' ME.
W.C. Hayden '74

1974

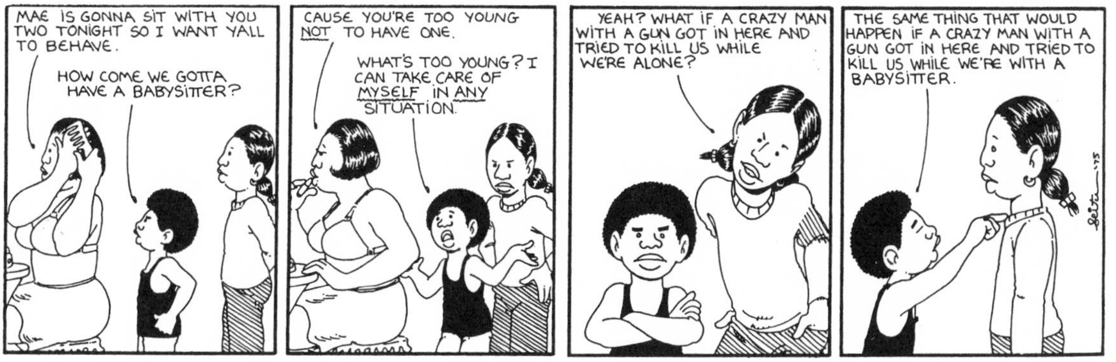
MAE IS GONNA SIT WITH YOU TWO TONIGHT SO I WANT YALL TO BEHAVE.
HOW COME WE GOTTA HAVE A BABYSITTER?
CAUSE YOU'RE TOO YOUNG NOT TO HAVE ONE.
WHAT'S TOO YOUNG? I CAN TAKE CARE OF MYSELF IN ANY SITUATION.
YEAH? WHAT IF A CRAZY MAN WITH A GUN GOT IN HERE AND TRIED TO KILL US WHILE WE'RE ALONE?
THE SAME THING THAT WOULD HAPPEN IF A CRAZY MAN WITH A GUN GOT IN HERE AND TRIED TO KILL US WHILE WE'RE WITH A BABYSITTER.

1975

JAY JACKSON
1908–1954

Photographer unknown. *The Chicago Defender*, June 5, 1954.

Born in Oberlin, Ohio, Jay Jackson was hammering railroad spikes near Columbus for ten hours a day at age thirteen, and soon after was working in a steel mill in Pittsburgh. After a year at Ohio Wesleyan University he became a sign painter, and in 1930 he moved to Chicago to be a poster artist and production director for a chain of movie theaters. In 1933 he began his cartooning career at the *Pittsburgh Courier*. Robert Sengstacke Abbott, founder of The *Chicago Defender*, brought him first to his illustrated magazine, *Abbott's Monthly*, and then to the newspaper itself in 1933, commissioning a strip that would address "the moral and ethical foibles of our people . . . an examination of the influences which have made it possible for malicious observers to label and libel us." This was *As Others See Us*, which took the form of lushly drawn observations of Black life in Chicago. In the following decade Jackson wrote and drew reams of comics, from the action strip *Speed Jaxon* to the romance *Tish Mingo*. In 1938 Jackson also began a five-year run of illustrations for Chicago-based science fiction pulps, including *Golden Fleece*, *Amazing*, and *Weird Tales*.

Created by Leslie Rogers in 1920, *Bungleton Green* ran in the *Defender* until 1968, making its protagonist the longest-running Black comic-strip character to date. Jackson's experience with science fiction may have fueled his narrative approach to the strip. He may also have been influenced by *Pittsburgh Courier* writer George Schuyler's 1931 satirical science-fiction novel *Black No More*, about Black people transforming into whites, and the serialized Black-independence story, *Black Empire*. He began his stories in 1936, gradually transforming it into an adventure serial about a group of kids called the Mystic Commandos. In 1943 the Mystic Commandos stumble across a plot by a German scientist to build a time machine. They are carried first back to 1778 and nearly executed as rebel slaves, and then travel one hundred years into the future, to 2044, where we find them in this excerpt. In 1947, *Bungleton Green* returned to its original format, with Jackson showing Bung awakening from a dream. Life and work continued for Jackson through the 1940s; he drew a *Bungleton Green* strip, a *Speed Jackson* strip, and two editorial cartoons every week, as well as advertisements for the Valmor line of Black cosmetics, and pinups for postcards and magazines. In the late 1940s Jackson and his family moved to Los Angeles. He took a staff cartoonist job at the *California Eagle* and continued freelancing until his sudden death in 1954. His final work for the *Defender* was *Home Folks*, which, like *As Others See Us*, was an observation-based strip. Though it only began the year of Jackson's death, he and his wife Eleanor produced enough installments that it ran until 1958.

Bungleton Green, The Chicago Defender, February 1944–November 1944.

BUNGLETON GREEN
AND THE
Mystic Commandos

BUD HAPPYHOLLOW, A MYSTIC COMMANDO, IS IN TWENTY FIRST CENTURY AMERICA WHERE COMPLETE EQUALITY REIGNS SUPREME! HOWEVER A NEW WORLD PEOPLED BY RUTHLESS GREEN MEN HAS ERUPTED FROM THE SEA! THE PRESIDENT OF THE U.S.A. SENT LOTTA, COLORED MAYOR OF MEMPHIS WITH A WHITE AND A YELLOW MAN TO TRAIN THEM IN THE WAYS OF PEACE, LOTTA TOOK BUD.

February 12, 1944

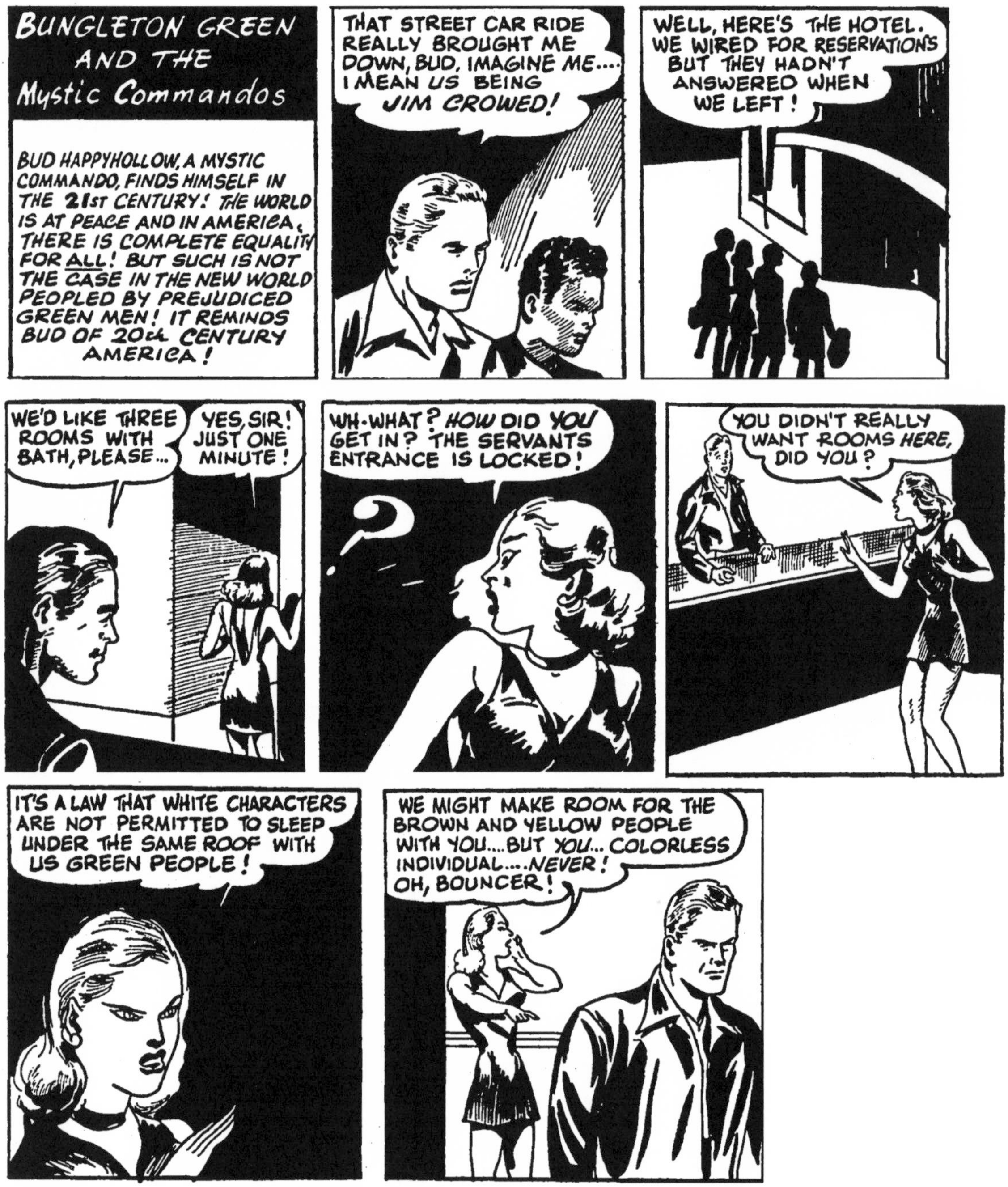
BUNGLETON GREEN AND THE Mystic Commandos
BUD HAPPYHOLLOW, A MYSTIC COMMANDO, FINDS HIMSELF IN THE 21ST CENTURY! THE WORLD IS AT PEACE AND IN AMERICA, THERE IS COMPLETE EQUALITY FOR ALL! BUT SUCH IS NOT THE CASE IN THE NEW WORLD PEOPLED BY PREJUDICED GREEN MEN! IT REMINDS BUD OF 20th CENTURY AMERICA!
THAT STREET CAR RIDE REALLY BROUGHT ME DOWN, BUD, IMAGINE ME.... I MEAN US BEING JIM CROWED!
WELL, HERE'S THE HOTEL. WE WIRED FOR RESERVATIONS BUT THEY HADN'T ANSWERED WHEN WE LEFT!
WE'D LIKE THREE ROOMS WITH BATH, PLEASE...
YES, SIR! JUST ONE MINUTE!
WH-WHAT? HOW DID YOU GET IN? THE SERVANTS ENTRANCE IS LOCKED!
?
YOU DIDN'T REALLY WANT ROOMS HERE, DID YOU?
IT'S A LAW THAT WHITE CHARACTERS ARE NOT PERMITTED TO SLEEP UNDER THE SAME ROOF WITH US GREEN PEOPLE!
WE MIGHT MAKE ROOM FOR THE BROWN AND YELLOW PEOPLE WITH YOU....BUT YOU... COLORLESS INDIVIDUAL....NEVER! OH, BOUNCER!

February 19, 1944

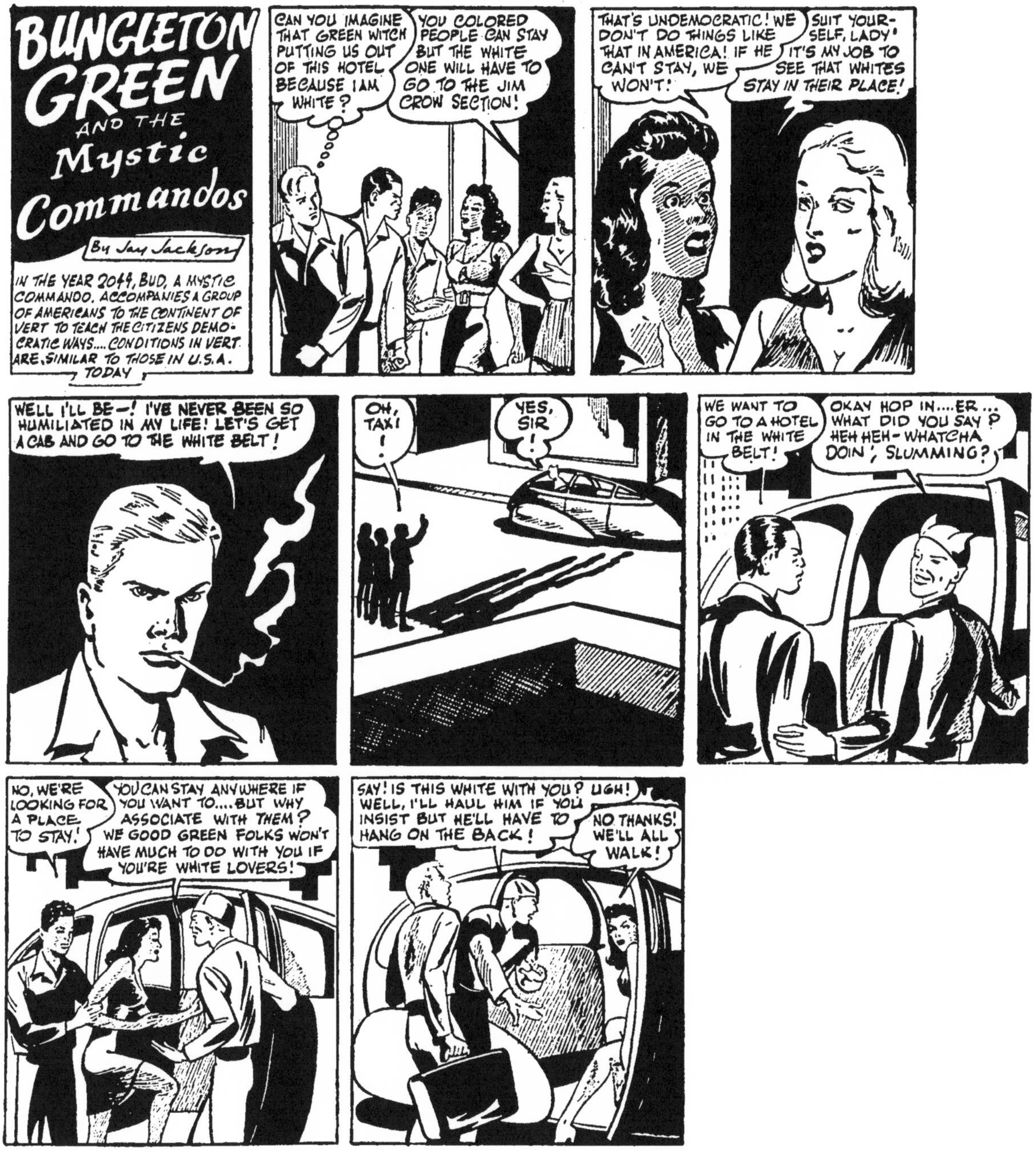
BUNGLETON GREEN AND THE Mystic Commandos
By Jay Jackson
IN THE YEAR 2044, BUD, A MYSTIC COMMANDO, ACCOMPANIES A GROUP OF AMERICANS TO THE CONTINENT OF VERT TO TEACH THE CITIZENS DEMOCRATIC WAYS.... CONDITIONS IN VERT ARE SIMILAR TO THOSE IN U.S.A. TODAY
CAN YOU IMAGINE THAT GREEN WITCH PUTTING US OUT OF THIS HOTEL BECAUSE I AM WHITE?
YOU COLORED PEOPLE CAN STAY BUT THE WHITE ONE WILL HAVE TO GO TO THE JIM CROW SECTION!
THAT'S UNDEMOCRATIC! WE DON'T DO THINGS LIKE THAT IN AMERICA! IF HE CAN'T STAY, WE WON'T!
SUIT YOURSELF, LADY! IT'S MY JOB TO SEE THAT WHITES STAY IN THEIR PLACE!
WELL I'LL BE—! I'VE NEVER BEEN SO HUMILIATED IN MY LIFE! LET'S GET A CAB AND GO TO THE WHITE BELT!
OH, TAXI!
YES, SIR!
WE WANT TO GO TO A HOTEL IN THE WHITE BELT!
OKAY HOP IN.... ER... WHAT DID YOU SAY? HEH HEH- WHATCHA DOIN', SLUMMING?
NO, WE'RE LOOKING FOR A PLACE TO STAY!
YOU CAN STAY ANYWHERE IF YOU WANT TO.... BUT WHY ASSOCIATE WITH THEM? WE GOOD GREEN FOLKS WON'T HAVE MUCH TO DO WITH YOU IF YOU'RE WHITE LOVERS!
SAY! IS THIS WHITE WITH YOU? UGH! WELL, I'LL HAUL HIM IF YOU INSIST BUT HE'LL HAVE TO HANG ON THE BACK!
NO THANKS! WE'LL ALL WALK!

February 26, 1944

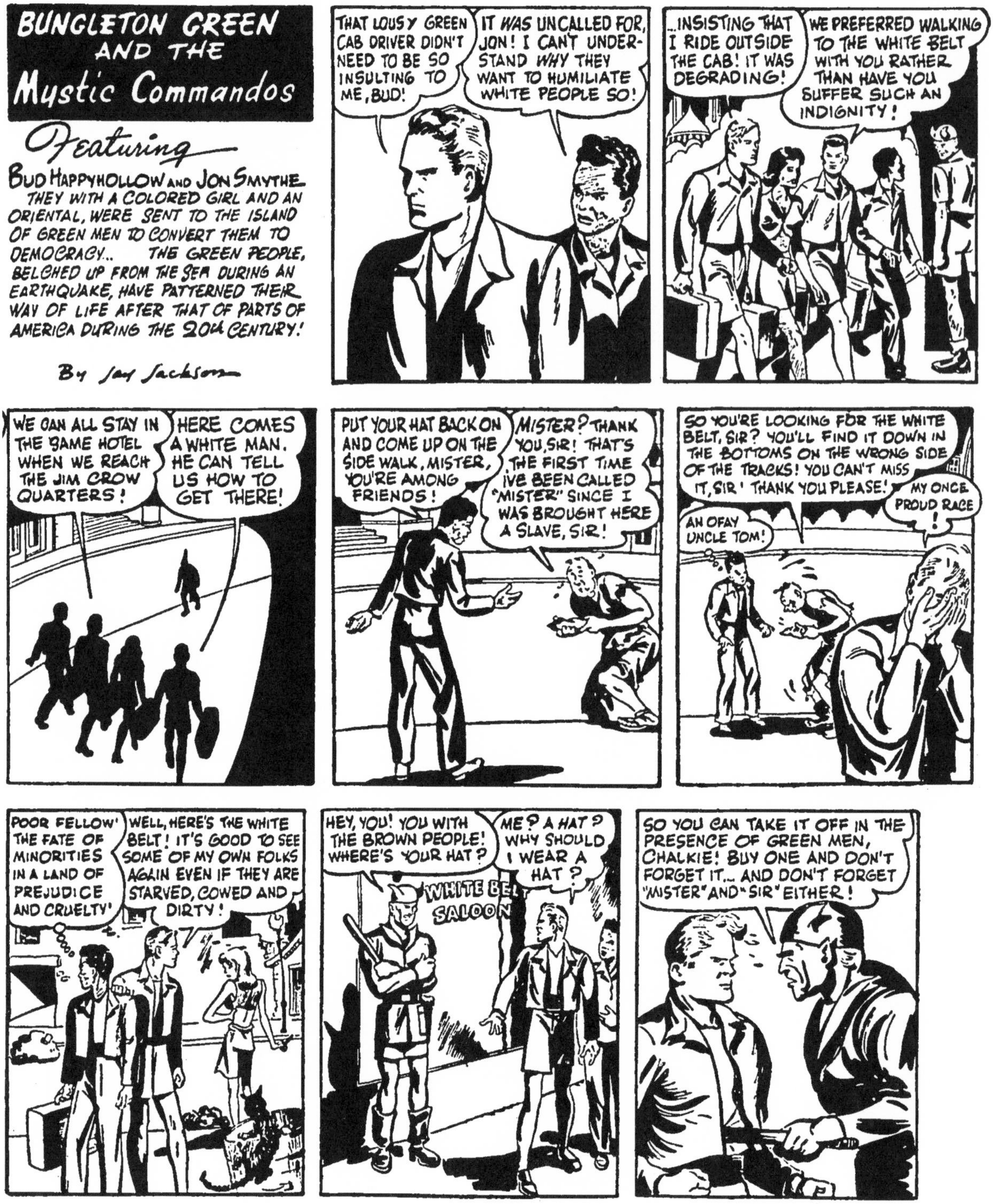

BUNGLETON GREEN AND THE Mystic Commandos
Featuring
BUD HAPPYHOLLOW AND JON SMYTHE THEY WITH A COLORED GIRL AND AN ORIENTAL, WERE SENT TO THE ISLAND OF GREEN MEN TO CONVERT THEM TO DEMOCRACY... THE GREEN PEOPLE, BELCHED UP FROM THE SEA DURING AN EARTHQUAKE, HAVE PATTERNED THEIR WAY OF LIFE AFTER THAT OF PARTS OF AMERICA DURING THE 20th CENTURY!
By Jay Jackson
THAT LOUSY GREEN CAB DRIVER DIDN'T NEED TO BE SO INSULTING TO ME, BUD!
IT WAS UNCALLED FOR, JON! I CAN'T UNDERSTAND WHY THEY WANT TO HUMILIATE WHITE PEOPLE SO!
...INSISTING THAT I RIDE OUTSIDE THE CAB! IT WAS DEGRADING!
WE PREFERRED WALKING TO THE WHITE BELT WITH YOU RATHER THAN HAVE YOU SUFFER SUCH AN INDIGNITY!
WE CAN ALL STAY IN THE SAME HOTEL WHEN WE REACH THE JIM CROW QUARTERS!
HERE COMES A WHITE MAN. HE CAN TELL US HOW TO GET THERE!
PUT YOUR HAT BACK ON AND COME UP ON THE SIDE WALK, MISTER, YOU'RE AMONG FRIENDS!
MISTER? THANK YOU, SIR! THAT'S THE FIRST TIME I'VE BEEN CALLED "MISTER" SINCE I WAS BROUGHT HERE A SLAVE, SIR!
SO YOU'RE LOOKING FOR THE WHITE BELT, SIR? YOU'LL FIND IT DOWN IN THE BOTTOMS ON THE WRONG SIDE OF THE TRACKS! YOU CAN'T MISS IT, SIR! THANK YOU PLEASE!
AN OFAY UNCLE TOM!
MY ONCE PROUD RACE!
POOR FELLOW! THE FATE OF MINORITIES IN A LAND OF PREJUDICE AND CRUELTY!
WELL, HERE'S THE WHITE BELT! IT'S GOOD TO SEE SOME OF MY OWN FOLKS AGAIN EVEN IF THEY ARE STARVED, COWED AND DIRTY!
HEY, YOU! YOU WITH THE BROWN PEOPLE! WHERE'S YOUR HAT?
ME? A HAT? WHY SHOULD I WEAR A HAT?
WHITE BEL
SALOON
SO YOU CAN TAKE IT OFF IN THE PRESENCE OF GREEN MEN, CHALKIE! BUY ONE AND DON'T FORGET IT... AND DON'T FORGET "MISTER" AND "SIR" EITHER!

March 4, 1944

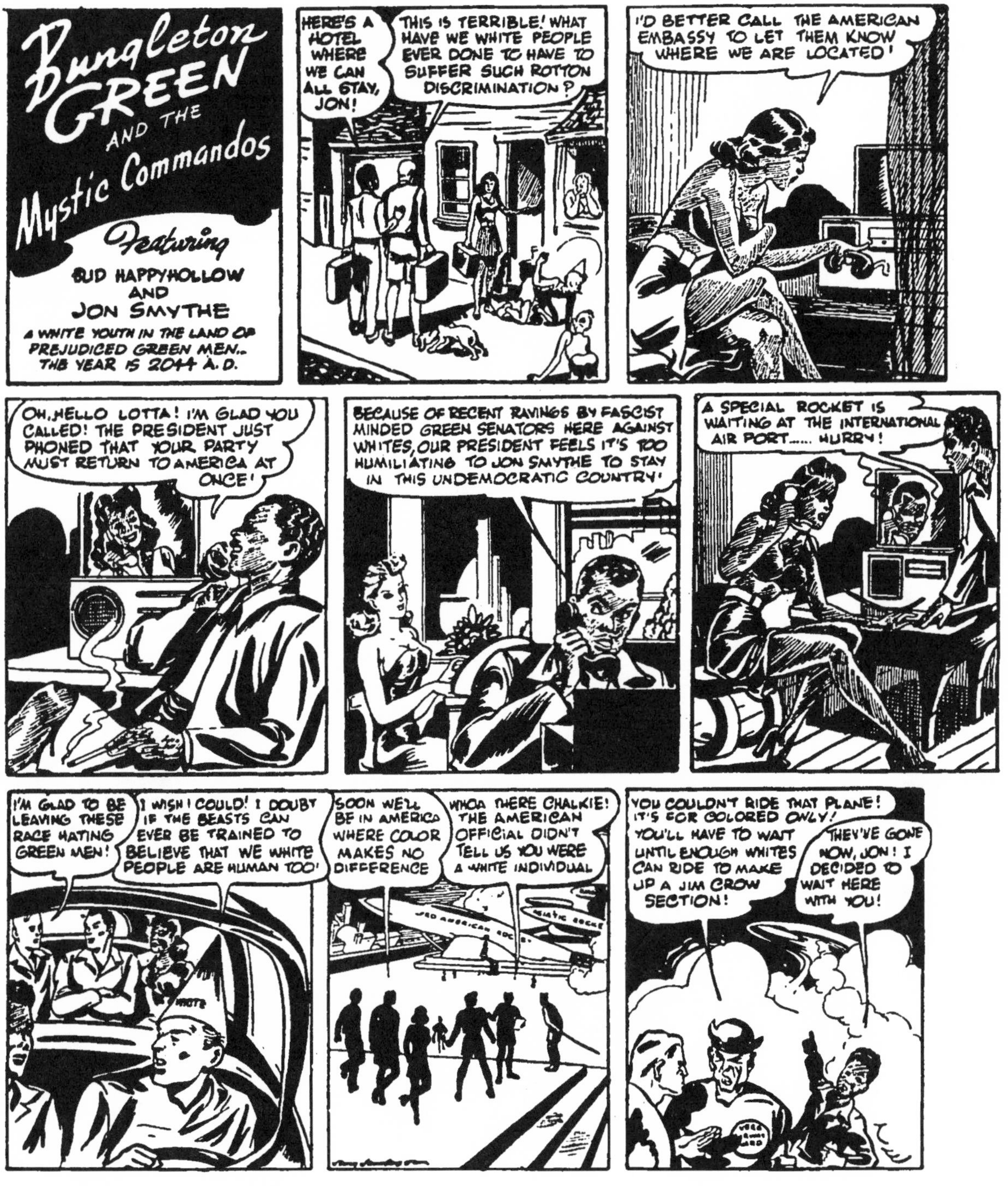
Bungleton GREEN AND THE Mystic Commandos
Featuring
BUD HAPPYHOLLOW AND JON SMYTHE
A WHITE YOUTH IN THE LAND OF PREJUDICED GREEN MEN.. THE YEAR IS 2044 A.D.
HERE'S A HOTEL WHERE WE CAN ALL STAY, JON!
THIS IS TERRIBLE! WHAT HAVE WE WHITE PEOPLE EVER DONE TO HAVE TO SUFFER SUCH ROTTON DISCRIMINATION?
I'D BETTER CALL THE AMERICAN EMBASSY TO LET THEM KNOW WHERE WE ARE LOCATED!
OH, HELLO LOTTA! I'M GLAD YOU CALLED! THE PRESIDENT JUST PHONED THAT YOUR PARTY MUST RETURN TO AMERICA AT ONCE!
BECAUSE OF RECENT RAVINGS BY FASCIST MINDED GREEN SENATORS HERE AGAINST WHITES, OUR PRESIDENT FEELS IT'S TOO HUMILIATING TO JON SMYTHE TO STAY IN THIS UNDEMOCRATIC COUNTRY!
A SPECIAL ROCKET IS WAITING AT THE INTERNATIONAL AIR PORT...... HURRY!
I'M GLAD TO BE LEAVING THESE RACE HATING GREEN MEN!
I WISH I COULD! I DOUBT IF THE BEASTS CAN EVER BE TRAINED TO BELIEVE THAT WE WHITE PEOPLE ARE HUMAN TOO!
WHITE
SOON WE'LL BE IN AMERICA WHERE COLOR MAKES NO DIFFERENCE
WHOA THERE CHALKIE! THE AMERICAN OFFICIAL DIDN'T TELL US YOU WERE A WHITE INDIVIDUAL
YOU COULDN'T RIDE THAT PLANE! IT'S FOR COLORED ONLY! YOU'LL HAVE TO WAIT UNTIL ENOUGH WHITES CAN RIDE TO MAKE UP A JIM CROW SECTION!
THEY'VE GONE NOW, JON! I DECIDED TO WAIT HERE WITH YOU!

March 11, 1944

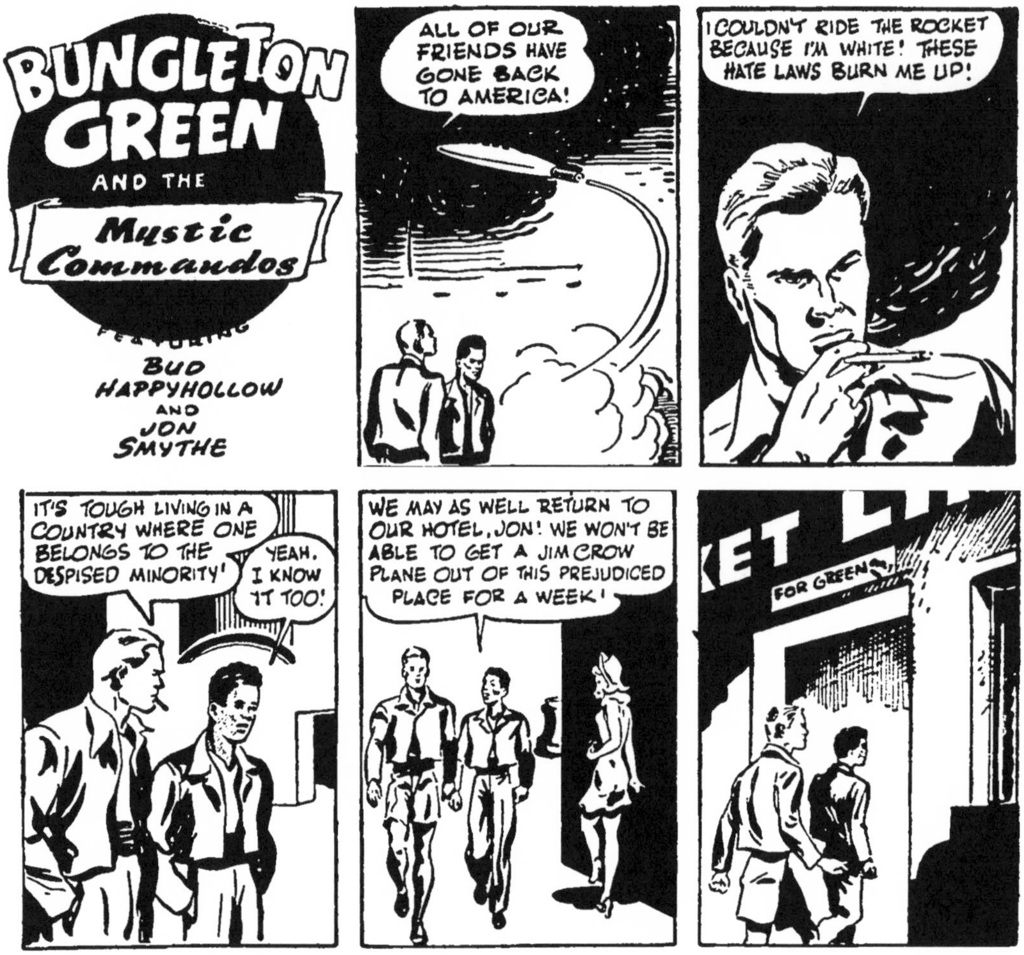
BUNGLETON GREEN
AND THE
Mystic Commandos
FEATURING
BUD HAPPYHOLLOW AND JON SMYTHE
ALL OF OUR FRIENDS HAVE GONE BACK TO AMERICA!
I COULDN'T RIDE THE ROCKET BECAUSE I'M WHITE! THESE HATE LAWS BURN ME UP!
IT'S TOUGH LIVING IN A COUNTRY WHERE ONE BELONGS TO THE DESPISED MINORITY!
YEAH. I KNOW IT TOO!
WE MAY AS WELL RETURN TO OUR HOTEL, JON! WE WON'T BE ABLE TO GET A JIM CROW PLANE OUT OF THIS PREJUDICED PLACE FOR A WEEK!
KET
FOR GREEN

March 18, 1944

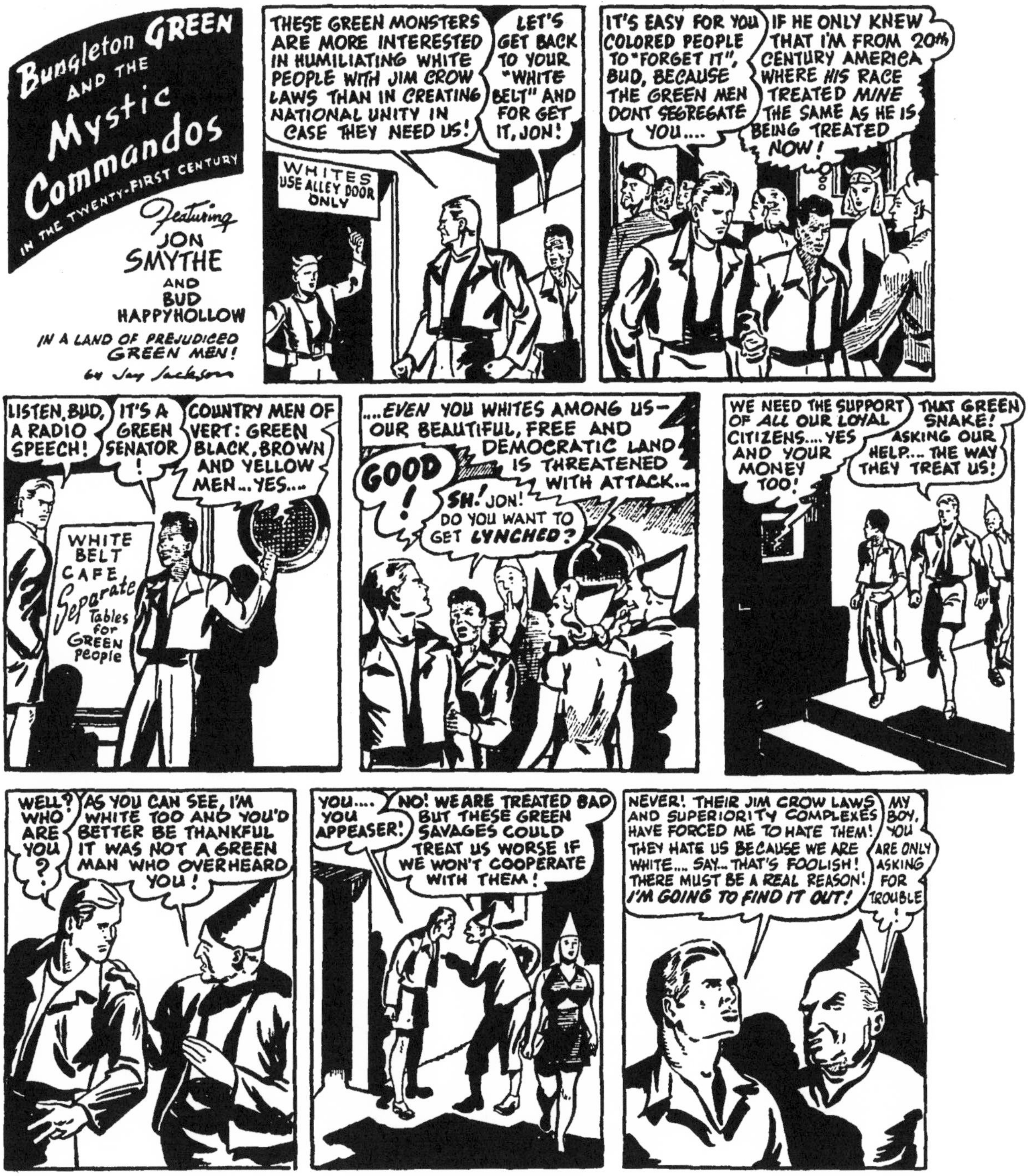

Bungleton GREEN AND THE Mystic Commandos
IN THE TWENTY-FIRST CENTURY
Featuring JON SMYTHE AND BUD HAPPYHOLLOW
IN A LAND OF PREJUDICED GREEN MEN!
by Jay Jackson
THESE GREEN MONSTERS ARE MORE INTERESTED IN HUMILIATING WHITE PEOPLE WITH JIM CROW LAWS THAN IN CREATING NATIONAL UNITY IN CASE THEY NEED US!
LET'S GET BACK TO YOUR "WHITE BELT" AND FOR GET IT, JON!
WHITES USE ALLEY DOOR ONLY
IT'S EASY FOR YOU COLORED PEOPLE TO "FORGET IT", BUD, BECAUSE THE GREEN MEN DONT SEGREGATE YOU....
IF HE ONLY KNEW THAT I'M FROM 20th CENTURY AMERICA WHERE HIS RACE TREATED MINE THE SAME AS HE IS BEING TREATED NOW!
LISTEN, BUD, A RADIO SPEECH!
IT'S A GREEN SENATOR!
COUNTRY MEN OF VERT: GREEN BLACK, BROWN AND YELLOW MEN...YES....
WHITE BELT CAFE Separate Tables for GREEN People
....EVEN YOU WHITES AMONG US—OUR BEAUTIFUL, FREE AND DEMOCRATIC LAND IS THREATENED WITH ATTACK...
GOOD!
SH! JON! DO YOU WANT TO GET LYNCHED?
WE NEED THE SUPPORT OF ALL OUR LOYAL CITIZENS....YES AND YOUR MONEY TOO!
THAT GREEN SNAKE! ASKING OUR HELP... THE WAY THEY TREAT US!
WELL? WHO ARE YOU?
AS YOU CAN SEE, I'M WHITE TOO AND YOU'D BETTER BE THANKFUL IT WAS NOT A GREEN MAN WHO OVERHEARD YOU!
YOU.... YOU APPEASER!
NO! WE ARE TREATED BAD BUT THESE GREEN SAVAGES COULD TREAT US WORSE IF WE WON'T COOPERATE WITH THEM!
NEVER! THEIR JIM CROW LAWS AND SUPERIORITY COMPLEXES HAVE FORCED ME TO HATE THEM! THEY HATE US BECAUSE WE ARE WHITE.... SAY... THAT'S FOOLISH! THERE MUST BE A REAL REASON! I'M GOING TO FIND IT OUT!
MY BOY, YOU ARE ONLY ASKING FOR TROUBLE!

March 25, 1944

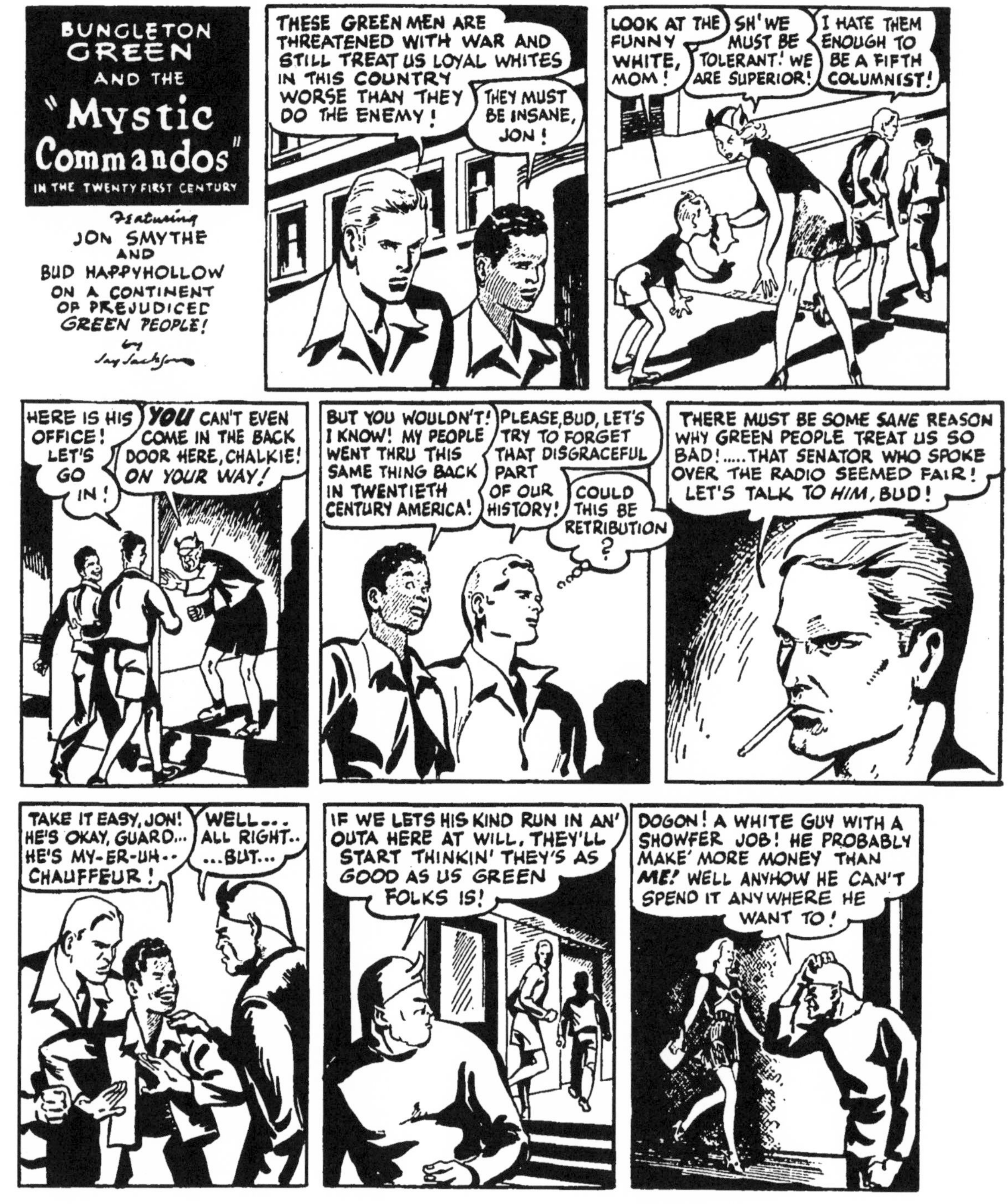
BUNGLETON GREEN AND THE "Mystic Commandos"
IN THE TWENTY FIRST CENTURY
Featuring JON SMYTHE AND BUD HAPPYHOLLOW ON A CONTINENT OF PREJUDICED GREEN PEOPLE!
by Jay Jackson
THESE GREEN MEN ARE THREATENED WITH WAR AND STILL TREAT US LOYAL WHITES IN THIS COUNTRY WORSE THAN THEY DO THE ENEMY!
THEY MUST BE INSANE, JON!
LOOK AT THE FUNNY WHITE, MOM!
SH' WE MUST BE TOLERANT! WE ARE SUPERIOR!
I HATE THEM ENOUGH TO BE A FIFTH COLUMNIST!
HERE IS HIS OFFICE! LET'S GO IN!
YOU CAN'T EVEN COME IN THE BACK DOOR HERE, CHALKIE! ON YOUR WAY!
BUT YOU WOULDN'T! I KNOW! MY PEOPLE WENT THRU THIS SAME THING BACK IN TWENTIETH CENTURY AMERICA!
PLEASE, BUD, LET'S TRY TO FORGET THAT DISGRACEFUL PART OF OUR HISTORY!
COULD THIS BE RETRIBUTION ?
THERE MUST BE SOME SANE REASON WHY GREEN PEOPLE TREAT US SO BAD!..... THAT SENATOR WHO SPOKE OVER THE RADIO SEEMED FAIR! LET'S TALK TO HIM, BUD!
TAKE IT EASY, JON! HE'S OKAY, GUARD... HE'S MY-ER-UH.. CHAUFFEUR!
WELL... ALL RIGHT.. ...BUT...
IF WE LETS HIS KIND RUN IN AN' OUTA HERE AT WILL, THEY'LL START THINKIN' THEY'S AS GOOD AS US GREEN FOLKS IS!
DOGON! A WHITE GUY WITH A SHOWFER JOB! HE PROBABLY MAKE' MORE MONEY THAN ME! WELL ANYHOW HE CAN'T SPEND IT ANYWHERE HE WANT TO!

April 1, 1944

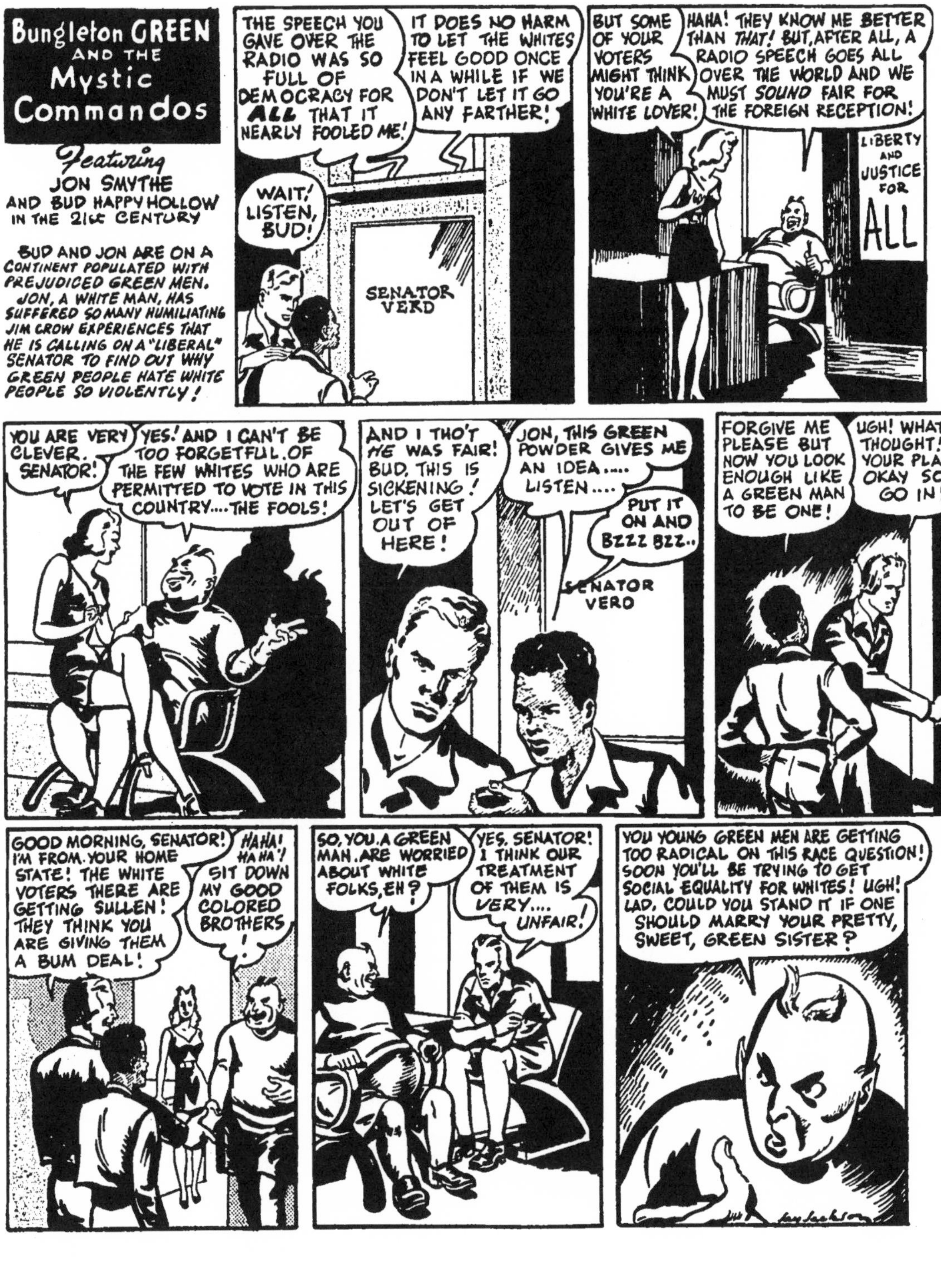
Bungleton GREEN AND THE Mystic Commandos
Featuring JON SMYTHE AND BUD HAPPY HOLLOW IN THE 21st CENTURY
BUD AND JON ARE ON A CONTINENT POPULATED WITH PREJUDICED GREEN MEN. JON, A WHITE MAN, HAS SUFFERED SO MANY HUMILIATING JIM CROW EXPERIENCES THAT HE IS CALLING ON A "LIBERAL" SENATOR TO FIND OUT WHY GREEN PEOPLE HATE WHITE PEOPLE SO VIOLENTLY!
THE SPEECH YOU GAVE OVER THE RADIO WAS SO FULL OF DEMOCRACY FOR ALL THAT IT NEARLY FOOLED ME!
IT DOES NO HARM TO LET THE WHITES FEEL GOOD ONCE IN A WHILE IF WE DON'T LET IT GO ANY FARTHER!
WAIT! LISTEN, BUD!
SENATOR VERD
BUT SOME OF YOUR VOTERS MIGHT THINK YOU'RE A WHITE LOVER!
HAHA! THEY KNOW ME BETTER THAN THAT! BUT, AFTER ALL, A RADIO SPEECH GOES ALL OVER THE WORLD AND WE MUST SOUND FAIR FOR THE FOREIGN RECEPTION!
LIBERTY AND JUSTICE FOR ALL
YOU ARE VERY CLEVER, SENATOR!
YES! AND I CAN'T BE TOO FORGETFUL OF THE FEW WHITES WHO ARE PERMITTED TO VOTE IN THIS COUNTRY.... THE FOOLS!
AND I THO'T HE WAS FAIR! BUD, THIS IS SICKENING! LET'S GET OUT OF HERE!
JON, THIS GREEN POWDER GIVES ME AN IDEA..... LISTEN....
PUT IT ON AND BZZZ BZZ..
SENATOR VERD
FORGIVE ME PLEASE BUT NOW YOU LOOK ENOUGH LIKE A GREEN MAN TO BE ONE!
UGH! WHAT A THOUGHT! BUT YOUR PLAN SEEMS OKAY SO LET'S GO IN!
GOOD MORNING, SENATOR! I'M FROM YOUR HOME STATE! THE WHITE VOTERS THERE ARE GETTING SULLEN! THEY THINK YOU ARE GIVING THEM A BUM DEAL!
HAHA! HAHA! SIT DOWN MY GOOD COLORED BROTHERS!
SO, YOU, A GREEN MAN, ARE WORRIED ABOUT WHITE FOLKS, EH?
YES, SENATOR! I THINK OUR TREATMENT OF THEM IS VERY.... UNFAIR!
YOU YOUNG GREEN MEN ARE GETTING TOO RADICAL ON THIS RACE QUESTION! SOON YOU'LL BE TRYING TO GET SOCIAL EQUALITY FOR WHITES! UGH! LAD, COULD YOU STAND IT IF ONE SHOULD MARRY YOUR PRETTY, SWEET, GREEN SISTER?
Jay Jackson

April 8, 1944

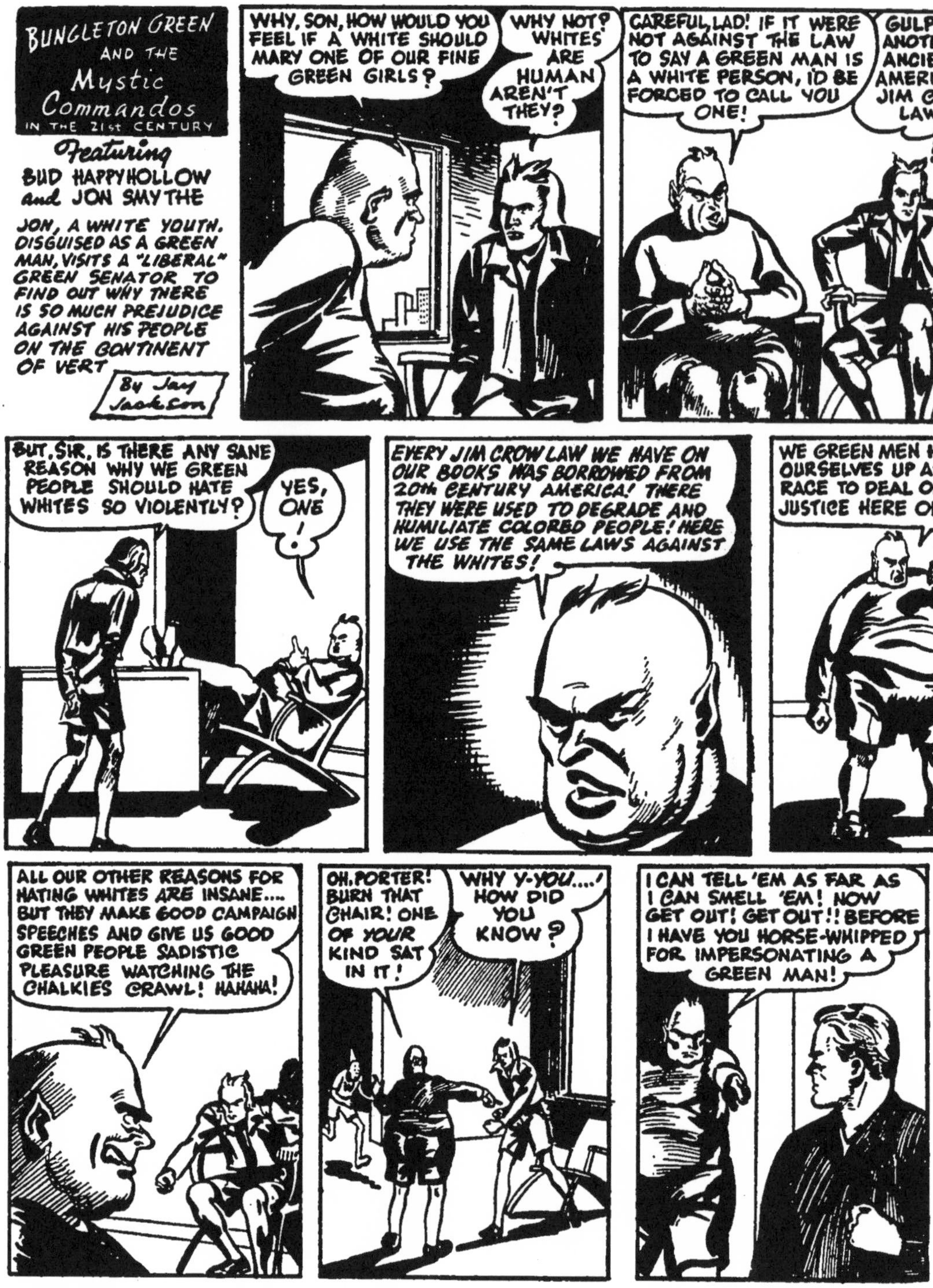
BUNGLETON GREEN AND THE Mystic Commandos IN THE 21st CENTURY
Featuring BUD HAPPYHOLLOW and JON SMYTHE
JON, A WHITE YOUTH, DISGUISED AS A GREEN MAN, VISITS A "LIBERAL" GREEN SENATOR TO FIND OUT WHY THERE IS SO MUCH PREJUDICE AGAINST HIS PEOPLE ON THE CONTINENT OF VERT
By Jay Jackson
WHY, SON, HOW WOULD YOU FEEL IF A WHITE SHOULD MARY ONE OF OUR FINE GREEN GIRLS?
WHY NOT? WHITES ARE HUMAN AREN'T THEY?
CAREFUL, LAD! IF IT WERE NOT AGAINST THE LAW TO SAY A GREEN MAN IS A WHITE PERSON, I'D BE FORCED TO CALL YOU ONE!
GULP! ANOTHER ANCIENT AMERICAN JIM CROW LAW!
BUT, SIR, IS THERE ANY SANE REASON WHY WE GREEN PEOPLE SHOULD HATE WHITES SO VIOLENTLY?
YES, ONE!
EVERY JIM CROW LAW WE HAVE ON OUR BOOKS WAS BORROWED FROM 20th CENTURY AMERICA! THERE THEY WERE USED TO DEGRADE AND HUMILIATE COLORED PEOPLE! HERE WE USE THE SAME LAWS AGAINST THE WHITES!
WE GREEN MEN HAVE SET OURSELVES UP AS A MASTER RACE TO DEAL OUT BELATED JUSTICE HERE ON EARTH!
ALL OUR OTHER REASONS FOR HATING WHITES ARE INSANE.... BUT THEY MAKE GOOD CAMPAIGN SPEECHES AND GIVE US GOOD GREEN PEOPLE SADISTIC PLEASURE WATCHING THE CHALKIES CRAWL! HAHAHA!
OH, PORTER! BURN THAT CHAIR! ONE OF YOUR KIND SAT IN IT!
WHY Y-YOU....! HOW DID YOU KNOW?
I CAN TELL 'EM AS FAR AS I CAN SMELL 'EM! NOW GET OUT! GET OUT!! BEFORE I HAVE YOU HORSE-WHIPPED FOR IMPERSONATING A GREEN MAN!

April 15, 1944

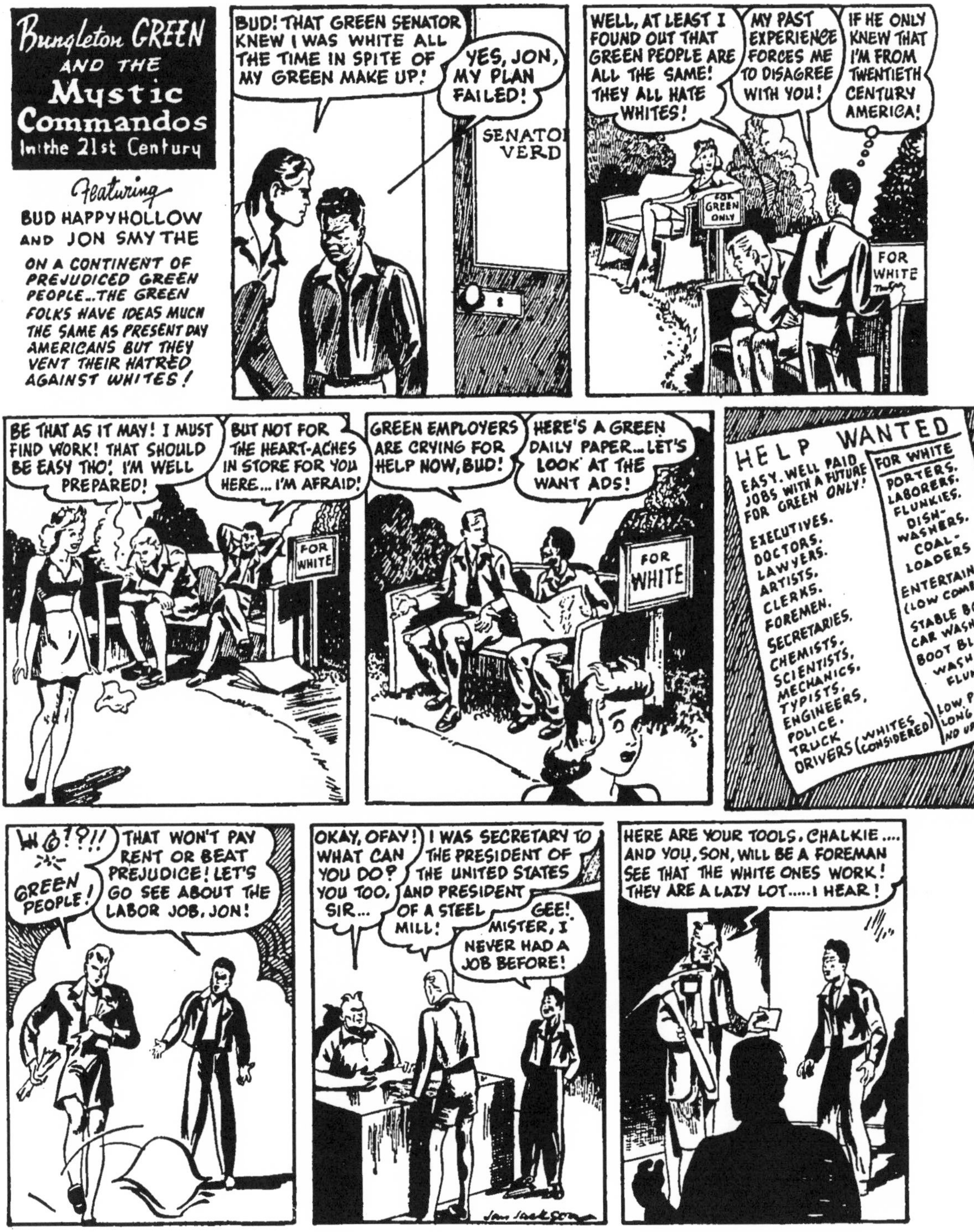
Bungleton GREEN AND THE Mystic Commandos In the 21st Century
Featuring BUD HAPPYHOLLOW AND JON SMYTHE
ON A CONTINENT OF PREJUDICED GREEN PEOPLE..THE GREEN FOLKS HAVE IDEAS MUCH THE SAME AS PRESENT DAY AMERICANS BUT THEY VENT THEIR HATRED AGAINST WHITES!
BUD! THAT GREEN SENATOR KNEW I WAS WHITE ALL THE TIME IN SPITE OF MY GREEN MAKE UP!
YES, JON, MY PLAN FAILED!
SENATO VERD
WELL, AT LEAST I FOUND OUT THAT GREEN PEOPLE ARE ALL THE SAME! THEY ALL HATE WHITES!
MY PAST EXPERIENCE FORCES ME TO DISAGREE WITH YOU!
IF HE ONLY KNEW THAT I'M FROM TWENTIETH CENTURY AMERICA!
FOR GREEN ONLY
FOR WHITE
BE THAT AS IT MAY! I MUST FIND WORK! THAT SHOULD BE EASY THO'! I'M WELL PREPARED!
BUT NOT FOR THE HEART-ACHES IN STORE FOR YOU HERE... I'M AFRAID!
FOR WHITE
GREEN EMPLOYERS ARE CRYING FOR HELP NOW, BUD!
HERE'S A GREEN DAILY PAPER... LET'S LOOK AT THE WANT ADS!
FOR WHITE
HELP WANTED
EASY. WELL PAID JOBS WITH A FUTURE FOR GREEN ONLY!
EXECUTIVES. DOCTORS. LAWYERS. ARTISTS. CLERKS. FOREMEN. SECRETARIES. CHEMISTS. SCIENTISTS. MECHANICS. TYPISTS. ENGINEERS. POLICE. TRUCK DRIVERS (WHITES CONSIDERED)
FOR WHITE
PORTERS. LABORERS. FLUNKIES. DISH-WASHERS. COAL-LOADERS
ENTERTAINER (LOW COMEDY)
STABLE BOY. CAR WASHER. BOOT BLACK. WASH ROOM FLUNKIE.
LOW PAY AN LONG HOUR ND UP-GRAD
W@!?!! GREEN PEOPLE!
THAT WON'T PAY RENT OR BEAT PREJUDICE! LET'S GO SEE ABOUT THE LABOR JOB, JON!
OKAY, OFAY! WHAT CAN YOU DO? YOU TOO, SIR...
I WAS SECRETARY TO THE PRESIDENT OF THE UNITED STATES AND PRESIDENT OF A STEEL MILL!
GEE! MISTER, I NEVER HAD A JOB BEFORE!
HERE ARE YOUR TOOLS, CHALKIE.... AND YOU, SON, WILL BE A FOREMAN SEE THAT THE WHITE ONES WORK! THEY ARE A LAZY LOT.....I HEAR!

April 22, 1944

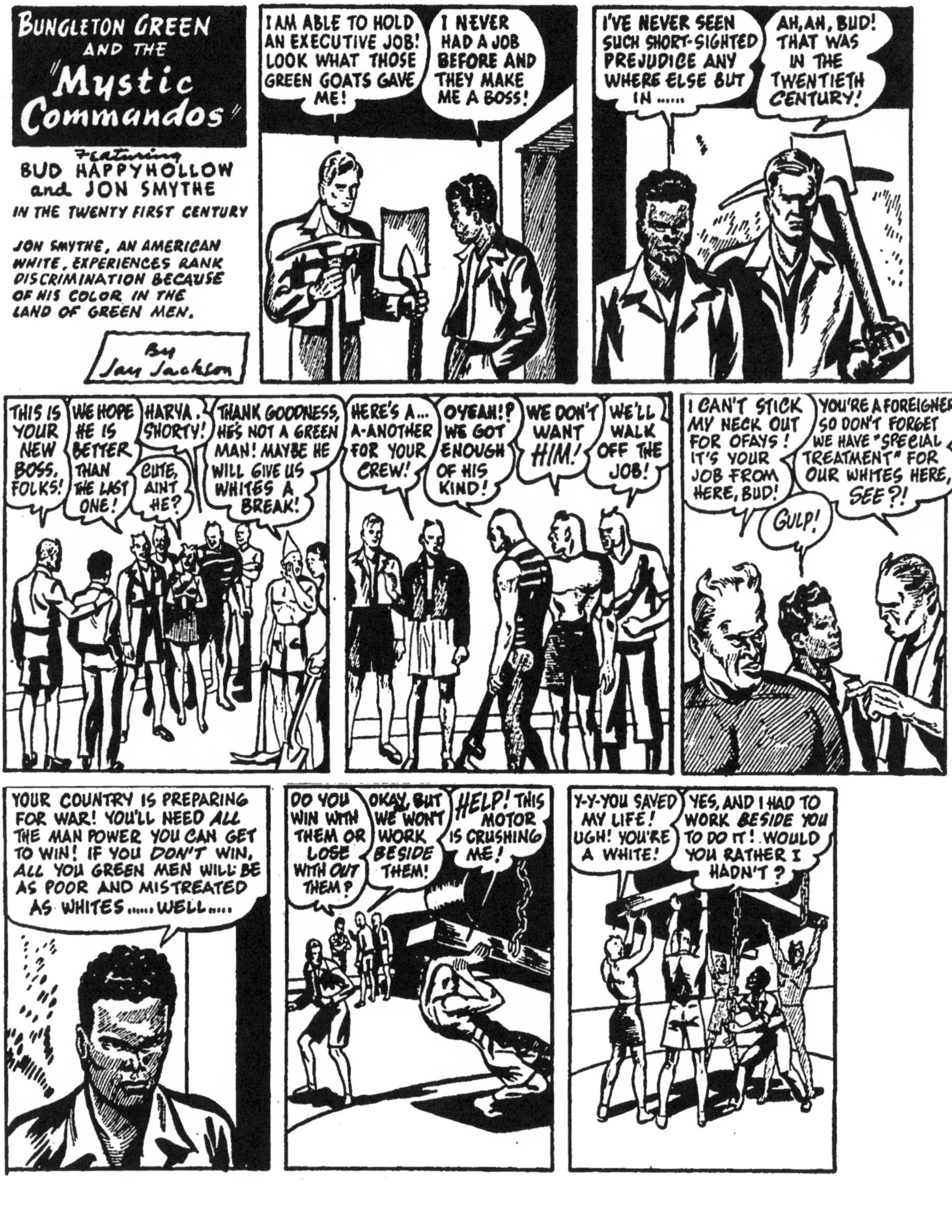
BUNGLETON GREEN AND THE "Mystic Commandos"
Featuring BUD HAPPYHOLLOW and JON SMYTHE IN THE TWENTY FIRST CENTURY
JON SMYTHE, AN AMERICAN WHITE, EXPERIENCES RANK DISCRIMINATION BECAUSE OF HIS COLOR IN THE LAND OF GREEN MEN.
By Jay Jackson
I AM ABLE TO HOLD AN EXECUTIVE JOB! LOOK WHAT THOSE GREEN GOATS GAVE ME!
I NEVER HAD A JOB BEFORE AND THEY MAKE ME A BOSS!
I'VE NEVER SEEN SUCH SHORT-SIGHTED PREJUDICE ANY WHERE ELSE BUT IN ......
AH, AH, BUD! THAT WAS IN THE TWENTIETH CENTURY!
THIS IS YOUR NEW BOSS, FOLKS!
WE HOPE HE IS BETTER THAN THE LAST ONE!
HARYA, SHORTY!
CUTE, AINT HE?
THANK GOODNESS, HE'S NOT A GREEN MAN! MAYBE HE WILL GIVE US WHITES A BREAK!
HERE'S A... A-ANOTHER FOR YOUR CREW!
OYEAH!? WE GOT ENOUGH OF HIS KIND!
WE DON'T WANT HIM!
WE'LL WALK OFF THE JOB!
I CAN'T STICK MY NECK OUT FOR OFAYS! IT'S YOUR JOB FROM HERE, BUD!
YOU'RE A FOREIGNER SO DON'T FORGET WE HAVE "SPECIAL TREATMENT" FOR OUR WHITES HERE, SEE?!
GULP!
YOUR COUNTRY IS PREPARING FOR WAR! YOU'LL NEED ALL THE MAN POWER YOU CAN GET TO WIN! IF YOU DON'T WIN, ALL YOU GREEN MEN WILL BE AS POOR AND MISTREATED AS WHITES...... WELL.....
DO YOU WIN WITH THEM OR LOSE WITH OUT THEM?
OKAY, BUT WE WON'T WORK BESIDE THEM!
HELP! THIS MOTOR IS CRUSHING ME!
Y-Y-YOU SAVED MY LIFE! UGH! YOU'RE A WHITE!
YES, AND I HAD TO WORK BESIDE YOU TO DO IT! WOULD YOU RATHER I HADN'T?

April 29, 1944

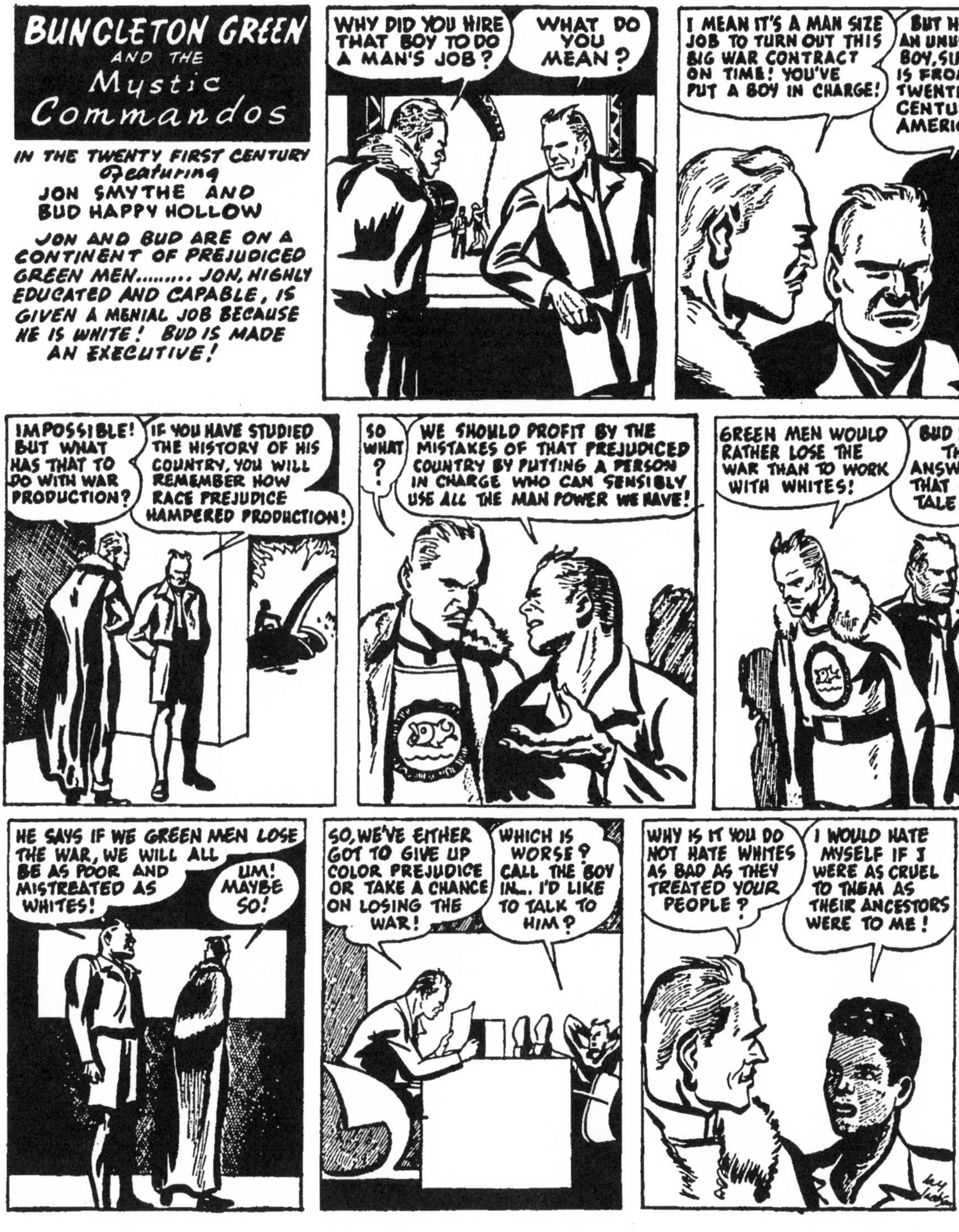
BUNGLETON GREEN AND THE Mystic Commandos
IN THE TWENTY FIRST CENTURY Featuring JON SMYTHE AND BUD HAPPY HOLLOW
JON AND BUD ARE ON A CONTINENT OF PREJUDICED GREEN MEN......... JON, HIGHLY EDUCATED AND CAPABLE, IS GIVEN A MENIAL JOB BECAUSE HE IS WHITE! BUD IS MADE AN EXECUTIVE!
WHY DID YOU HIRE THAT BOY TO DO A MAN'S JOB?
WHAT DO YOU MEAN?
I MEAN IT'S A MAN SIZE JOB TO TURN OUT THIS BIG WAR CONTRACT ON TIME! YOU'VE PUT A BOY IN CHARGE!
BUT HE'S AN UNUSUAL BOY, SIR! HE IS FROM TWENTIETH CENTURY AMERICA!
IMPOSSIBLE! BUT WHAT HAS THAT TO DO WITH WAR PRODUCTION?
IF YOU HAVE STUDIED THE HISTORY OF HIS COUNTRY, YOU WILL REMEMBER HOW RACE PREJUDICE HAMPERED PRODUCTION!
SO WHAT?
WE SHOULD PROFIT BY THE MISTAKES OF THAT PREJUDICED COUNTRY BY PUTTING A PERSON IN CHARGE WHO CAN SENSIBLY USE ALL THE MAN POWER WE HAVE!
GREEN MEN WOULD RATHER LOSE THE WAR THAN TO WORK WITH WHITES!
BUD KNEW THE ANSWER TO THAT FRAIL TALE TOO!
HE SAYS IF WE GREEN MEN LOSE THE WAR, WE WILL ALL BE AS POOR AND MISTREATED AS WHITES!
UM! MAYBE SO!
SO, WE'VE EITHER GOT TO GIVE UP COLOR PREJUDICE OR TAKE A CHANCE ON LOSING THE WAR!
WHICH IS WORSE? CALL THE BOY IN... I'D LIKE TO TALK TO HIM?
WHY IS IT YOU DO NOT HATE WHITES AS BAD AS THEY TREATED YOUR PEOPLE?
I WOULD HATE MYSELF IF I WERE AS CRUEL TO THEM AS THEIR ANCESTORS WERE TO ME!

May 6, 1944

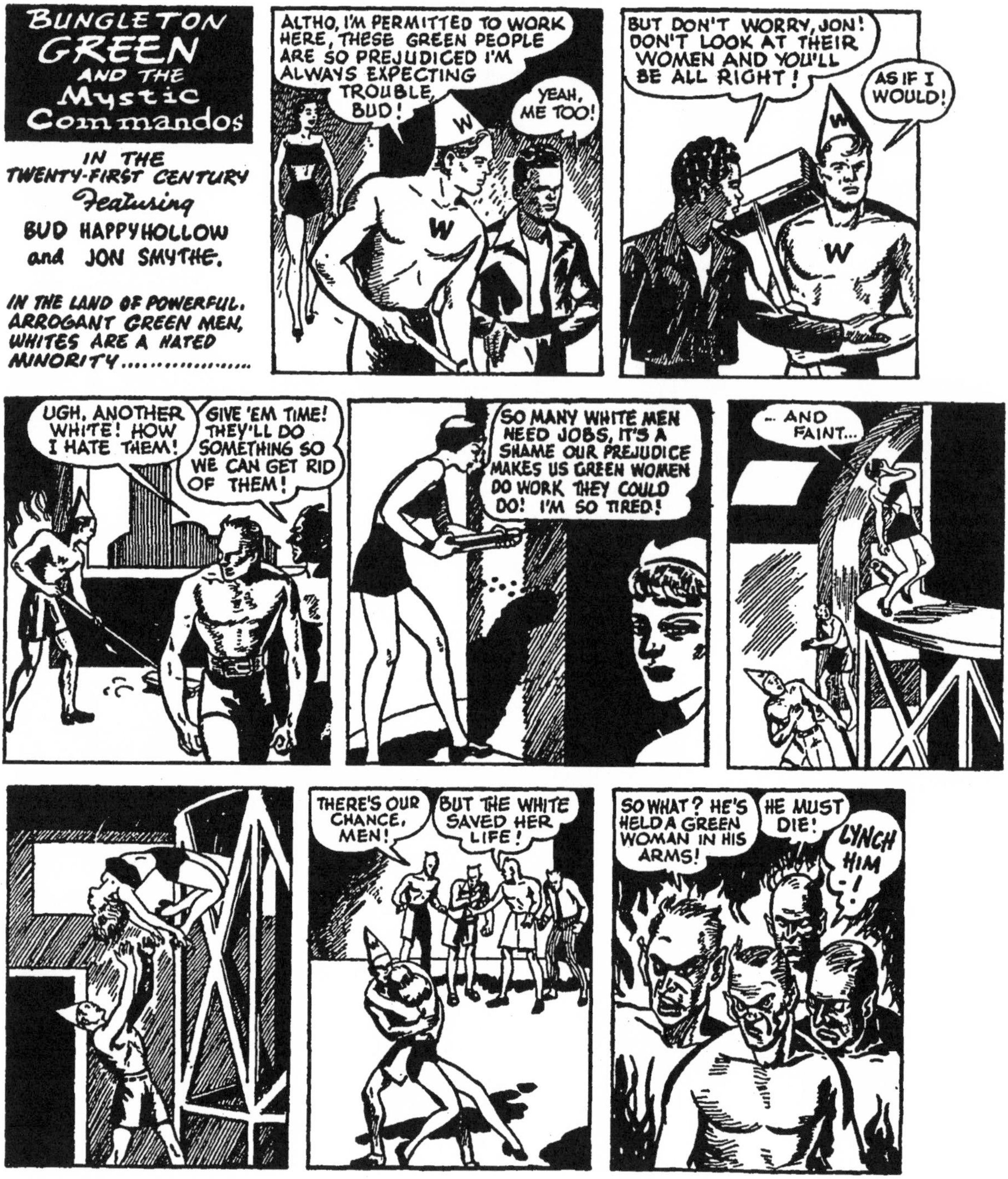
BUNGLETON GREEN AND THE Mystic Commandos
IN THE TWENTY-FIRST CENTURY Featuring BUD HAPPYHOLLOW and JON SMYTHE.
IN THE LAND OF POWERFUL, ARROGANT GREEN MEN, WHITES ARE A HATED MINORITY..................
ALTHO, I'M PERMITTED TO WORK HERE, THESE GREEN PEOPLE ARE SO PREJUDICED I'M ALWAYS EXPECTING TROUBLE, BUD!
YEAH, ME TOO!
W
W
BUT DON'T WORRY, JON! DON'T LOOK AT THEIR WOMEN AND YOU'LL BE ALL RIGHT!
AS IF I WOULD!
W
W
UGH, ANOTHER WHITE! HOW I HATE THEM!
GIVE 'EM TIME! THEY'LL DO SOMETHING SO WE CAN GET RID OF THEM!
SO MANY WHITE MEN NEED JOBS, IT'S A SHAME OUR PREJUDICE MAKES US GREEN WOMEN DO WORK THEY COULD DO! I'M SO TIRED!
... AND FAINT...
THERE'S OUR CHANCE, MEN!
BUT THE WHITE SAVED HER LIFE!
SO WHAT? HE'S HELD A GREEN WOMAN IN HIS ARMS!
HE MUST DIE!
LYNCH HIM -!

May 13, 1944

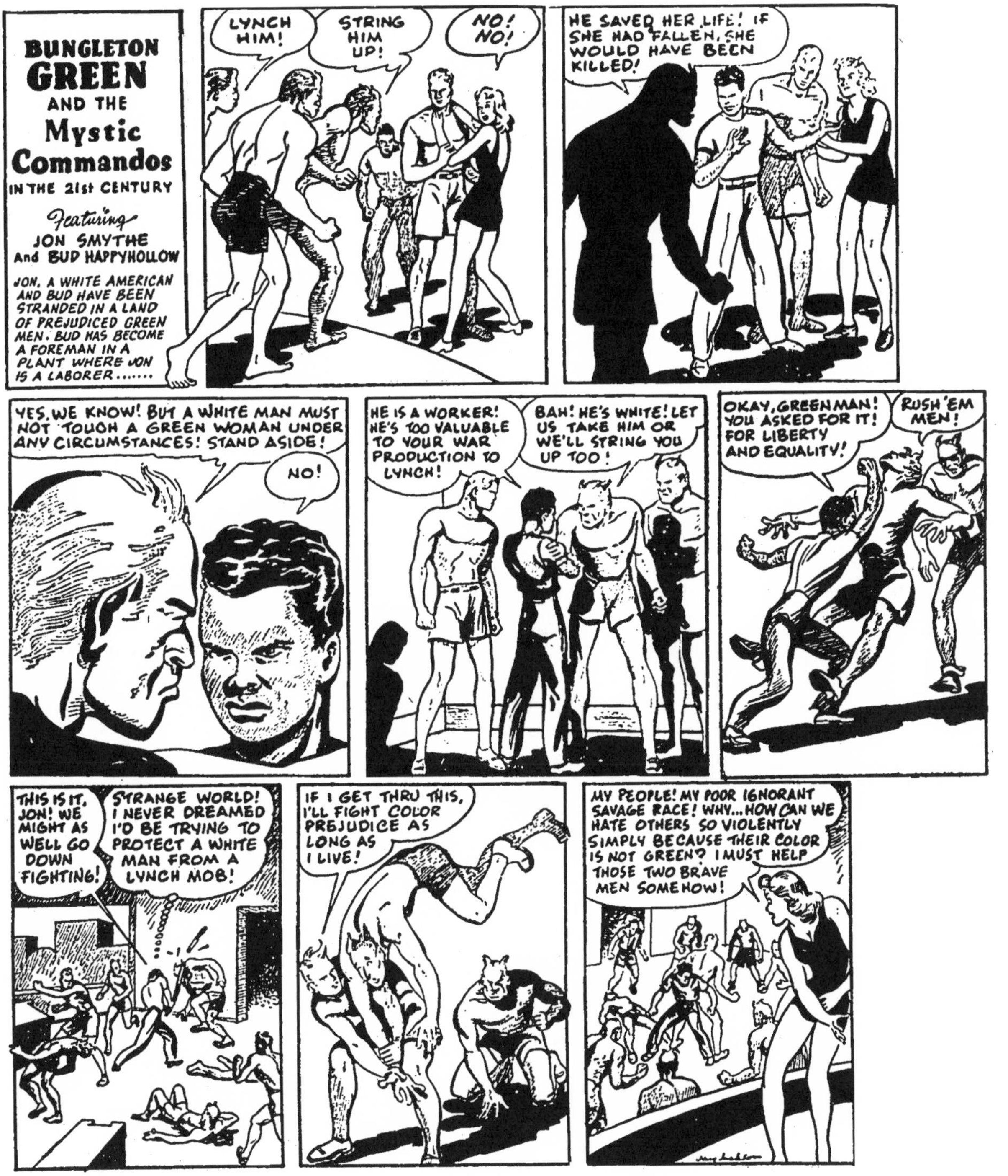
BUNGLETON GREEN AND THE Mystic Commandos IN THE 21st CENTURY
Featuring JON SMYTHE And BUD HAPPYHOLLOW
JON, A WHITE AMERICAN AND BUD HAVE BEEN STRANDED IN A LAND OF PREJUDICED GREEN MEN. BUD HAS BECOME A FOREMAN IN A PLANT WHERE JON IS A LABORER.......
LYNCH HIM!
STRING HIM UP!
NO! NO!
HE SAVED HER LIFE! IF SHE HAD FALLEN, SHE WOULD HAVE BEEN KILLED!
YES, WE KNOW! BUT A WHITE MAN MUST NOT TOUCH A GREEN WOMAN UNDER ANY CIRCUMSTANCES! STAND ASIDE!
NO!
HE IS A WORKER! HE'S TOO VALUABLE TO YOUR WAR PRODUCTION TO LYNCH!
BAH! HE'S WHITE! LET US TAKE HIM OR WE'LL STRING YOU UP TOO!
OKAY, GREEN MAN! YOU ASKED FOR IT! FOR LIBERTY AND EQUALITY!
RUSH 'EM MEN!
THIS IS IT, JON! WE MIGHT AS WELL GO DOWN FIGHTING!
STRANGE WORLD! I NEVER DREAMED I'D BE TRYING TO PROTECT A WHITE MAN FROM A LYNCH MOB!
IF I GET THRU THIS, I'LL FIGHT COLOR PREJUDICE AS LONG AS I LIVE!
MY PEOPLE! MY POOR IGNORANT SAVAGE RACE! WHY...HOW CAN WE HATE OTHERS SO VIOLENTLY SIMPLY BECAUSE THEIR COLOR IS NOT GREEN? I MUST HELP THOSE TWO BRAVE MEN SOMEHOW!

May 20, 1944

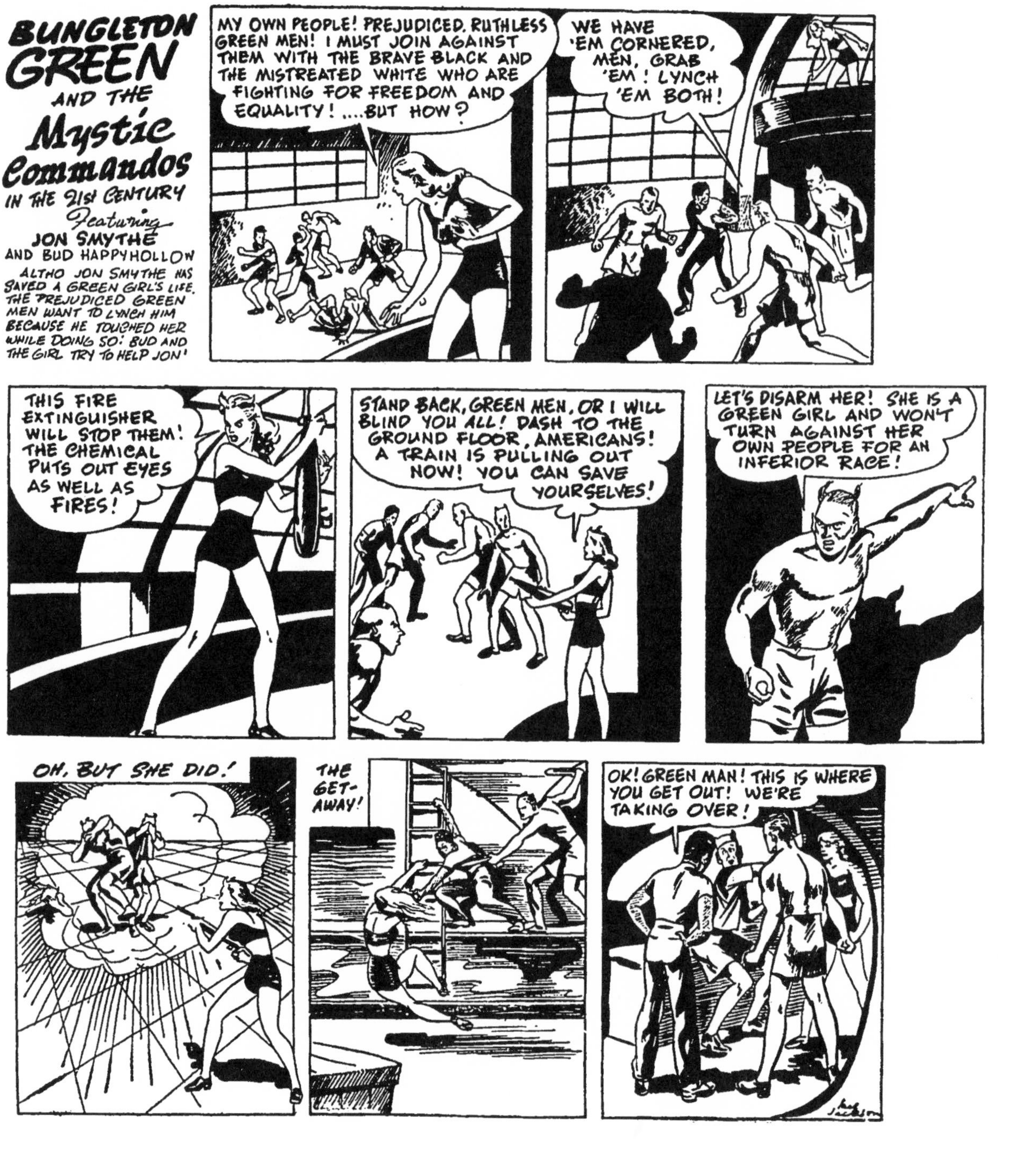

BUNGLETON GREEN AND THE Mystic Commandos IN THE 21st CENTURY
Featuring JON SMYTHE AND BUD HAPPYHOLLOW
ALTHO JON SMYTHE HAS SAVED A GREEN GIRL'S LIFE, THE PREJUDICED GREEN MEN WANT TO LYNCH HIM BECAUSE HE TOUCHED HER WHILE DOING SO: BUD AND THE GIRL TRY TO HELP JON'
MY OWN PEOPLE! PREJUDICED, RUTHLESS GREEN MEN! I MUST JOIN AGAINST THEM WITH THE BRAVE BLACK AND THE MISTREATED WHITE WHO ARE FIGHTING FOR FREEDOM AND EQUALITY! ....BUT HOW?
WE HAVE 'EM CORNERED, MEN, GRAB 'EM! LYNCH 'EM BOTH!
THIS FIRE EXTINGUISHER WILL STOP THEM! THE CHEMICAL PUTS OUT EYES AS WELL AS FIRES!
STAND BACK, GREEN MEN, OR I WILL BLIND YOU ALL! DASH TO THE GROUND FLOOR, AMERICANS! A TRAIN IS PULLING OUT NOW! YOU CAN SAVE YOURSELVES!
LET'S DISARM HER! SHE IS A GREEN GIRL AND WON'T TURN AGAINST HER OWN PEOPLE FOR AN INFERIOR RACE!
OH, BUT SHE DID!
THE GET-AWAY!
OK! GREEN MAN! THIS IS WHERE YOU GET OUT! WE'RE TAKING OVER!

May 27, 1944

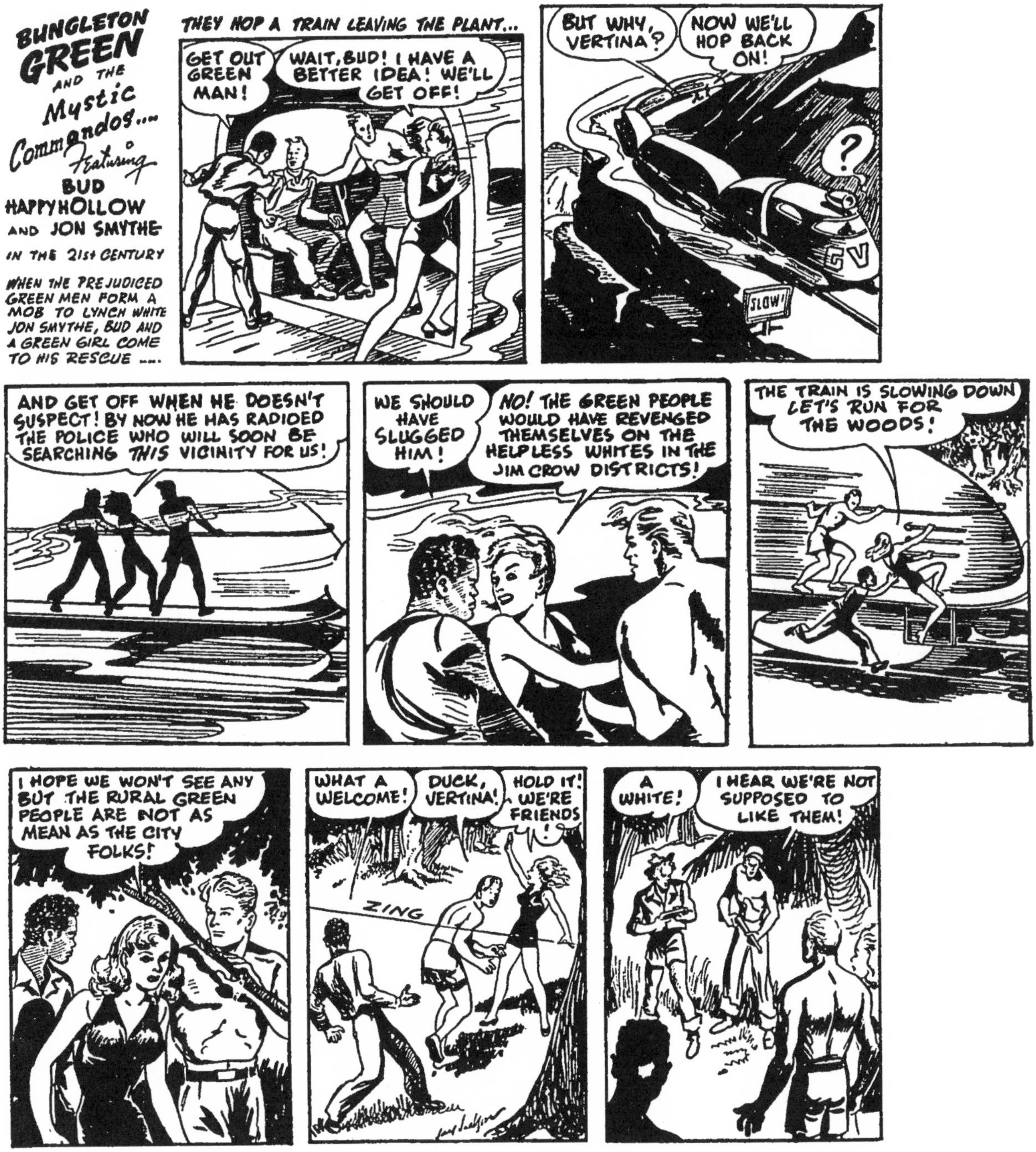
BUNGLETON GREEN AND THE Mystic Commandos.... Featuring BUD HAPPYHOLLOW AND JON SMYTHE IN THE 21st CENTURY
WHEN THE PREJUDICED GREEN MEN FORM A MOB TO LYNCH WHITE JON SMYTHE, BUD AND A GREEN GIRL COME TO HIS RESCUE ....
THEY HOP A TRAIN LEAVING THE PLANT...
GET OUT GREEN MAN!
WAIT, BUD! I HAVE A BETTER IDEA! WE'LL GET OFF!
BUT WHY, VERTINA?
NOW WE'LL HOP BACK ON!
?
GV
SLOW!
AND GET OFF WHEN HE DOESN'T SUSPECT! BY NOW HE HAS RADIOED THE POLICE WHO WILL SOON BE SEARCHING THIS VICINITY FOR US!
WE SHOULD HAVE SLUGGED HIM!
NO! THE GREEN PEOPLE WOULD HAVE REVENGED THEMSELVES ON THE HELPLESS WHITES IN THE JIM CROW DISTRICTS!
THE TRAIN IS SLOWING DOWN LET'S RUN FOR THE WOODS!
I HOPE WE WON'T SEE ANY BUT THE RURAL GREEN PEOPLE ARE NOT AS MEAN AS THE CITY FOLKS!
WHAT A WELCOME!
DUCK, VERTINA!
HOLD IT! WE'RE FRIENDS!
ZING
A WHITE!
I HEAR WE'RE NOT SUPPOSED TO LIKE THEM!

June 3, 1944

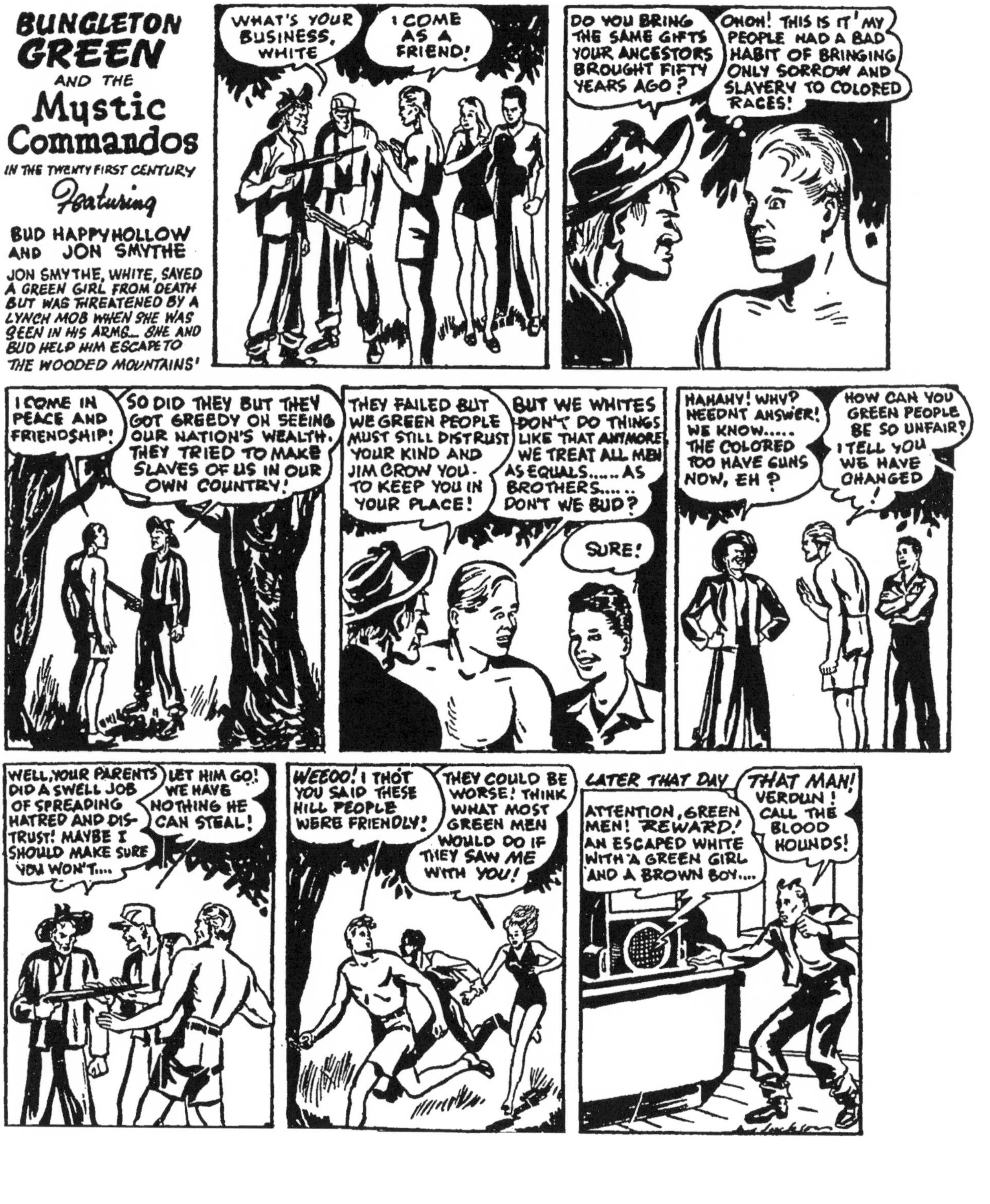
BUNGLETON GREEN
AND THE
Mystic Commandos
IN THE TWENTY FIRST CENTURY
Featuring
BUD HAPPYHOLLOW AND JON SMYTHE
JON SMYTHE, WHITE, SAVED A GREEN GIRL FROM DEATH BUT WAS THREATENED BY A LYNCH MOB WHEN SHE WAS SEEN IN HIS ARMS... SHE AND BUD HELP HIM ESCAPE TO THE WOODED MOUNTAINS'
WHAT'S YOUR BUSINESS, WHITE
I COME AS A FRIEND!
DO YOU BRING THE SAME GIFTS YOUR ANCESTORS BROUGHT FIFTY YEARS AGO?
OHOH! THIS IS IT! MY PEOPLE HAD A BAD HABIT OF BRINGING ONLY SORROW AND SLAVERY TO COLORED RACES!
I COME IN PEACE AND FRIENDSHIP!
SO DID THEY BUT THEY GOT GREEDY ON SEEING OUR NATION'S WEALTH. THEY TRIED TO MAKE SLAVES OF US IN OUR OWN COUNTRY!
THEY FAILED BUT WE GREEN PEOPLE MUST STILL DISTRUST YOUR KIND AND JIM CROW YOU. TO KEEP YOU IN YOUR PLACE!
BUT WE WHITES DON'T DO THINGS LIKE THAT ANYMORE. WE TREAT ALL MEN AS EQUALS...... AS BROTHERS...... DON'T WE BUD?
SURE!
HAHAHY! WHY? NEEDNT ANSWER! WE KNOW..... THE COLORED TOO HAVE GUNS NOW, EH?
HOW CAN YOU GREEN PEOPLE BE SO UNFAIR? I TELL YOU WE HAVE CHANGED!
WELL, YOUR PARENTS DID A SWELL JOB OF SPREADING HATRED AND DISTRUST! MAYBE I SHOULD MAKE SURE YOU WON'T....
LET HIM GO! WE HAVE NOTHING HE CAN STEAL!
WEEOO! I THOT YOU SAID THESE HILL PEOPLE WERE FRIENDLY!
THEY COULD BE WORSE! THINK WHAT MOST GREEN MEN WOULD DO IF THEY SAW ME WITH YOU!
LATER THAT DAY
ATTENTION, GREEN MEN! REWARD! AN ESCAPED WHITE WITH A GREEN GIRL AND A BROWN BOY....
THAT MAN! VERDUN! CALL THE BLOOD HOUNDS!

June 10, 1944

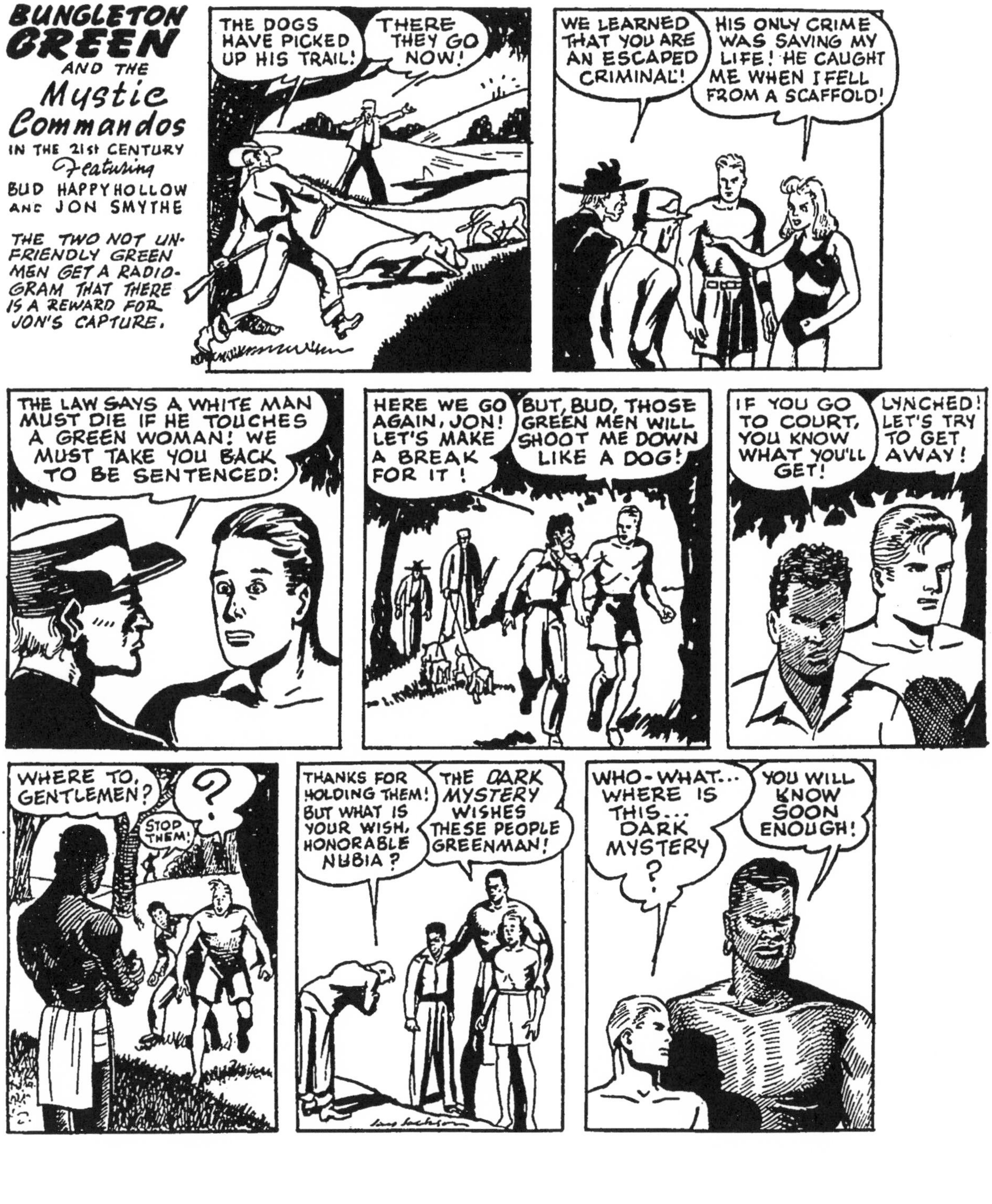
BUNGLETON GREEN AND THE Mystic Commandos IN THE 21st CENTURY Featuring BUD HAPPYHOLLOW AND JON SMYTHE
THE TWO NOT UN-FRIENDLY GREEN MEN GET A RADIOGRAM THAT THERE IS A REWARD FOR JON'S CAPTURE.
THE DOGS HAVE PICKED UP HIS TRAIL!
THERE THEY GO NOW!
WE LEARNED THAT YOU ARE AN ESCAPED CRIMINAL!
HIS ONLY CRIME WAS SAVING MY LIFE! HE CAUGHT ME WHEN I FELL FROM A SCAFFOLD!
THE LAW SAYS A WHITE MAN MUST DIE IF HE TOUCHES A GREEN WOMAN! WE MUST TAKE YOU BACK TO BE SENTENCED!
HERE WE GO AGAIN, JON! LET'S MAKE A BREAK FOR IT!
BUT, BUD, THOSE GREEN MEN WILL SHOOT ME DOWN LIKE A DOG!
IF YOU GO TO COURT, YOU KNOW WHAT YOU'LL GET!
LYNCHED! LET'S TRY TO GET AWAY!
WHERE TO, GENTLEMEN?
?
STOP THEM!
THANKS FOR HOLDING THEM! BUT WHAT IS YOUR WISH, HONORABLE NUBIA?
THE DARK MYSTERY WISHES THESE PEOPLE GREENMAN!
WHO-WHAT... WHERE IS THIS... DARK MYSTERY ?
YOU WILL KNOW SOON ENOUGH!

June 17, 1944

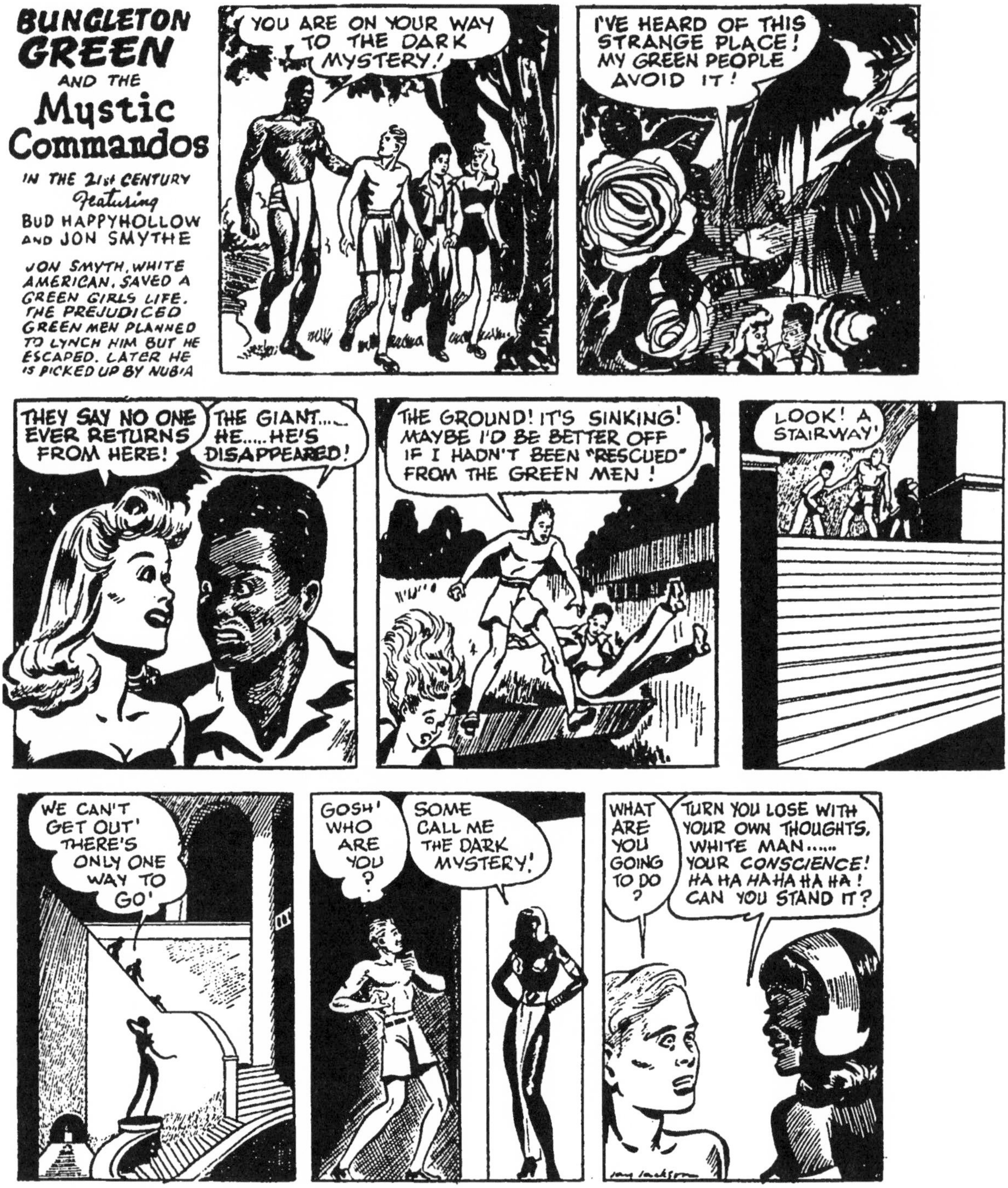
BUNGLETON GREEN AND THE Mystic Commandos
IN THE 21st CENTURY Featuring BUD HAPPYHOLLOW AND JON SMYTHE
JON SMYTH, WHITE AMERICAN, SAVED A GREEN GIRLS LIFE. THE PREJUDICED GREEN MEN PLANNED TO LYNCH HIM BUT HE ESCAPED. LATER HE IS PICKED UP BY NUBIA
YOU ARE ON YOUR WAY TO THE DARK MYSTERY!
I'VE HEARD OF THIS STRANGE PLACE! MY GREEN PEOPLE AVOID IT!
THEY SAY NO ONE EVER RETURNS FROM HERE!
THE GIANT..... HE.....HE'S DISAPPEARED!
THE GROUND! IT'S SINKING! MAYBE I'D BE BETTER OFF IF I HADN'T BEEN "RESCUED" FROM THE GREEN MEN!
LOOK! A STAIRWAY'
WE CAN'T GET OUT' THERE'S ONLY ONE WAY TO GO'
GOSH' WHO ARE YOU ?
SOME CALL ME THE DARK MYSTERY!
WHAT ARE YOU GOING TO DO ?
TURN YOU LOSE WITH YOUR OWN THOUGHTS, WHITE MAN...... YOUR CONSCIENCE! HA HA HA HA HA HA! CAN YOU STAND IT?

June 24, 1944

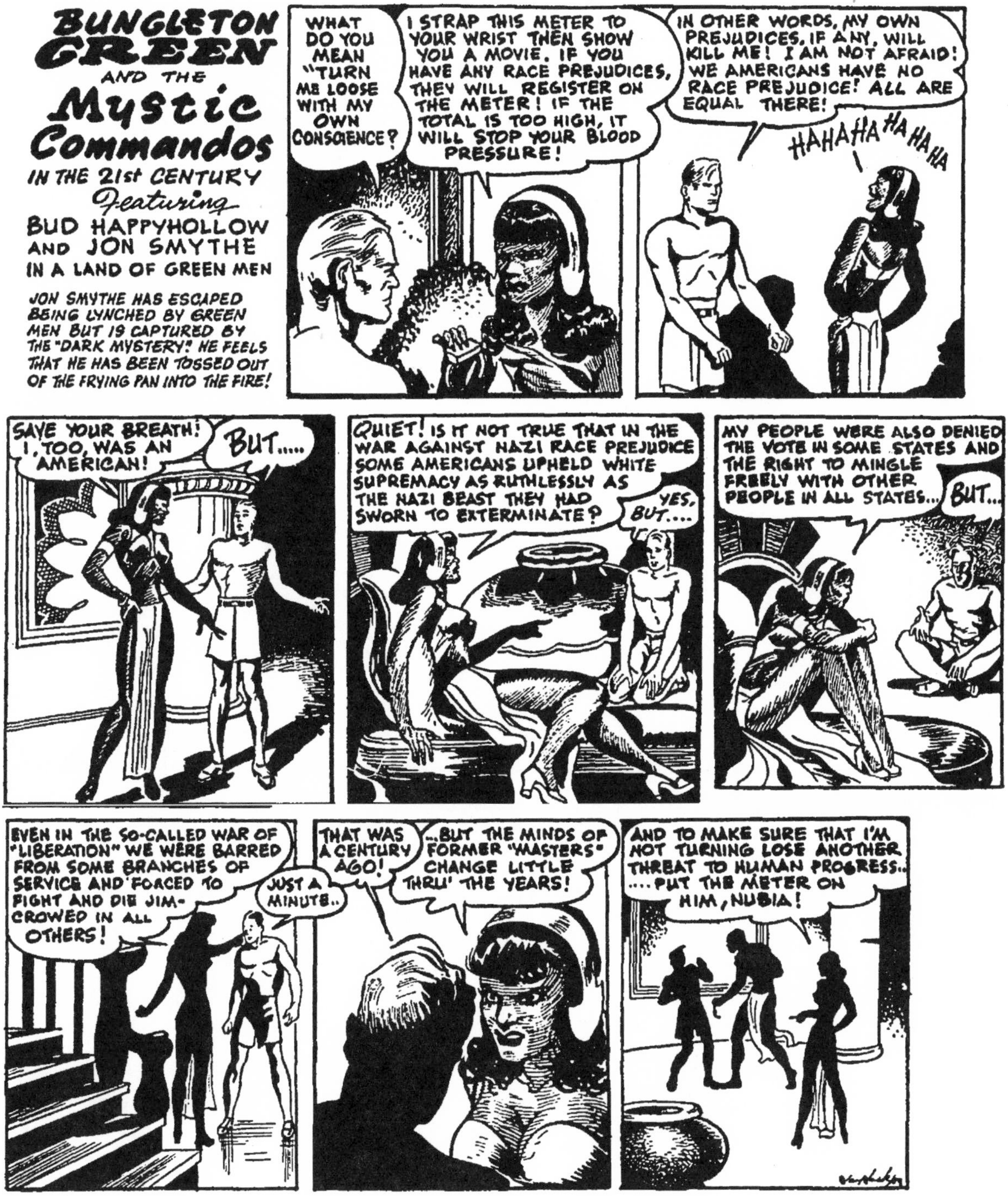
BUNGLETON GREEN AND THE Mystic Commandos IN THE 21st CENTURY
Featuring BUD HAPPYHOLLOW AND JON SMYTHE IN A LAND OF GREEN MEN
JON SMYTHE HAS ESCAPED BEING LYNCHED BY GREEN MEN BUT IS CAPTURED BY THE "DARK MYSTERY." HE FEELS THAT HE HAS BEEN TOSSED OUT OF THE FRYING PAN INTO THE FIRE!
WHAT DO YOU MEAN "TURN ME LOOSE WITH MY OWN CONSCIENCE?
I STRAP THIS METER TO YOUR WRIST THEN SHOW YOU A MOVIE. IF YOU HAVE ANY RACE PREJUDICES, THEY WILL REGISTER ON THE METER! IF THE TOTAL IS TOO HIGH, IT WILL STOP YOUR BLOOD PRESSURE!
IN OTHER WORDS, MY OWN PREJUDICES, IF ANY, WILL KILL ME! I AM NOT AFRAID! WE AMERICANS HAVE NO RACE PREJUDICE! ALL ARE EQUAL THERE!
HAHAHA HA HA HA HA
SAVE YOUR BREATH! I, TOO, WAS AN AMERICAN!
BUT.....
QUIET! IS IT NOT TRUE THAT IN THE WAR AGAINST NAZI RACE PREJUDICE SOME AMERICANS UPHELD WHITE SUPREMACY AS RUTHLESSLY AS THE NAZI BEAST THEY HAD SWORN TO EXTERMINATE?
YES, BUT....
MY PEOPLE WERE ALSO DENIED THE VOTE IN SOME STATES AND THE RIGHT TO MINGLE FREELY WITH OTHER PEOPLE IN ALL STATES...
BUT...
EVEN IN THE SO-CALLED WAR OF "LIBERATION" WE WERE BARRED FROM SOME BRANCHES OF SERVICE AND FORCED TO FIGHT AND DIE JIM-CROWED IN ALL OTHERS!
JUST A MINUTE..
THAT WAS A CENTURY AGO!
...BUT THE MINDS OF FORMER "MASTERS" CHANGE LITTLE THRU' THE YEARS!
AND TO MAKE SURE THAT I'M NOT TURNING LOSE ANOTHER THREAT TO HUMAN PROGRESS.. ....PUT THE METER ON HIM, NUBIA!

July 1, 1944

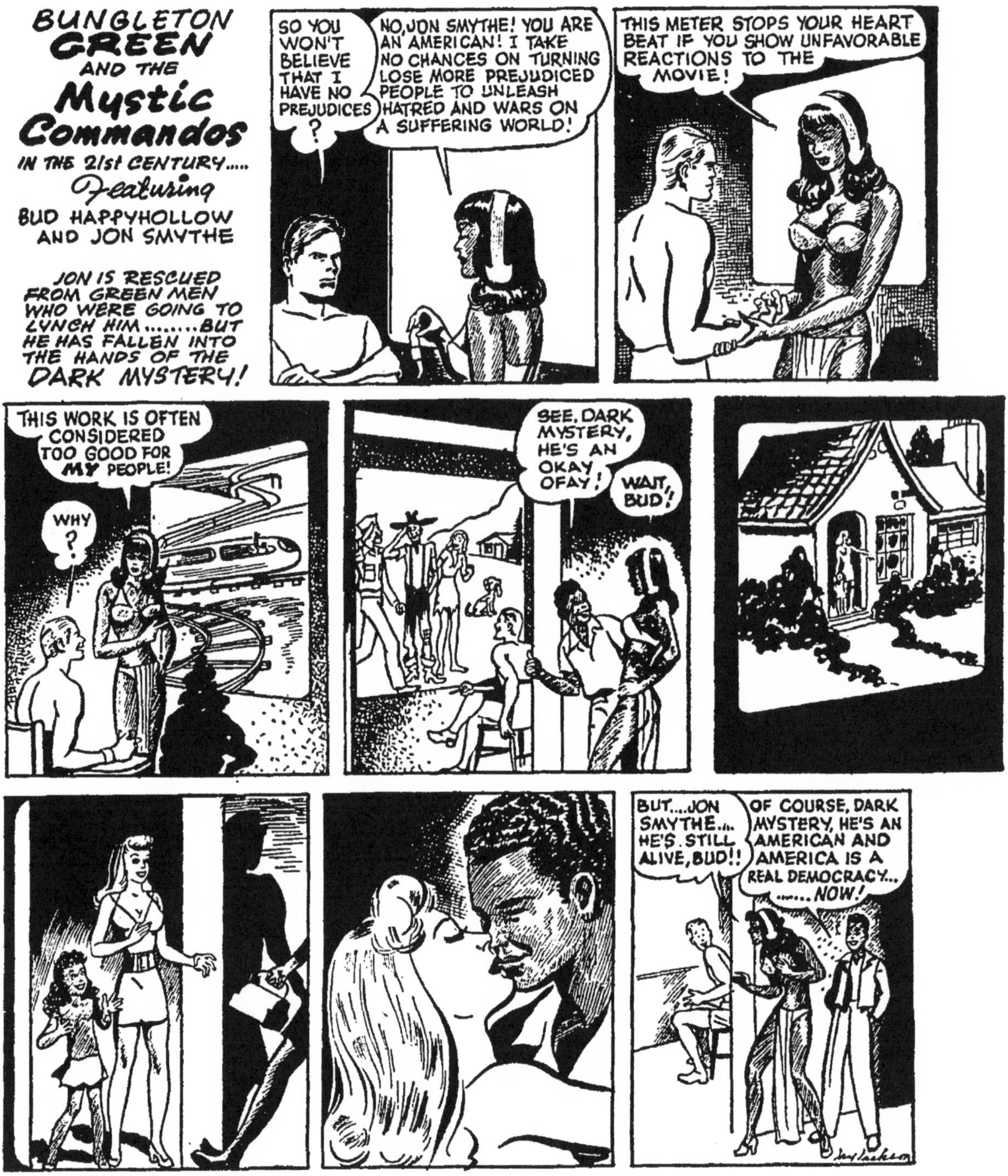
BUNGLETON GREEN AND THE Mystic Commandos IN THE 21st CENTURY..... Featuring BUD HAPPYHOLLOW AND JON SMYTHE
JON IS RESCUED FROM GREEN MEN WHO WERE GOING TO LYNCH HIM........BUT HE HAS FALLEN INTO THE HANDS OF THE DARK MYSTERY!
SO YOU WON'T BELIEVE THAT I HAVE NO PREJUDICES ?
NO, JON SMYTHE! YOU ARE AN AMERICAN! I TAKE NO CHANCES ON TURNING LOSE MORE PREJUDICED PEOPLE TO UNLEASH HATRED AND WARS ON A SUFFERING WORLD!
THIS METER STOPS YOUR HEART BEAT IF YOU SHOW UNFAVORABLE REACTIONS TO THE MOVIE!
THIS WORK IS OFTEN CONSIDERED TOO GOOD FOR MY PEOPLE!
WHY ?
SEE, DARK MYSTERY, HE'S AN OKAY OFAY!
WAIT, BUD!
BUT....JON SMYTHE.... HE'S STILL ALIVE, BUD!!
OF COURSE, DARK MYSTERY, HE'S AN AMERICAN AND AMERICA IS A REAL DEMOCRACY... ......NOW!

July 8, 1944

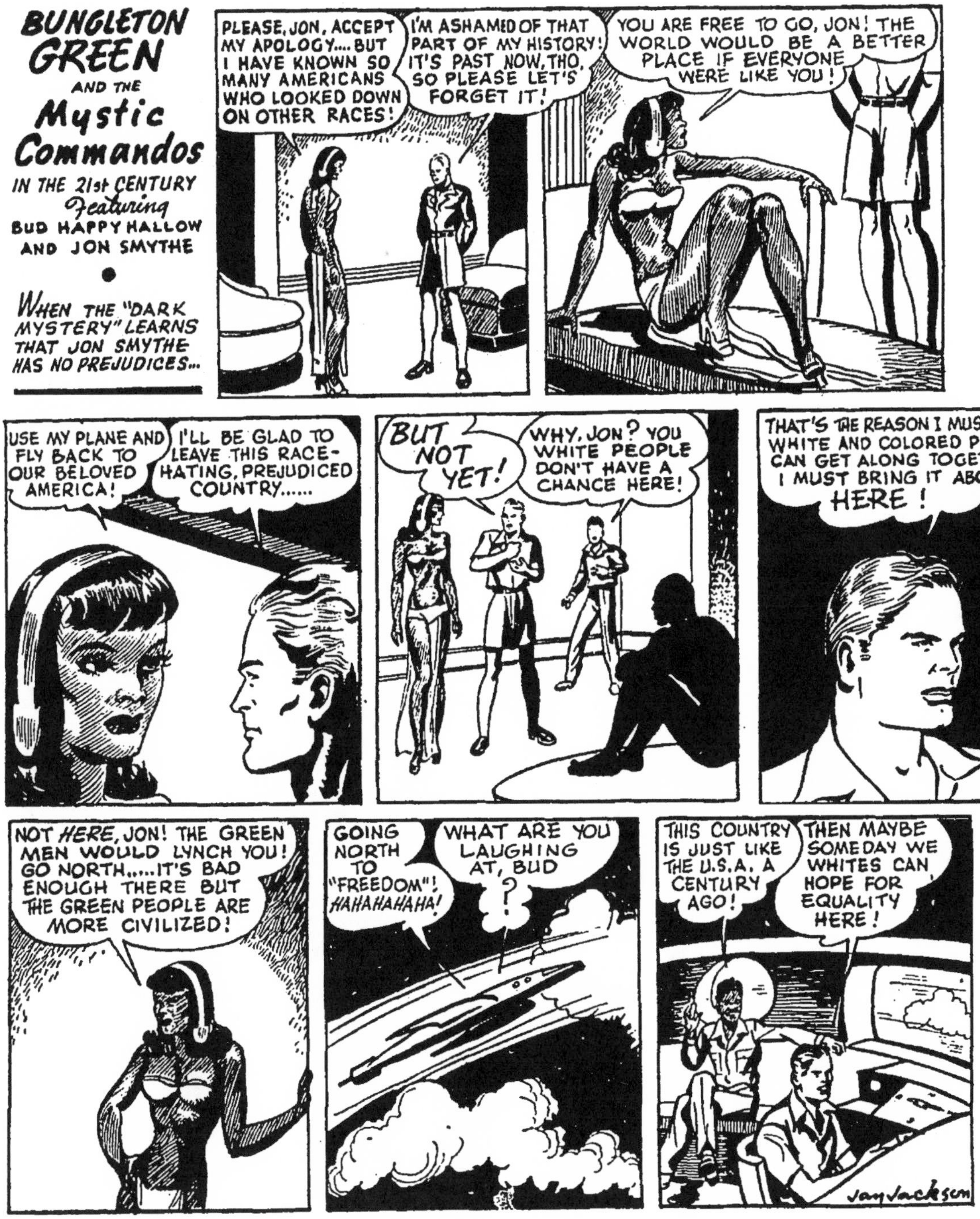
BUNGLETON GREEN AND THE Mystic Commandos IN THE 21st CENTURY Featuring BUD HAPPY HALLOW AND JON SMYTHE
WHEN THE "DARK MYSTERY" LEARNS THAT JON SMYTHE HAS NO PREJUDICES...
PLEASE, JON, ACCEPT MY APOLOGY.... BUT I HAVE KNOWN SO MANY AMERICANS WHO LOOKED DOWN ON OTHER RACES!
I'M ASHAMED OF THAT PART OF MY HISTORY! IT'S PAST NOW, THO, SO PLEASE LET'S FORGET IT!
YOU ARE FREE TO GO, JON! THE WORLD WOULD BE A BETTER PLACE IF EVERYONE WERE LIKE YOU!
USE MY PLANE AND FLY BACK TO OUR BELOVED AMERICA!
I'LL BE GLAD TO LEAVE THIS RACE-HATING, PREJUDICED COUNTRY......
BUT NOT YET!
WHY, JON? YOU WHITE PEOPLE DON'T HAVE A CHANCE HERE!
THAT'S THE REASON I MUST STAY! WHITE AND COLORED PEOPLE CAN GET ALONG TOGETHER! I MUST BRING IT ABOUT HERE!
NOT HERE, JON! THE GREEN MEN WOULD LYNCH YOU! GO NORTH.....IT'S BAD ENOUGH THERE BUT THE GREEN PEOPLE ARE MORE CIVILIZED!
GOING NORTH TO "FREEDOM"! HAHAHAHAHA!
WHAT ARE YOU LAUGHING AT, BUD?
THIS COUNTRY IS JUST LIKE THE U.S.A. A CENTURY AGO!
THEN MAYBE SOMEDAY WE WHITES CAN HOPE FOR EQUALITY HERE!
Jay Jackson

July 15, 1944

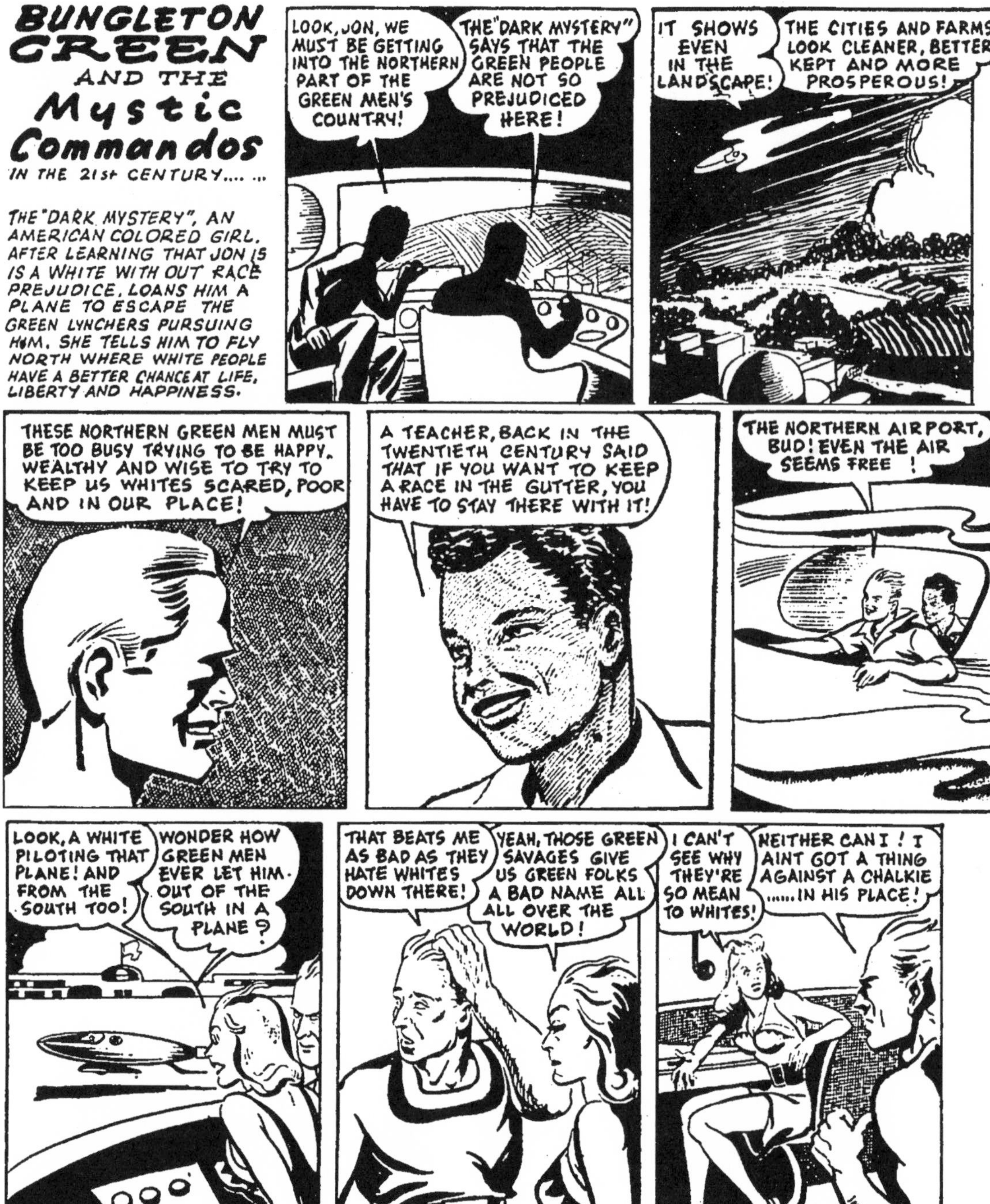
BUNGLETON GREEN AND THE Mystic Commandos
IN THE 21st CENTURY.... ...
THE "DARK MYSTERY", AN AMERICAN COLORED GIRL. AFTER LEARNING THAT JON IS IS A WHITE WITH OUT RACE PREJUDICE, LOANS HIM A PLANE TO ESCAPE THE GREEN LYNCHERS PURSUING HIM. SHE TELLS HIM TO FLY NORTH WHERE WHITE PEOPLE HAVE A BETTER CHANCE AT LIFE, LIBERTY AND HAPPINESS.
LOOK, JON, WE MUST BE GETTING INTO THE NORTHERN PART OF THE GREEN MEN'S COUNTRY!
THE "DARK MYSTERY" SAYS THAT THE GREEN PEOPLE ARE NOT SO PREJUDICED HERE!
IT SHOWS EVEN IN THE LANDSCAPE!
THE CITIES AND FARMS LOOK CLEANER, BETTER KEPT AND MORE PROSPEROUS!
THESE NORTHERN GREEN MEN MUST BE TOO BUSY TRYING TO BE HAPPY, WEALTHY AND WISE TO TRY TO KEEP US WHITES SCARED, POOR AND IN OUR PLACE!
A TEACHER, BACK IN THE TWENTIETH CENTURY SAID THAT IF YOU WANT TO KEEP A RACE IN THE GUTTER, YOU HAVE TO STAY THERE WITH IT!
THE NORTHERN AIRPORT, BUD! EVEN THE AIR SEEMS FREE !
LOOK, A WHITE PILOTING THAT PLANE! AND FROM THE SOUTH TOO!
WONDER HOW GREEN MEN EVER LET HIM OUT OF THE SOUTH IN A PLANE ?
THAT BEATS ME AS BAD AS THEY HATE WHITES DOWN THERE!
YEAH, THOSE GREEN SAVAGES GIVE US GREEN FOLKS A BAD NAME ALL ALL OVER THE WORLD!
I CAN'T SEE WHY THEY'RE SO MEAN TO WHITES!
NEITHER CAN I ! I AINT GOT A THING AGAINST A CHALKIE ......IN HIS PLACE!

July 22, 1944

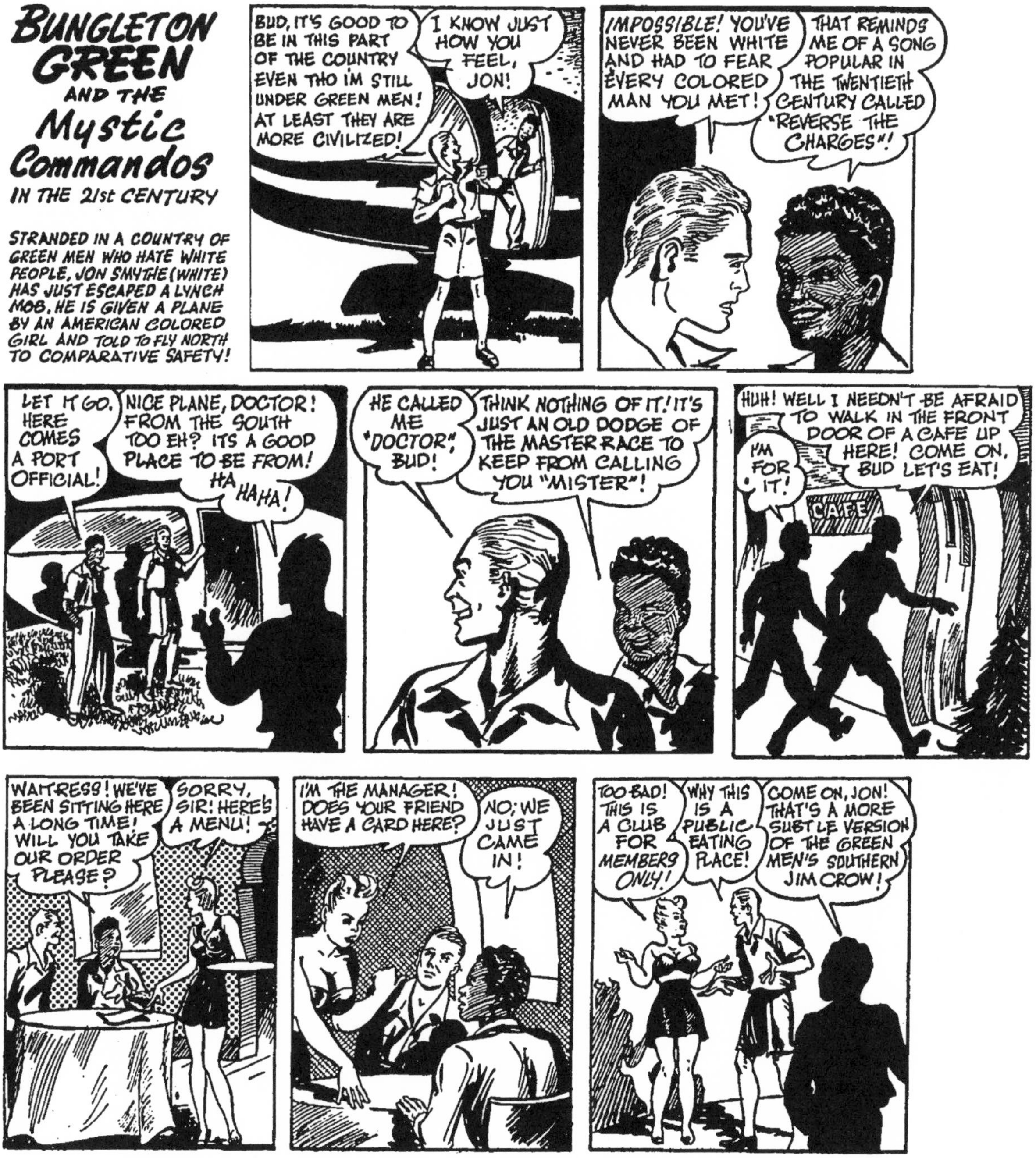
BUNGLETON GREEN AND THE Mystic Commandos IN THE 21st CENTURY
STRANDED IN A COUNTRY OF GREEN MEN WHO HATE WHITE PEOPLE, JON SMYTHE (WHITE) HAS JUST ESCAPED A LYNCH MOB. HE IS GIVEN A PLANE BY AN AMERICAN COLORED GIRL AND TOLD TO FLY NORTH TO COMPARATIVE SAFETY!
BUD, IT'S GOOD TO BE IN THIS PART OF THE COUNTRY EVEN THO I'M STILL UNDER GREEN MEN! AT LEAST THEY ARE MORE CIVILIZED!
I KNOW JUST HOW YOU FEEL, JON!
IMPOSSIBLE! YOU'VE NEVER BEEN WHITE AND HAD TO FEAR EVERY COLORED MAN YOU MET!
THAT REMINDS ME OF A SONG POPULAR IN THE TWENTIETH CENTURY CALLED "REVERSE THE CHARGES"!
LET IT GO. HERE COMES A PORT OFFICIAL!
NICE PLANE, DOCTOR! FROM THE SOUTH TOO EH? ITS A GOOD PLACE TO BE FROM! HA HAHA!
HE CALLED ME "DOCTOR", BUD!
THINK NOTHING OF IT! IT'S JUST AN OLD DODGE OF THE MASTER RACE TO KEEP FROM CALLING YOU "MISTER"!
HUH! WELL I NEEDN'T BE AFRAID TO WALK IN THE FRONT DOOR OF A CAFE UP HERE! COME ON, BUD LET'S EAT!
I'M FOR IT!
CAFE
WAITRESS! WE'VE BEEN SITTING HERE A LONG TIME! WILL YOU TAKE OUR ORDER PLEASE?
SORRY, SIR! HERE'S A MENU!
I'M THE MANAGER! DOES YOUR FRIEND HAVE A CARD HERE?
NO; WE JUST CAME IN!
TOO BAD! THIS IS A CLUB FOR MEMBERS ONLY!
WHY THIS IS A PUBLIC EATING PLACE!
COME ON, JON! THAT'S A MORE SUBTLE VERSION OF THE GREEN MEN'S SOUTHERN JIM CROW!

July 29, 1944

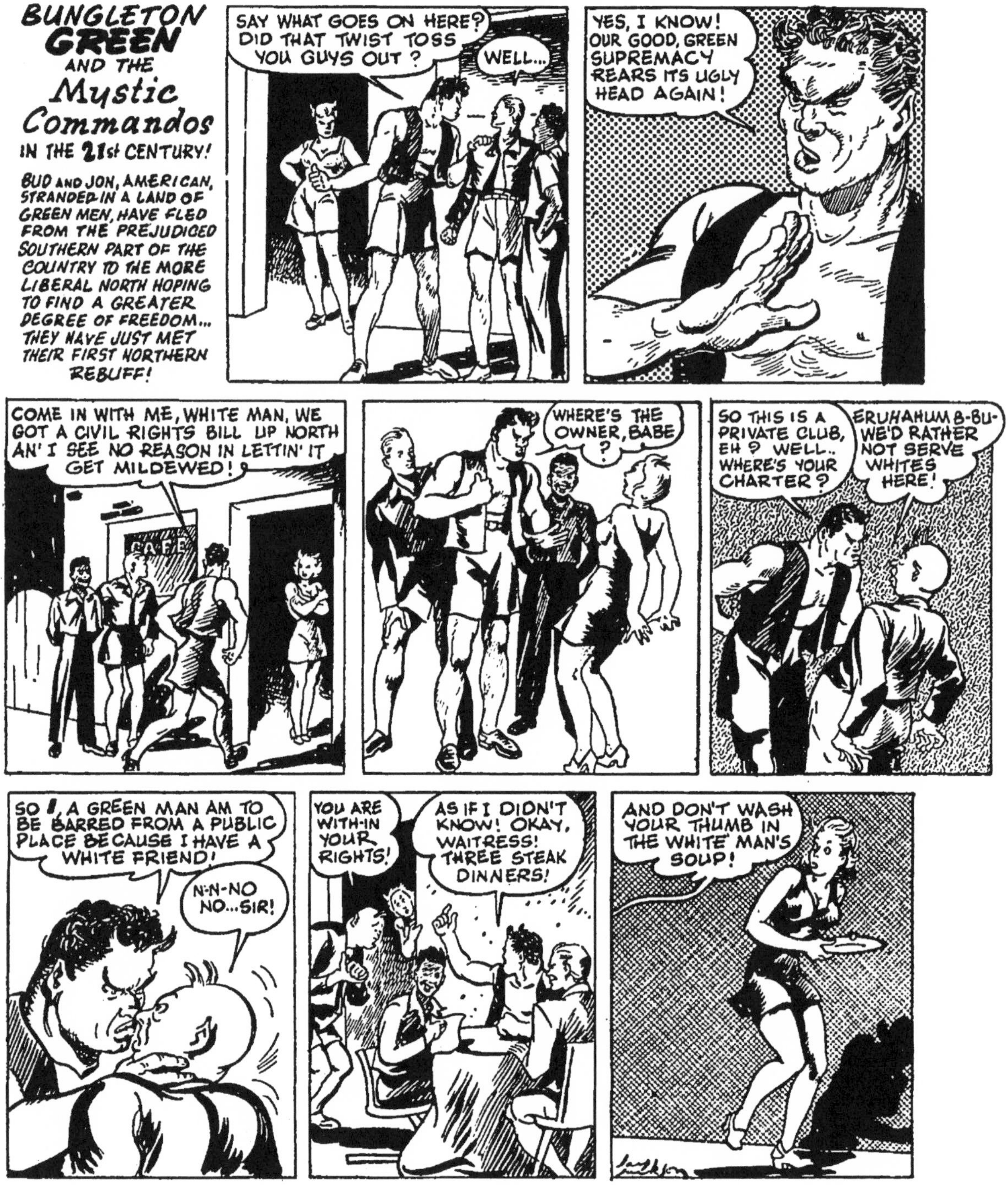
BUNGLETON GREEN AND THE Mystic Commandos IN THE 21st CENTURY!
BUD AND JON, AMERICAN, STRANDED IN A LAND OF GREEN MEN, HAVE FLED FROM THE PREJUDICED SOUTHERN PART OF THE COUNTRY TO THE MORE LIBERAL NORTH HOPING TO FIND A GREATER DEGREE OF FREEDOM... THEY HAVE JUST MET THEIR FIRST NORTHERN REBUFF!
SAY WHAT GOES ON HERE? DID THAT TWIST TOSS YOU GUYS OUT ?
WELL...
YES, I KNOW! OUR GOOD, GREEN SUPREMACY REARS ITS UGLY HEAD AGAIN!
COME IN WITH ME, WHITE MAN, WE GOT A CIVIL RIGHTS BILL UP NORTH AN' I SEE NO REASON IN LETTIN' IT GET MILDEWED!
CAFE
WHERE'S THE OWNER, BABE ?
SO THIS IS A PRIVATE CLUB, EH ? WELL.. WHERE'S YOUR CHARTER ?
ERUHAHUM B-BU- WE'D RATHER NOT SERVE WHITES HERE!
SO I, A GREEN MAN AM TO BE BARRED FROM A PUBLIC PLACE BECAUSE I HAVE A WHITE FRIEND!
N-N-NO NO...SIR!
YOU ARE WITH-IN YOUR RIGHTS!
AS IF I DIDN'T KNOW! OKAY, WAITRESS! THREE STEAK DINNERS!
AND DON'T WASH YOUR THUMB IN THE WHITE MAN'S SOUP!

August 5, 1944

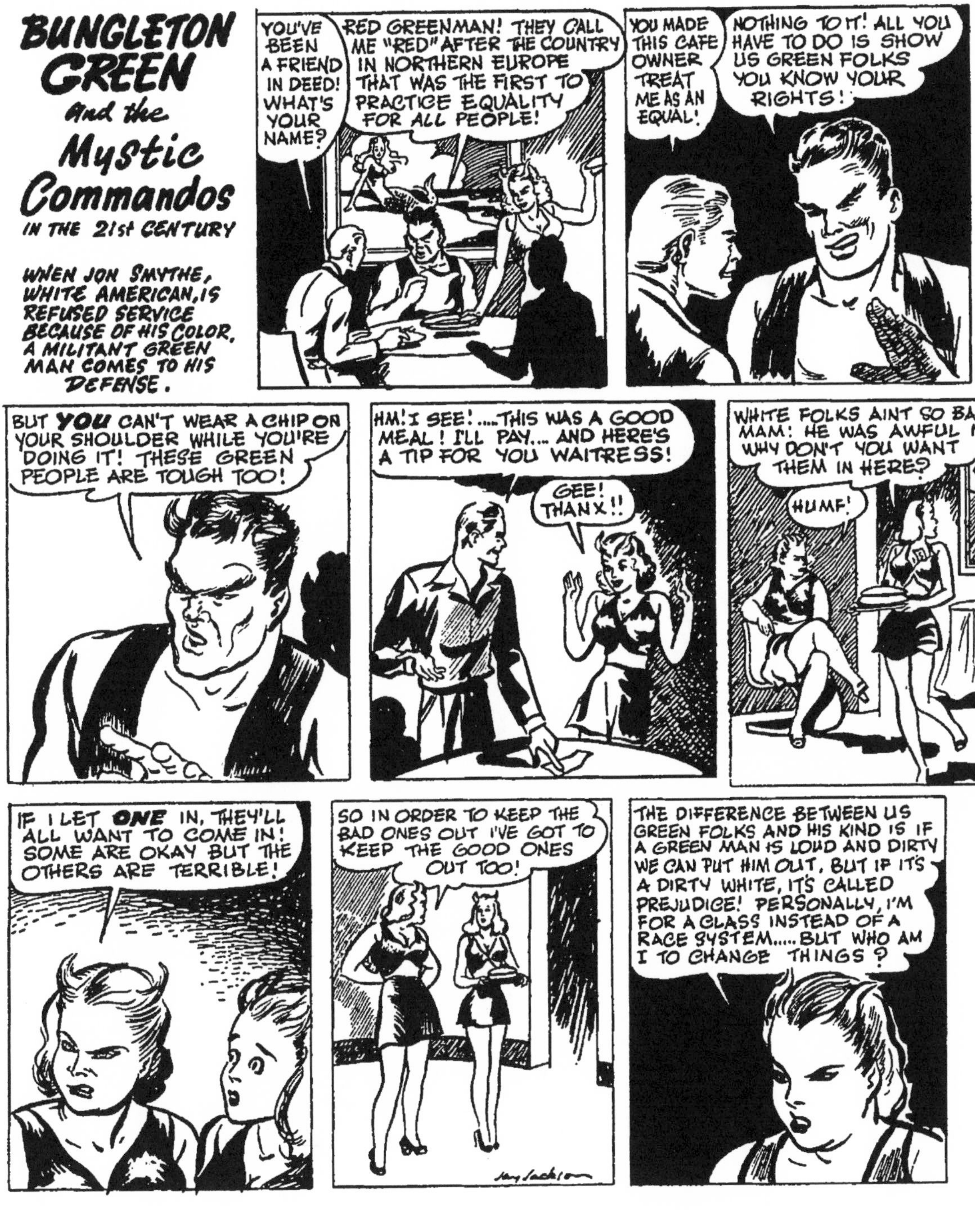
BUNGLETON GREEN and the Mystic Commandos IN THE 21st CENTURY
WHEN JON SMYTHE, WHITE AMERICAN, IS REFUSED SERVICE BECAUSE OF HIS COLOR, A MILITANT GREEN MAN COMES TO HIS DEFENSE.
YOU'VE BEEN A FRIEND IN DEED! WHAT'S YOUR NAME?
RED GREENMAN! THEY CALL ME "RED" AFTER THE COUNTRY IN NORTHERN EUROPE THAT WAS THE FIRST TO PRACTICE EQUALITY FOR ALL PEOPLE!
YOU MADE THIS CAFE OWNER TREAT ME AS AN EQUAL!
NOTHING TO IT! ALL YOU HAVE TO DO IS SHOW US GREEN FOLKS YOU KNOW YOUR RIGHTS!
BUT YOU CAN'T WEAR A CHIP ON YOUR SHOULDER WHILE YOU'RE DOING IT! THESE GREEN PEOPLE ARE TOUGH TOO!
HM! I SEE! ....THIS WAS A GOOD MEAL! I'LL PAY... AND HERE'S A TIP FOR YOU WAITRESS!
GEE! THANX!!
WHITE FOLKS AINT SO BAD, MAM: HE WAS AWFUL NICE! WHY DON'T YOU WANT THEM IN HERE?
HUMF!
IF I LET ONE IN, THEY'LL ALL WANT TO COME IN! SOME ARE OKAY BUT THE OTHERS ARE TERRIBLE!
SO IN ORDER TO KEEP THE BAD ONES OUT I'VE GOT TO KEEP THE GOOD ONES OUT TOO!
THE DIFFERENCE BETWEEN US GREEN FOLKS AND HIS KIND IS IF A GREEN MAN IS LOUD AND DIRTY WE CAN PUT HIM OUT, BUT IF IT'S A DIRTY WHITE, IT'S CALLED PREJUDICE! PERSONALLY, I'M FOR A CLASS INSTEAD OF A RACE SYSTEM..... BUT WHO AM I TO CHANGE THINGS?
Jay Jackson

August 12, 1944

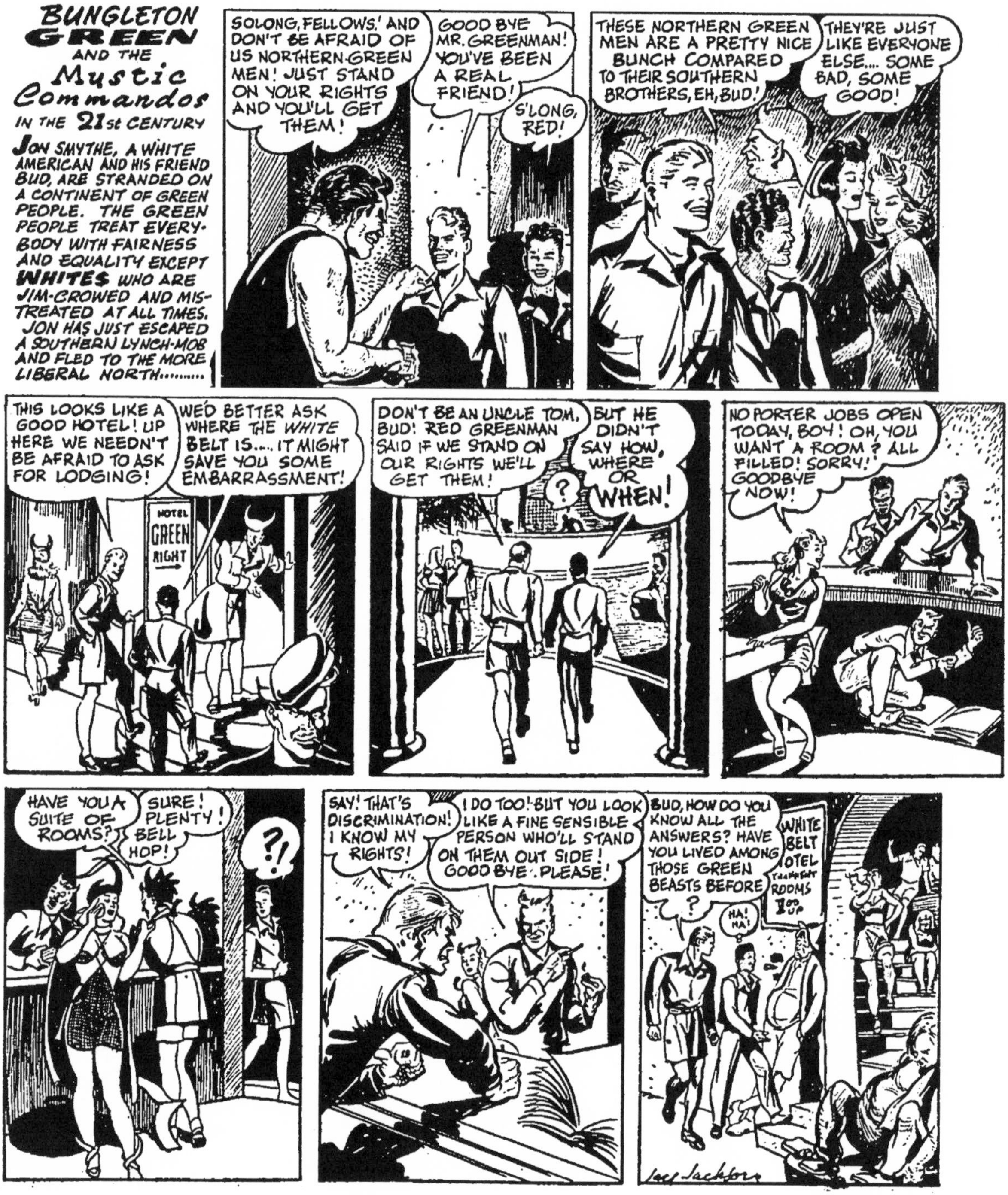

BUNGLETON GREEN AND THE Mystic Commandos IN THE 21st CENTURY
JON SMYTHE, A WHITE AMERICAN AND HIS FRIEND BUD, ARE STRANDED ON A CONTINENT OF GREEN PEOPLE. THE GREEN PEOPLE TREAT EVERYBODY WITH FAIRNESS AND EQUALITY EXCEPT WHITES WHO ARE JIM-CROWED AND MISTREATED AT ALL TIMES. JON HAS JUST ESCAPED A SOUTHERN LYNCH-MOB AND FLED TO THE MORE LIBERAL NORTH.........
SOLONG, FELLOWS! AND DON'T BE AFRAID OF US NORTHERN-GREEN MEN! JUST STAND ON YOUR RIGHTS AND YOU'LL GET THEM!
GOOD BYE MR. GREENMAN! YOU'VE BEEN A REAL FRIEND!
S'LONG, RED!
THESE NORTHERN GREEN MEN ARE A PRETTY NICE BUNCH COMPARED TO THEIR SOUTHERN BROTHERS, EH, BUD!
THEY'RE JUST LIKE EVERYONE ELSE.... SOME BAD, SOME GOOD!
THIS LOOKS LIKE A GOOD HOTEL! UP HERE WE NEEDN'T BE AFRAID TO ASK FOR LODGING!
WE'D BETTER ASK WHERE THE WHITE BELT IS.... IT MIGHT SAVE YOU SOME EMBARRASSMENT!
HOTEL GREEN RIGHT
DON'T BE AN UNCLE TOM, BUD! RED GREENMAN SAID IF WE STAND ON OUR RIGHTS WE'LL GET THEM!
BUT HE DIDN'T SAY HOW, WHERE OR WHEN!
?
NO PORTER JOBS OPEN TODAY, BOY! OH, YOU WANT A ROOM? ALL FILLED! SORRY! GOODBYE NOW!
HAVE YOU A SUITE OF ROOMS?
SURE! PLENTY! BELL HOP!
?!
SAY! THAT'S DISCRIMINATION! I KNOW MY RIGHTS!
I DO TOO! BUT YOU LOOK LIKE A FINE SENSIBLE PERSON WHO'LL STAND ON THEM OUT SIDE! GOOD BYE. PLEASE!
BUD, HOW DO YOU KNOW ALL THE ANSWERS? HAVE YOU LIVED AMONG THOSE GREEN BEASTS BEFORE
?
HA! HA!
WHITE BELT HOTEL ROOMS

August 19, 1944

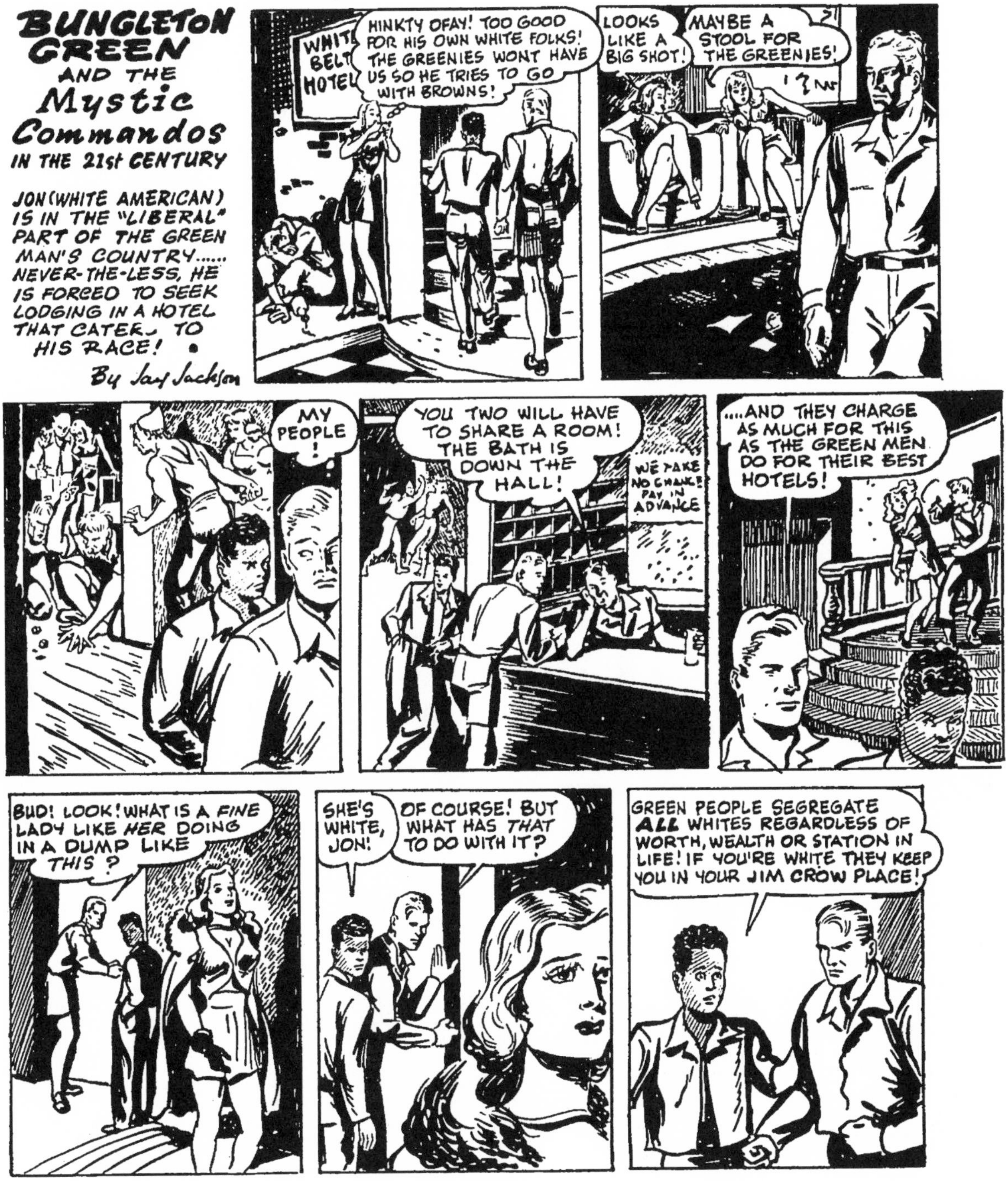

BUNGLETON GREEN AND THE Mystic Commandos IN THE 21st CENTURY
JON (WHITE AMERICAN) IS IN THE "LIBERAL" PART OF THE GREEN MAN'S COUNTRY..... NEVER-THE-LESS, HE IS FORCED TO SEEK LODGING IN A HOTEL THAT CATERS TO HIS RACE!
By Jay Jackson
HINKTY OFAY! TOO GOOD FOR HIS OWN WHITE FOLKS! THE GREENIES WONT HAVE US SO HE TRIES TO GO WITH BROWNS!
LOOKS LIKE A BIG SHOT!
MAYBE A STOOL FOR THE GREENIES!
MY PEOPLE!
YOU TWO WILL HAVE TO SHARE A ROOM! THE BATH IS DOWN THE HALL!
....AND THEY CHARGE AS MUCH FOR THIS AS THE GREEN MEN DO FOR THEIR BEST HOTELS!
BUD! LOOK! WHAT IS A FINE LADY LIKE HER DOING IN A DUMP LIKE THIS?
SHE'S WHITE, JON!
OF COURSE! BUT WHAT HAS THAT TO DO WITH IT?
GREEN PEOPLE SEGREGATE ALL WHITES REGARDLESS OF WORTH, WEALTH OR STATION IN LIFE! IF YOU'RE WHITE THEY KEEP YOU IN YOUR JIM CROW PLACE!

August 26, 1944

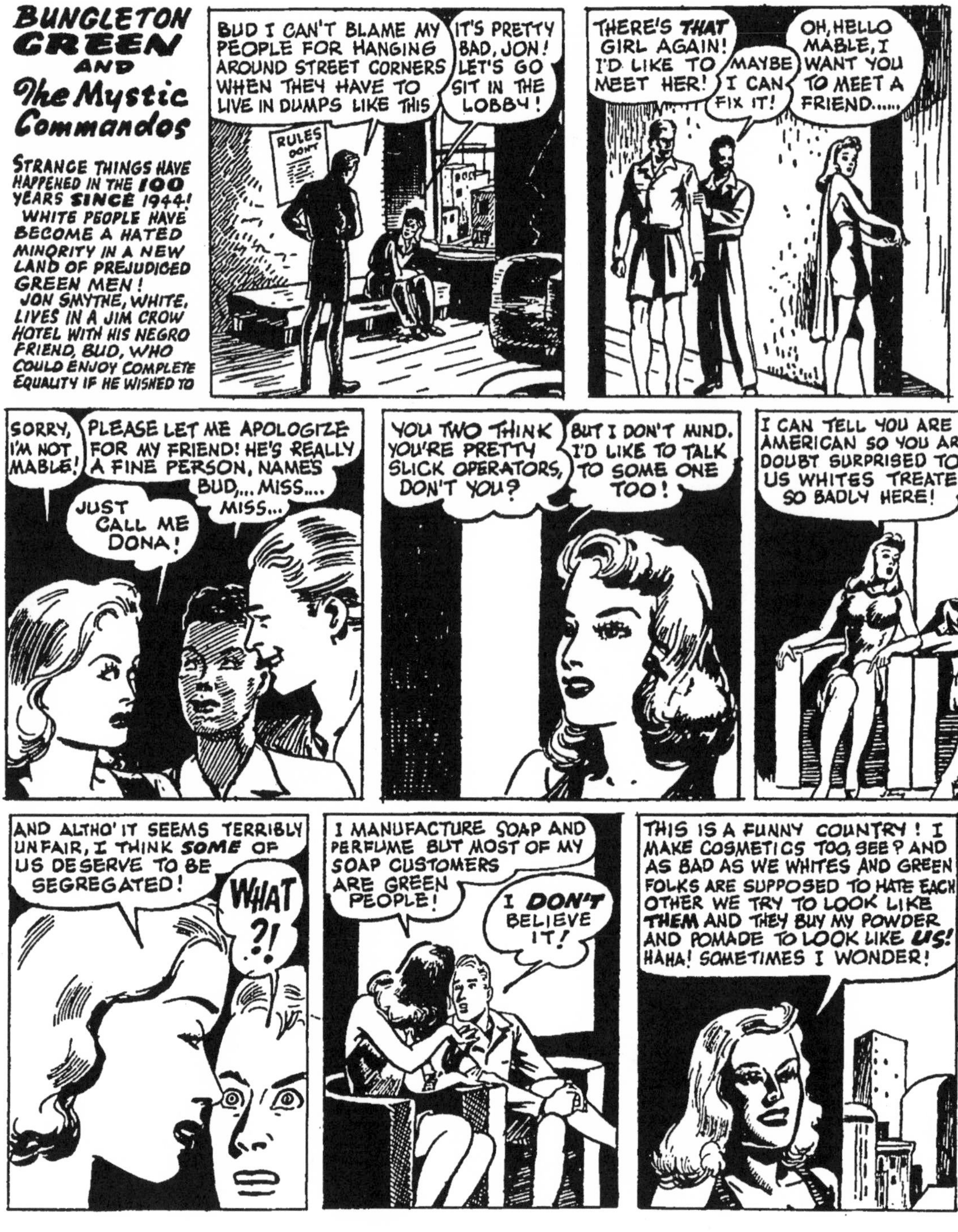
BUNGLETON GREEN AND The Mystic Commandos
STRANGE THINGS HAVE HAPPENED IN THE 100 YEARS SINCE 1944! WHITE PEOPLE HAVE BECOME A HATED MINORITY IN A NEW LAND OF PREJUDICED GREEN MEN! JON SMYTHE, WHITE, LIVES IN A JIM CROW HOTEL WITH HIS NEGRO FRIEND, BUD, WHO COULD ENJOY COMPLETE EQUALITY IF HE WISHED TO
BUD I CAN'T BLAME MY PEOPLE FOR HANGING AROUND STREET CORNERS WHEN THEY HAVE TO LIVE IN DUMPS LIKE THIS
IT'S PRETTY BAD, JON! LET'S GO SIT IN THE LOBBY!
RULES
THERE'S THAT GIRL AGAIN! I'D LIKE TO MEET HER!
MAYBE I CAN FIX IT!
OH, HELLO MABLE, I WANT YOU TO MEET A FRIEND......
SORRY, I'M NOT MABLE!
PLEASE LET ME APOLOGIZE FOR MY FRIEND! HE'S REALLY A FINE PERSON, NAMES BUD,... MISS.... MISS...
JUST CALL ME DONA!
YOU TWO THINK YOU'RE PRETTY SLICK OPERATORS, DON'T YOU?
BUT I DON'T MIND. I'D LIKE TO TALK TO SOME ONE TOO!
I CAN TELL YOU ARE AN AMERICAN SO YOU ARE NO DOUBT SURPRISED TO SEE US WHITES TREATED SO BADLY HERE!
AND ALTHO' IT SEEMS TERRIBLY UNFAIR, I THINK SOME OF US DESERVE TO BE SEGREGATED!
WHAT ?!
I MANUFACTURE SOAP AND PERFUME BUT MOST OF MY SOAP CUSTOMERS ARE GREEN PEOPLE!
I DON'T BELIEVE IT!
THIS IS A FUNNY COUNTRY! I MAKE COSMETICS TOO, SEE? AND AS BAD AS WE WHITES AND GREEN FOLKS ARE SUPPOSED TO HATE EACH OTHER WE TRY TO LOOK LIKE THEM AND THEY BUY MY POWDER AND POMADE TO LOOK LIKE US! HAHA! SOMETIMES I WONDER!

September 2, 1944

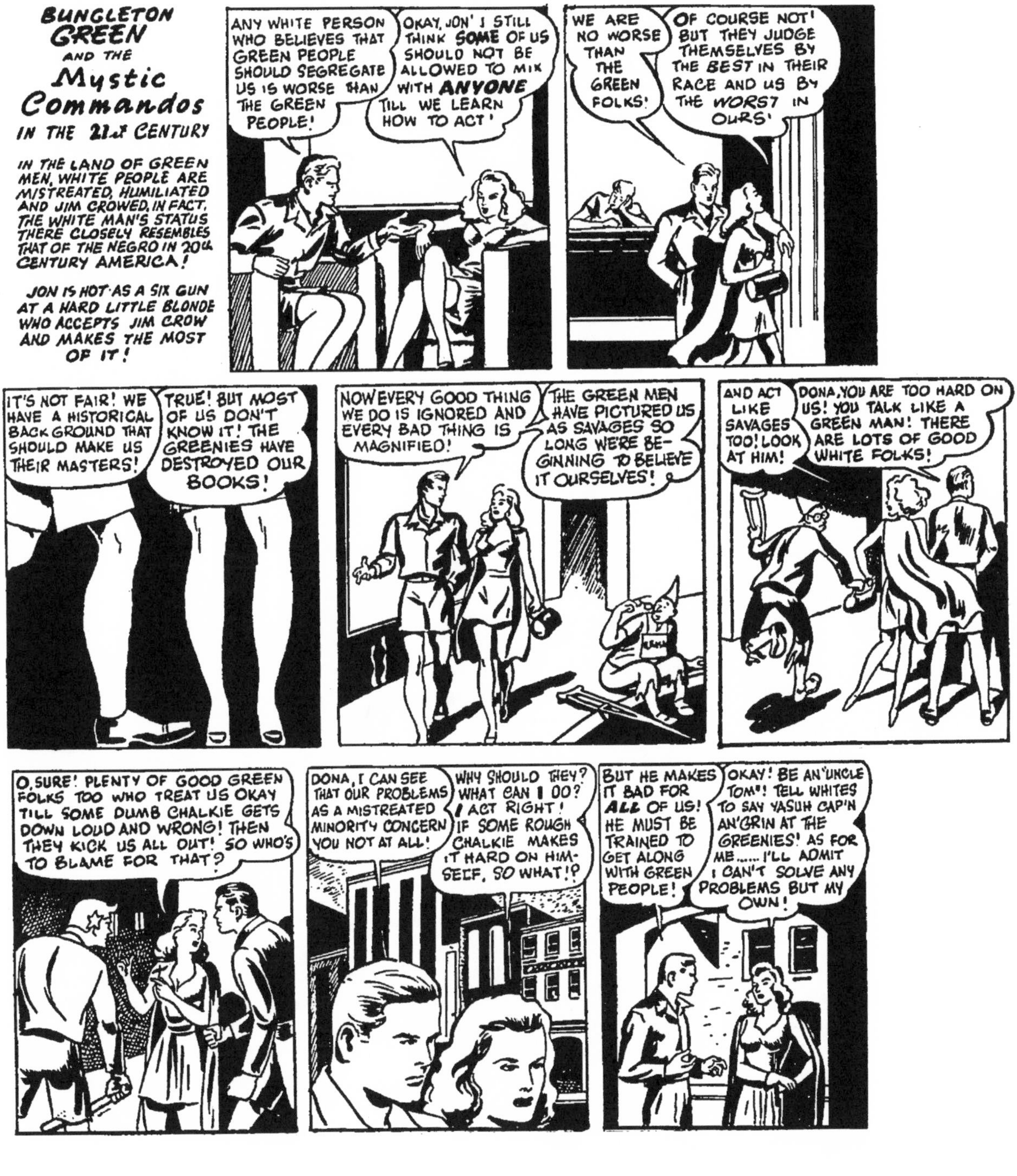

BUNGLETON GREEN AND THE Mystic Commandos IN THE 21st CENTURY
IN THE LAND OF GREEN MEN, WHITE PEOPLE ARE MISTREATED, HUMILIATED AND JIM CROWED. IN FACT, THE WHITE MAN'S STATUS THERE CLOSELY RESEMBLES THAT OF THE NEGRO IN 20th CENTURY AMERICA!
JON IS HOT AS A SIX GUN AT A HARD LITTLE BLONDE WHO ACCEPTS JIM CROW AND MAKES THE MOST OF IT!
ANY WHITE PERSON WHO BELIEVES THAT GREEN PEOPLE SHOULD SEGREGATE US IS WORSE THAN THE GREEN PEOPLE!
OKAY, JON! I STILL THINK SOME OF US SHOULD NOT BE ALLOWED TO MIX WITH ANYONE TILL WE LEARN HOW TO ACT!
WE ARE NO WORSE THAN THE GREEN FOLKS!
OF COURSE NOT! BUT THEY JUDGE THEMSELVES BY THE BEST IN THEIR RACE AND US BY THE WORST IN OURS!
IT'S NOT FAIR! WE HAVE A HISTORICAL BACKGROUND THAT SHOULD MAKE US THEIR MASTERS!
TRUE! BUT MOST OF US DON'T KNOW IT! THE GREENIES HAVE DESTROYED OUR BOOKS!
NOW EVERY GOOD THING WE DO IS IGNORED AND EVERY BAD THING IS MAGNIFIED!
THE GREEN MEN HAVE PICTURED US AS SAVAGES SO LONG WE'RE BEGINNING TO BELIEVE IT OURSELVES!
AND ACT LIKE SAVAGES TOO! LOOK AT HIM!
DONA, YOU ARE TOO HARD ON US! YOU TALK LIKE A GREEN MAN! THERE ARE LOTS OF GOOD WHITE FOLKS!
O, SURE! PLENTY OF GOOD GREEN FOLKS TOO WHO TREAT US OKAY TILL SOME DUMB CHALKIE GETS DOWN LOUD AND WRONG! THEN THEY KICK US ALL OUT! SO WHO'S TO BLAME FOR THAT?
DONA, I CAN SEE THAT OUR PROBLEMS AS A MISTREATED MINORITY CONCERN YOU NOT AT ALL!
WHY SHOULD THEY? WHAT CAN I DO? I ACT RIGHT! IF SOME ROUGH CHALKIE MAKES IT HARD ON HIMSELF, SO WHAT!?
BUT HE MAKES IT BAD FOR ALL OF US! HE MUST BE TRAINED TO GET ALONG WITH GREEN PEOPLE!
OKAY! BE AN 'UNCLE TOM'! TELL WHITES TO SAY YASUH CAP'N AN' GRIN AT THE GREENIES! AS FOR ME...... I'LL ADMIT I CAN'T SOLVE ANY PROBLEMS BUT MY OWN!

September 9, 1944

THE GREEN MAN REACHES HIS OFFICE

September 16, 1944

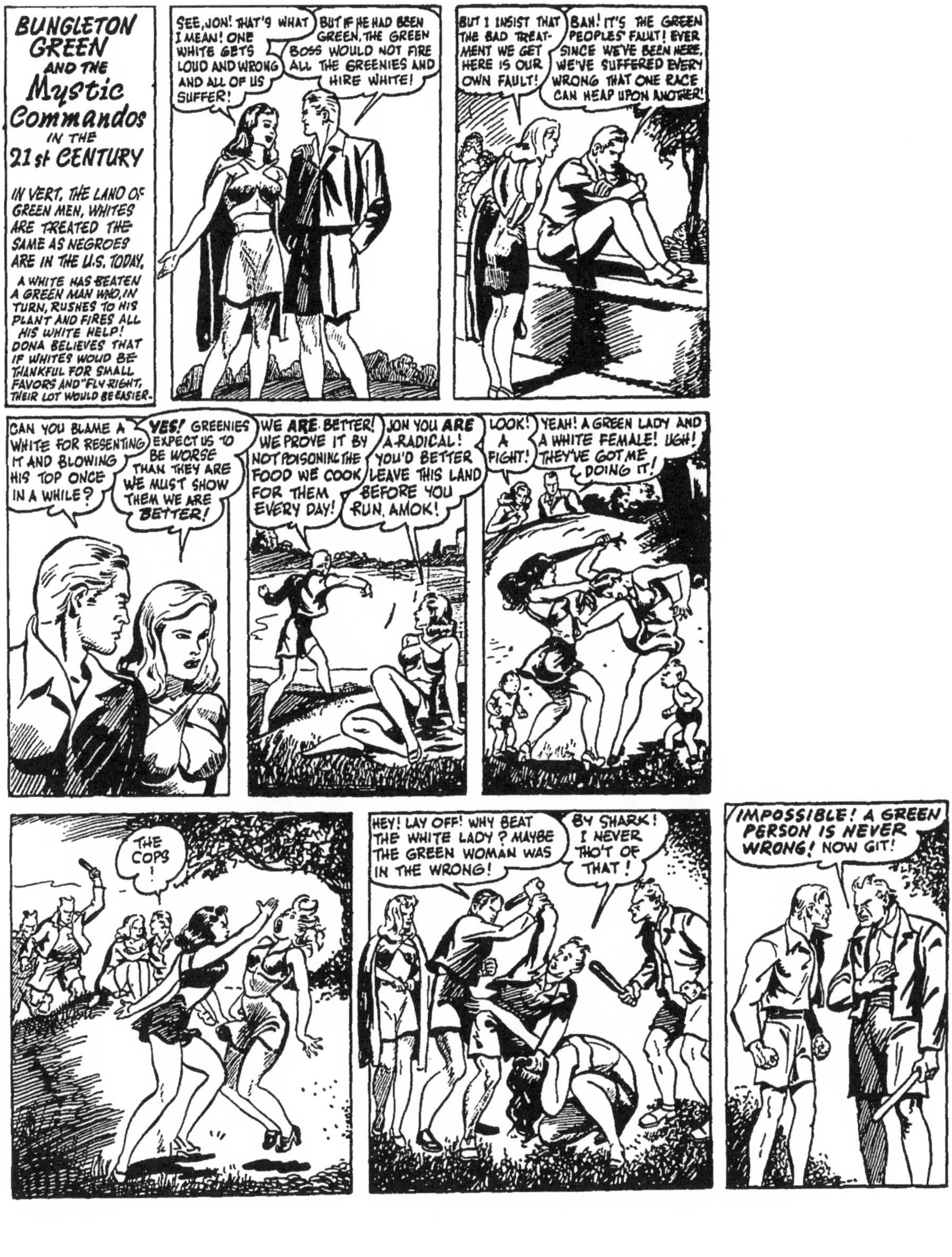
BUNGLETON GREEN AND THE Mystic Commandos IN THE 21st CENTURY
IN VERT, THE LAND OF GREEN MEN, WHITES ARE TREATED THE SAME AS NEGROES ARE IN THE U.S. TODAY.
A WHITE HAS BEATEN A GREEN MAN WHO, IN TURN, RUSHES TO HIS PLANT AND FIRES ALL HIS WHITE HELP! DONA BELIEVES THAT IF WHITES WOUD BE THANKFUL FOR SMALL FAVORS AND "FLY RIGHT," THEIR LOT WOULD BE EASIER.
SEE, JON! THAT'S WHAT I MEAN! ONE WHITE GETS LOUD AND WRONG AND ALL OF US SUFFER!
BUT IF HE HAD BEEN GREEN, THE GREEN BOSS WOULD NOT FIRE ALL THE GREENIES AND HIRE WHITE!
BUT I INSIST THAT THE BAD TREATMENT WE GET HERE IS OUR OWN FAULT!
BAH! IT'S THE GREEN PEOPLES' FAULT! EVER SINCE WE'VE BEEN HERE, WE'VE SUFFERED EVERY WRONG THAT ONE RACE CAN HEAP UPON ANOTHER!
CAN YOU BLAME A WHITE FOR RESENTING IT AND BLOWING HIS TOP ONCE IN A WHILE?
YES! GREENIES EXPECT US TO BE WORSE THAN THEY ARE WE MUST SHOW THEM WE ARE BETTER!
WE ARE BETTER! WE PROVE IT BY NOT POISONING THE FOOD WE COOK FOR THEM EVERY DAY!
JON YOU ARE A RADICAL! YOU'D BETTER LEAVE THIS LAND BEFORE YOU RUN, AMOK!
LOOK! A FIGHT!
YEAH! A GREEN LADY AND A WHITE FEMALE! UGH! THEY'VE GOT ME DOING IT!
THE COPS!
HEY! LAY OFF! WHY BEAT THE WHITE LADY? MAYBE THE GREEN WOMAN WAS IN THE WRONG!
BY SHARK! I NEVER THO'T OF THAT!
IMPOSSIBLE! A GREEN PERSON IS NEVER WRONG! NOW GIT!

September 23, 1944

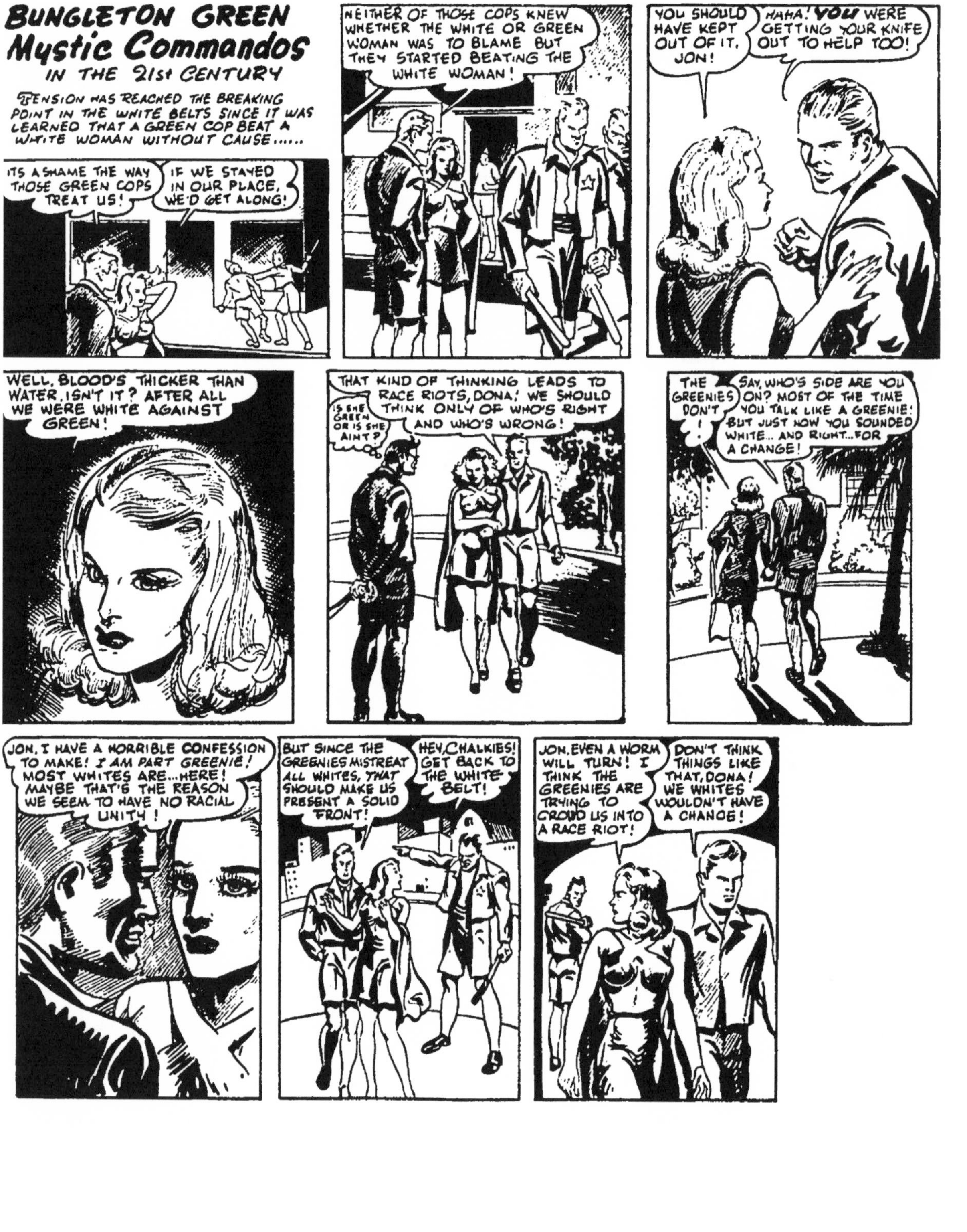
BUNGLETON GREEN
Mystic Commandos
IN THE 21st CENTURY
TENSION HAS REACHED THE BREAKING POINT IN THE WHITE BELTS SINCE IT WAS LEARNED THAT A GREEN COP BEAT A WHITE WOMAN WITHOUT CAUSE......
ITS A SHAME THE WAY THOSE GREEN COPS TREAT US!
IF WE STAYED IN OUR PLACE, WE'D GET ALONG!
NEITHER OF THOSE COPS KNEW WHETHER THE WHITE OR GREEN WOMAN WAS TO BLAME BUT THEY STARTED BEATING THE WHITE WOMAN!
YOU SHOULD HAVE KEPT OUT OF IT, JON!
HAHA! YOU WERE GETTING YOUR KNIFE OUT TO HELP TOO!
WELL, BLOOD'S THICKER THAN WATER, ISN'T IT? AFTER ALL WE WERE WHITE AGAINST GREEN!
THAT KIND OF THINKING LEADS TO RACE RIOTS, DONA! WE SHOULD THINK ONLY OF WHO'S RIGHT AND WHO'S WRONG!
IS SHE GREEN OR IS SHE AINT?
THE GREENIES DON'T!
SAY, WHO'S SIDE ARE YOU ON? MOST OF THE TIME YOU TALK LIKE A GREENIE! BUT JUST NOW YOU SOUNDED WHITE... AND RIGHT... FOR A CHANGE!
JON, I HAVE A HORRIBLE CONFESSION TO MAKE! I AM PART GREENIE! MOST WHITES ARE... HERE! MAYBE THAT'S THE REASON WE SEEM TO HAVE NO RACIAL UNITY!
BUT SINCE THE GREENIES MISTREAT ALL WHITES, THAT SHOULD MAKE US PRESENT A SOLID FRONT!
HEY, CHALKIES! GET BACK TO THE WHITE BELT!
JON, EVEN A WORM WILL TURN! I THINK THE GREENIES ARE TRYING TO CROWD US INTO A RACE RIOT!
DON'T THINK THINGS LIKE THAT, DONA! WE WHITES WOULDN'T HAVE A CHANCE!

September 30, 1944

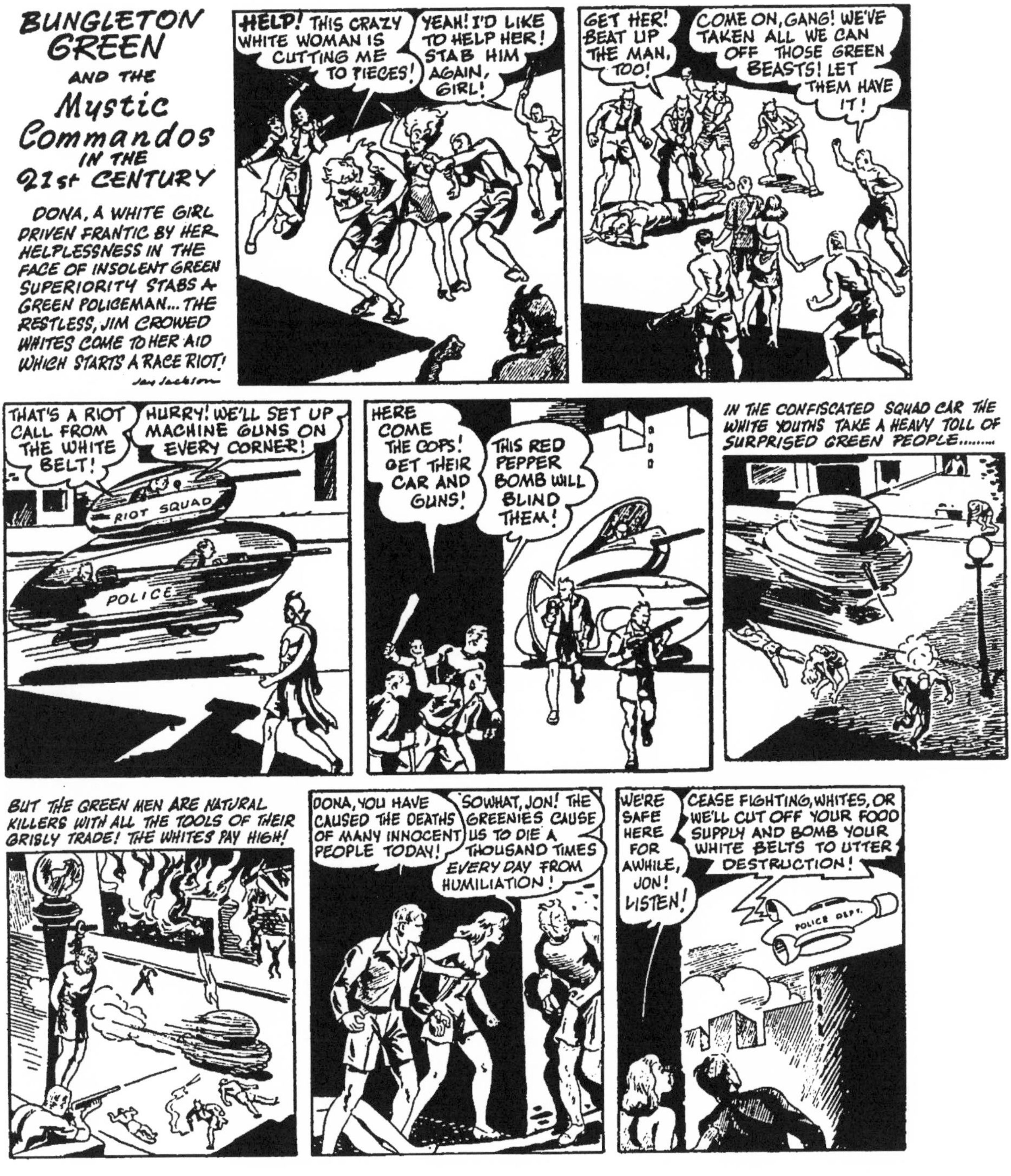
BUNGLETON GREEN AND THE Mystic Commandos IN THE 21st CENTURY
DONA, A WHITE GIRL DRIVEN FRANTIC BY HER HELPLESSNESS IN THE FACE OF INSOLENT GREEN SUPERIORITY STABS A GREEN POLICEMAN... THE RESTLESS, JIM CROWED WHITES COME TO HER AID WHICH STARTS A RACE RIOT!
HELP! THIS CRAZY WHITE WOMAN IS CUTTING ME TO PIECES!
YEAH! I'D LIKE TO HELP HER! STAB HIM AGAIN, GIRL!
GET HER! BEAT UP THE MAN, TOO!
COME ON, GANG! WE'VE TAKEN ALL WE CAN OFF THOSE GREEN BEASTS! LET THEM HAVE IT!
THAT'S A RIOT CALL FROM THE WHITE BELT!
HURRY! WE'LL SET UP MACHINE GUNS ON EVERY CORNER!
RIOT SQUAD
POLICE
HERE COME THE COPS! GET THEIR CAR AND GUNS!
THIS RED PEPPER BOMB WILL BLIND THEM!
IN THE CONFISCATED SQUAD CAR THE WHITE YOUTHS TAKE A HEAVY TOLL OF SURPRISED GREEN PEOPLE........
BUT THE GREEN MEN ARE NATURAL KILLERS WITH ALL THE TOOLS OF THEIR GRISLY TRADE! THE WHITES PAY HIGH!
DONA, YOU HAVE CAUSED THE DEATHS OF MANY INNOCENT PEOPLE TODAY!
SO WHAT, JON! THE GREENIES CAUSE US TO DIE A THOUSAND TIMES EVERY DAY FROM HUMILIATION!
WE'RE SAFE HERE FOR AWHILE, JON! LISTEN!
CEASE FIGHTING, WHITES, OR WE'LL CUT OFF YOUR FOOD SUPPLY AND BOMB YOUR WHITE BELTS TO UTTER DESTRUCTION!
POLICE DEPT.

October 14, 1944

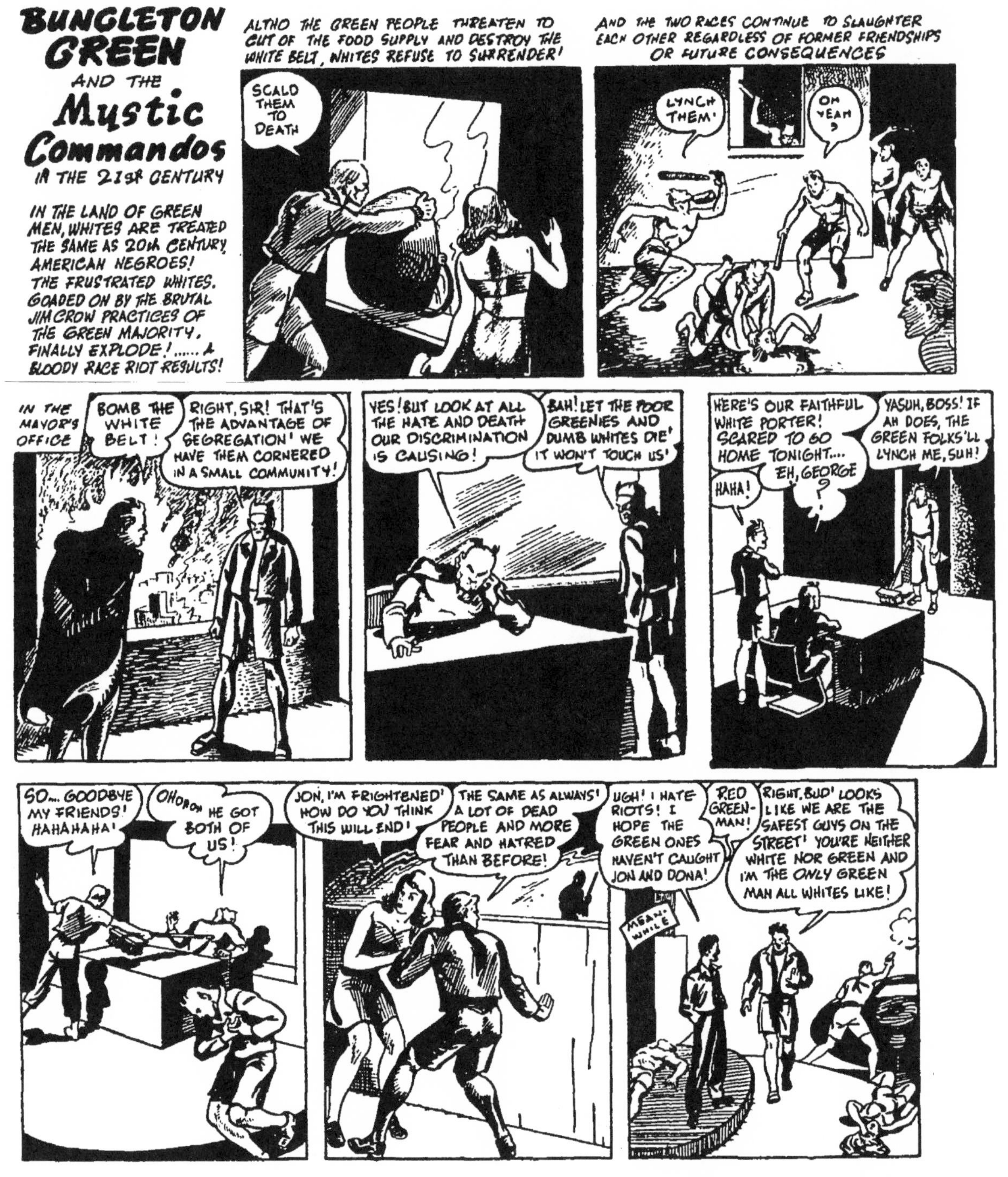
BUNGLETON GREEN AND THE Mystic Commandos IN THE 21ST CENTURY
IN THE LAND OF GREEN MEN, WHITES ARE TREATED THE SAME AS 20TH CENTURY AMERICAN NEGROES! THE FRUSTRATED WHITES, GOADED ON BY THE BRUTAL JIM CROW PRACTICES OF THE GREEN MAJORITY, FINALLY EXPLODE! ...... A BLOODY RACE RIOT RESULTS!
ALTHO THE GREEN PEOPLE THREATEN TO CUT OF THE FOOD SUPPLY AND DESTROY THE WHITE BELT, WHITES REFUSE TO SURRENDER!
SCALD THEM TO DEATH
AND THE TWO RACES CONTINUE TO SLAUGHTER EACH OTHER REGARDLESS OF FORMER FRIENDSHIPS OR FUTURE CONSEQUENCES
LYNCH THEM!
OH YEAH?
IN THE MAYOR'S OFFICE
BOMB THE WHITE BELT!
RIGHT, SIR! THAT'S THE ADVANTAGE OF SEGREGATION! WE HAVE THEM CORNERED IN A SMALL COMMUNITY!
YES! BUT LOOK AT ALL THE HATE AND DEATH OUR DISCRIMINATION IS CAUSING!
BAH! LET THE POOR GREENIES AND DUMB WHITES DIE! IT WON'T TOUCH US!
HERE'S OUR FAITHFUL WHITE PORTER! SCARED TO GO HOME TONIGHT.... EH, GEORGE?
HAHA!
YASUH, BOSS! IF AH DOES, THE GREEN FOLKS'LL LYNCH ME, SUH!
SO... GOODBYE MY FRIENDS! HAHAHAHA!
OHOHOH HE GOT BOTH OF US!
JON, I'M FRIGHTENED! HOW DO YOU THINK THIS WILL END!
THE SAME AS ALWAYS! A LOT OF DEAD PEOPLE AND MORE FEAR AND HATRED THAN BEFORE!
MEAN-WHILE
UGH! I HATE RIOTS! I HOPE THE GREEN ONES HAVEN'T CAUGHT JON AND DONA!
RED GREEN-MAN!
RIGHT, BUD! LOOKS LIKE WE ARE THE SAFEST GUYS ON THE STREET! YOU'RE NEITHER WHITE NOR GREEN AND I'M THE ONLY GREEN MAN ALL WHITES LIKE!

October 21, 1944

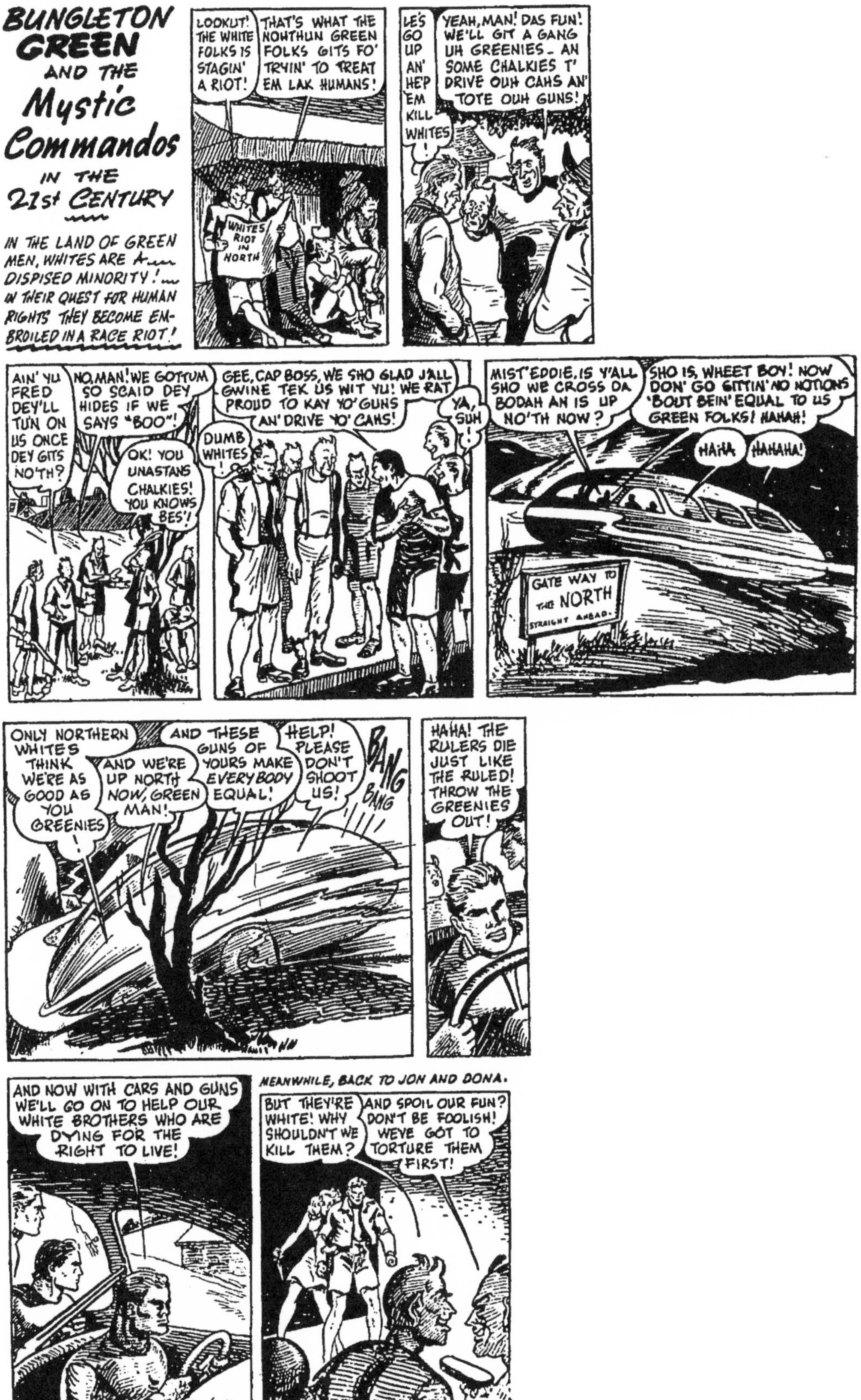
BUNGLETON GREEN AND THE Mystic Commandos IN THE 21st CENTURY
IN THE LAND OF GREEN MEN, WHITES ARE A DISPISED MINORITY! IN THEIR QUEST FOR HUMAN RIGHTS THEY BECOME EMBROILED IN A RACE RIOT!
LOOKUT! THE WHITE FOLKS IS STAGIN' A RIOT!
THAT'S WHAT THE NOHTHUN GREEN FOLKS GITS FO' TRYIN' TO TREAT EM LAK HUMANS!
WHITES RIOT IN NORTH
LE'S GO UP AN' HEP' EM KILL WHITES!
YEAH, MAN! DAS FUN! WE'LL GIT A GANG UH GREENIES - AN SOME CHALKIES T' DRIVE OUH CAHS AN' TOTE OUH GUNS!
AIN' YU FRED DEY'LL TUN ON US ONCE DEY GITS NO'TH?
NO, MAN! WE GOTTUM SO SCAID DEY HIDES IF WE SAYS "BOO"!
OK! YOU UNASTANS CHALKIES! YOU KNOWS BES'!
GEE, CAP BOSS, WE SHO GLAD J'ALL GWINE TEK US WIT YU! WE RAT PROUD TO KAY YO' GUNS AN' DRIVE YO' CAHS!
YA, SUH!
DUMB WHITES!
MIST' EDDIE, IS Y'ALL SHO WE CROSS DA BODAH AN IS UP NO'TH NOW?
SHO IS, WHEET BOY! NOW DON' GO GITTIN' NO NOTIONS 'BOUT BEIN' EQUAL TO US GREEN FOLKS! HAHAH!
HAHA
HAHAHA!
GATE WAY TO THE NORTH STRAIGHT AHEAD.
ONLY NORTHERN WHITES THINK WE'RE AS GOOD AS YOU GREENIES!
AND WE'RE UP NORTH NOW, GREEN MAN!
AND THESE GUNS OF YOURS MAKE EVERYBODY EQUAL!
HELP! PLEASE DON'T SHOOT US!
BANG
BANG
HAHA! THE RULERS DIE JUST LIKE THE RULED! THROW THE GREENIES OUT!
AND NOW WITH CARS AND GUNS WE'LL GO ON TO HELP OUR WHITE BROTHERS WHO ARE DYING FOR THE RIGHT TO LIVE!
MEANWHILE, BACK TO JON AND DONA.
BUT THEY'RE WHITE! WHY SHOULDN'T WE KILL THEM?
AND SPOIL OUR FUN? DON'T BE FOOLISH! WE'VE GOT TO TORTURE THEM FIRST!

October 28, 1944

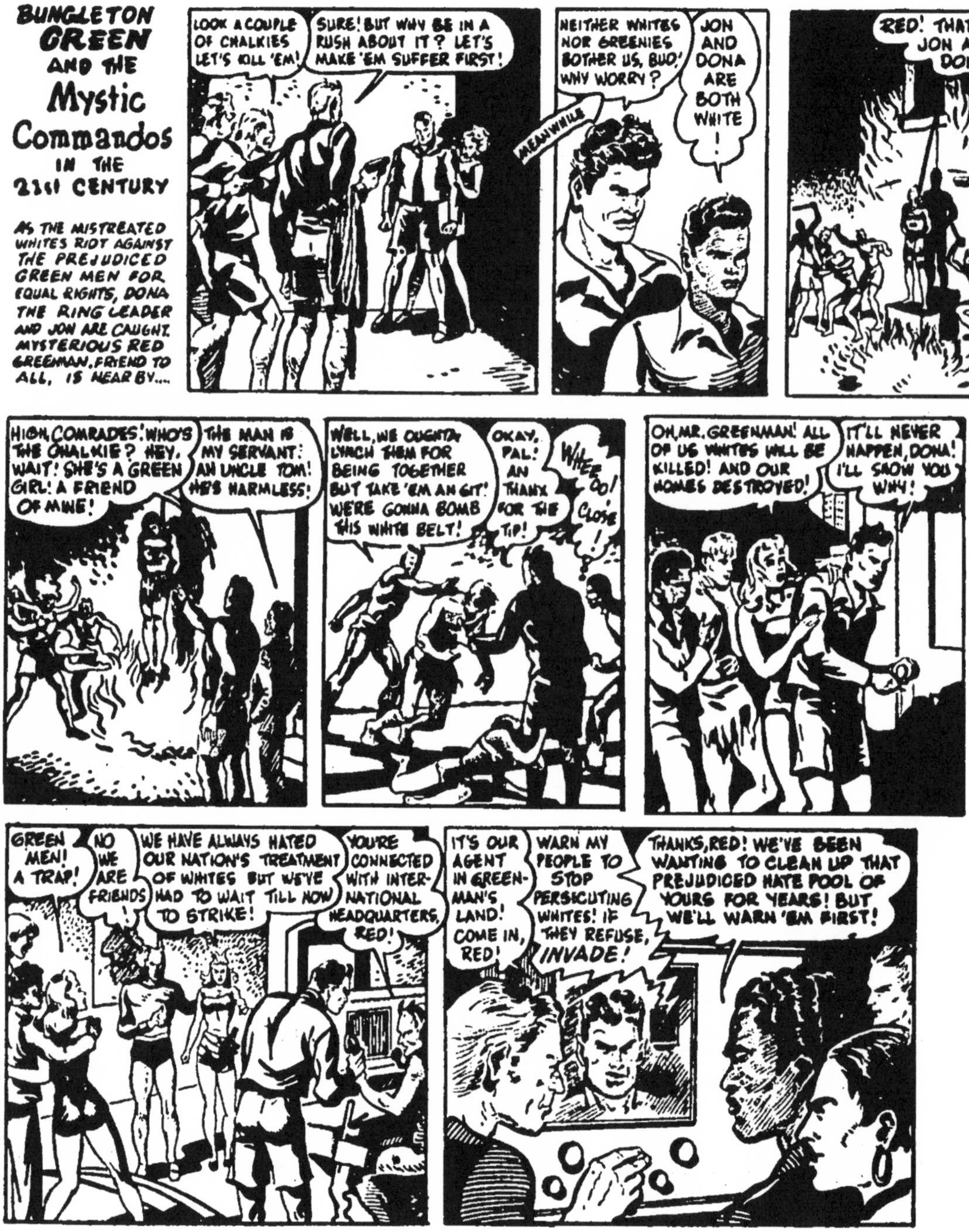
BUNGLETON GREEN AND THE Mystic Commandos IN THE 21st CENTURY
AS THE MISTREATED WHITES RIOT AGAINST THE PREJUDICED GREEN MEN FOR EQUAL RIGHTS, DONA THE RING LEADER AND JON ARE CAUGHT. MYSTERIOUS RED GREENMAN, FRIEND TO ALL, IS NEAR BY....
LOOK A COUPLE OF CHALKIES LET'S KILL 'EM!
SURE! BUT WHY BE IN A RUSH ABOUT IT? LET'S MAKE 'EM SUFFER FIRST!
MEANWHILE
NEITHER WHITES NOR GREENIES BOTHER US, BUD! WHY WORRY?
JON AND DONA ARE BOTH WHITE!
RED! THAT'S JON AND DONA!
WE MUST THINK FAST TO SAVE THEM!
HIGH, COMRADES! WHO'S THE CHALKIE? HEY. WAIT! SHE'S A GREEN GIRL! A FRIEND OF MINE!
THE MAN IS MY SERVANT! AN UNCLE TOM! HE'S HARMLESS!
WELL, WE OUGHTA LYNCH THEM FOR BEING TOGETHER BUT TAKE 'EM AN GIT! WE'RE GONNA BOMB THIS WHITE BELT!
OKAY, PAL! AN THANX FOR THE TIP!
WHEE-OO! CLOSE!
OH, MR. GREENMAN! ALL OF US WHITES WILL BE KILLED! AND OUR HOMES DESTROYED!
IT'LL NEVER HAPPEN, DONA! I'LL SHOW YOU WHY!
GREEN MEN! A TRAP!
NO WE ARE FRIENDS!
WE HAVE ALWAYS HATED OUR NATION'S TREATMENT OF WHITES BUT WE'VE HAD TO WAIT TILL NOW TO STRIKE!
YOU'RE CONNECTED WITH INTER-NATIONAL HEADQUARTERS, RED!
IT'S OUR AGENT IN GREEN-MAN'S LAND! COME IN, RED!
WARN MY PEOPLE TO STOP PERSECUTING WHITES! IF THEY REFUSE, INVADE!
THANKS, RED! WE'VE BEEN WANTING TO CLEAN UP THAT PREJUDICED HATE POOL OF YOURS FOR YEARS! BUT WE'LL WARN 'EM FIRST!

November 4, 1944

BUNGLETON **GREEN**
AND THE
Mystic Commandos
IN THE
21st CENTURY

IN THE LAND OF GREEN MEN WHITES RECEIVE THE SAME TREATMENT NEGROES GET IN AMERICA! THEIR RESENTMENT OVERFLOWS INTO A RACE RIOT! MYSTERIOUS RED GREENMAN CALLS INTERNATIONAL HEADQUARTERS TO MOVE IN AND RESTORE ORDER!

STOP RIOTING OR WE'LL BLAST YOUR ISLAND INTO THE SEA!

NOW THAT YOU'VE COME TO YOUR SENSES, WE'RE SENDING IN MEN TO ESTABLISH ORDER!

IF THEY ARE HARMED, YOUR DESTRUCTION WILL BE COMPLETE!

WHAT IF IT'S AN INVASION BY A WHITE COUNTRY?

QUIET! DON'T EVEN *THINK* SUCH THINGS!

OUR AGENT HERE ASKED US TO INVESTIGATE THIS RIOT AND YOUR MISTREATMENT OF WHITES!

GET OUT!

AS PRESIDENT AND A GREEN MAN, I REFUSE TO LET OUTSIDERS TELL ME HOW TO RUN MY COUNTRY! WE INTEND TO TREAT WHITES ANY WAY WE PLEASE!

EVEN THO YOU WISH TO KEEP YOUR LAND THE MOST HATED... THE LAUGHING STOCK OF CIVILIZED NATIONS BY YOUR RACE PREJUDICE, WE WILL *NOT* PERMIT IT!

HOWEVER WE *COULD* ARM THE WHITE RACES OF THE WORLD AND LOOSE THEM UPON YOU GREEN PEOPLE!

NO! NO! ANYTHING BUT THAT! WHAT ARE YOUR TERMS?

COMPLETE EQUALITY FOR WHITES! AND OUR AGENTS HERE.... YOUR OWN GREEN MEN... WILL ADVISE US OF ANY INJUSTICES!

OUR OWN PREJUDICES HAVE REDUCED US TO A SECOND CLASS NATION!

November 11, 1944

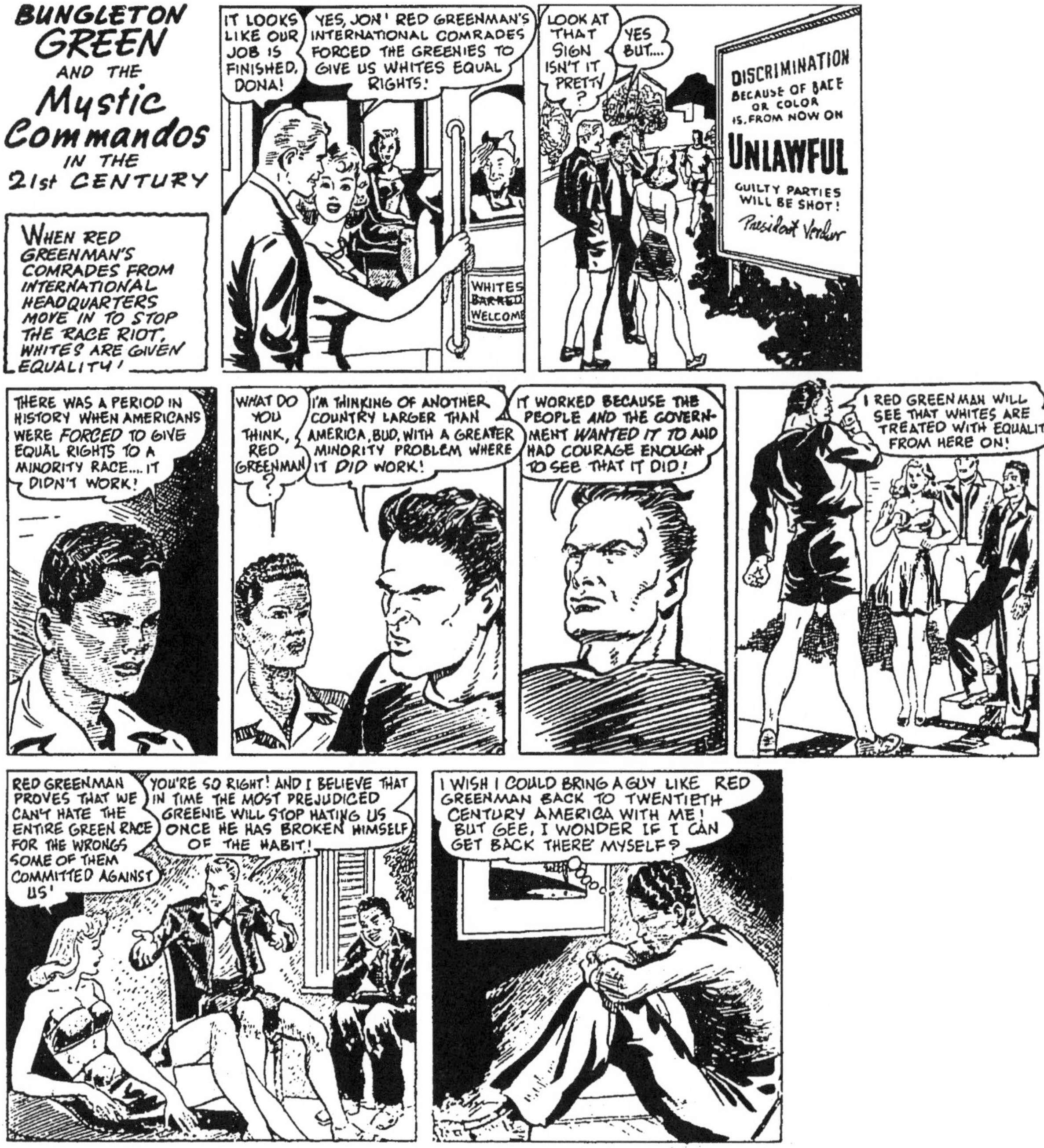
BUNGLETON GREEN AND THE Mystic Commandos IN THE 21st CENTURY
WHEN RED GREENMAN'S COMRADES FROM INTERNATIONAL HEADQUARTERS MOVE IN TO STOP THE RACE RIOT, WHITES ARE GIVEN EQUALITY!
IT LOOKS LIKE OUR JOB IS FINISHED, DONA!
YES, JON! RED GREENMAN'S INTERNATIONAL COMRADES FORCED THE GREENIES TO GIVE US WHITES EQUAL RIGHTS!
WHITES BARRED WELCOME
LOOK AT THAT SIGN ISN'T IT PRETTY?
YES BUT....
DISCRIMINATION BECAUSE OF RACE OR COLOR IS, FROM NOW ON UNLAWFUL GUILTY PARTIES WILL BE SHOT! President Verdur
THERE WAS A PERIOD IN HISTORY WHEN AMERICANS WERE FORCED TO GIVE EQUAL RIGHTS TO A MINORITY RACE.... IT DIDN'T WORK!
WHAT DO YOU THINK, RED GREENMAN?
I'M THINKING OF ANOTHER COUNTRY LARGER THAN AMERICA, BUD, WITH A GREATER MINORITY PROBLEM WHERE IT DID WORK!
IT WORKED BECAUSE THE PEOPLE AND THE GOVERNMENT WANTED IT TO AND HAD COURAGE ENOUGH TO SEE THAT IT DID!
I RED GREENMAN WILL SEE THAT WHITES ARE TREATED WITH EQUALITY FROM HERE ON!
RED GREENMAN PROVES THAT WE CAN'T HATE THE ENTIRE GREEN RACE FOR THE WRONGS SOME OF THEM COMMITTED AGAINST US!
YOU'RE SO RIGHT! AND I BELIEVE THAT IN TIME THE MOST PREJUDICED GREENIE WILL STOP HATING US ONCE HE HAS BROKEN HIMSELF OF THE HABIT!
I WISH I COULD BRING A GUY LIKE RED GREENMAN BACK TO TWENTIETH CENTURY AMERICA WITH ME! BUT GEE, I WONDER IF I CAN GET BACK THERE MYSELF?

November 18, 1944

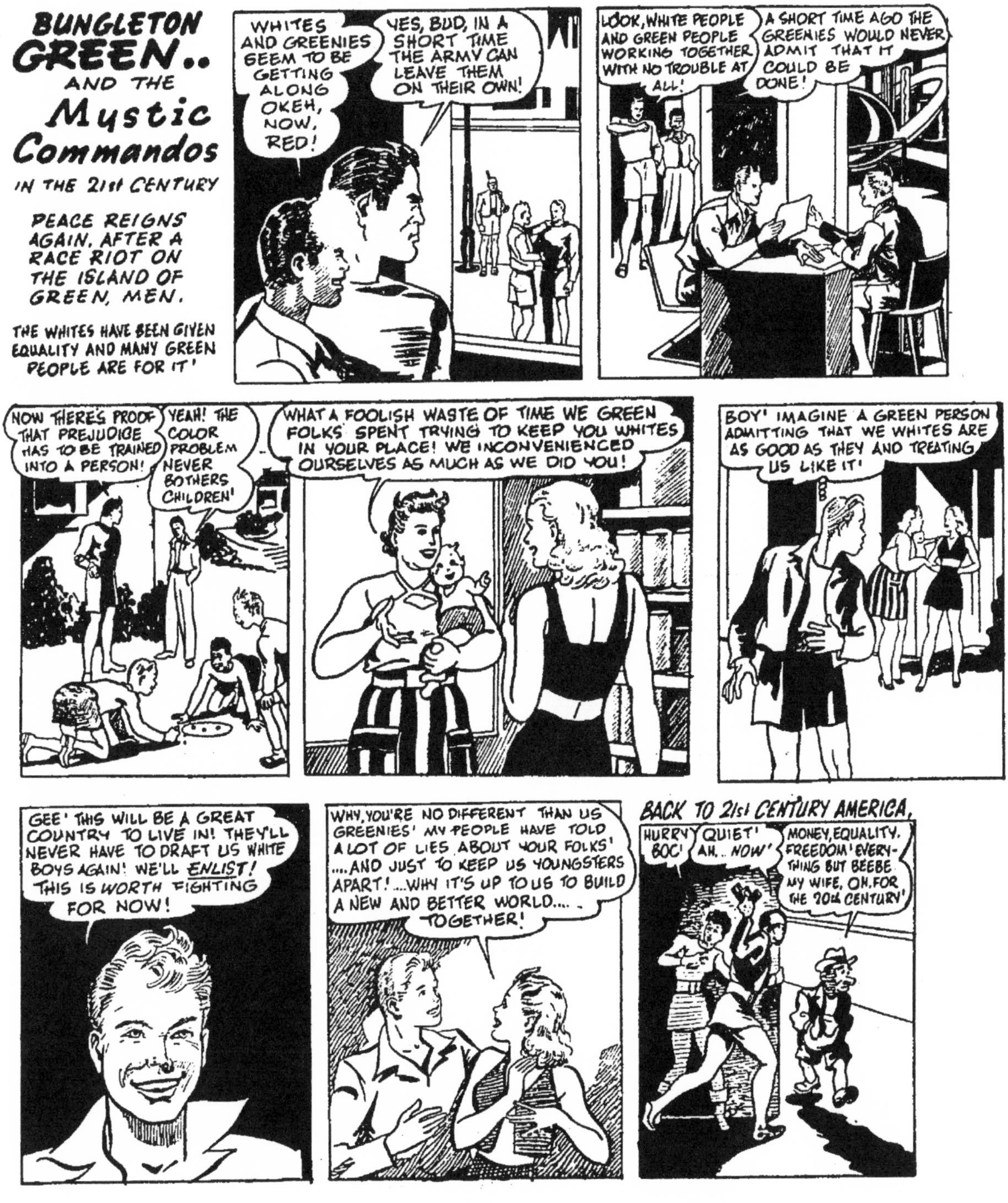
BUNGLETON GREEN.. AND THE Mystic Commandos IN THE 21st CENTURY
PEACE REIGNS AGAIN, AFTER A RACE RIOT ON THE ISLAND OF GREEN MEN.
THE WHITES HAVE BEEN GIVEN EQUALITY AND MANY GREEN PEOPLE ARE FOR IT!
WHITES AND GREENIES SEEM TO BE GETTING ALONG OKEH, NOW, RED!
YES, BUD, IN A SHORT TIME THE ARMY CAN LEAVE THEM ON THEIR OWN!
LOOK, WHITE PEOPLE AND GREEN PEOPLE WORKING TOGETHER WITH NO TROUBLE AT ALL!
A SHORT TIME AGO THE GREENIES WOULD NEVER ADMIT THAT IT COULD BE DONE!
NOW THERE'S PROOF THAT PREJUDICE HAS TO BE TRAINED INTO A PERSON!
YEAH! THE COLOR PROBLEM NEVER BOTHERS CHILDREN!
WHAT A FOOLISH WASTE OF TIME WE GREEN FOLKS SPENT TRYING TO KEEP YOU WHITES IN YOUR PLACE! WE INCONVENIENCED OURSELVES AS MUCH AS WE DID YOU!
BOY! IMAGINE A GREEN PERSON ADMITTING THAT WE WHITES ARE AS GOOD AS THEY AND TREATING US LIKE IT!
GEE! THIS WILL BE A GREAT COUNTRY TO LIVE IN! THEY'LL NEVER HAVE TO DRAFT US WHITE BOYS AGAIN! WE'LL ENLIST! THIS IS WORTH FIGHTING FOR NOW!
WHY, YOU'RE NO DIFFERENT THAN US GREENIES! MY PEOPLE HAVE TOLD A LOT OF LIES ABOUT YOUR FOLKS! ....AND JUST TO KEEP US YOUNGSTERS APART! ...WHY IT'S UP TO US TO BUILD A NEW AND BETTER WORLD.... TOGETHER!
BACK TO 21st CENTURY AMERICA,
HURRY BOC!
QUIET! AH... NOW!
MONEY, EQUALITY, FREEDOM! EVERY-THING BUT BEEBE MY WIFE. OH, FOR THE 20th CENTURY!

November 25, 1944

CHARLES JOHNSON
b. 1948

Promotional photo for *Charlie's Pad*, circa 1970. Courtesy of Charles Johnson.

Charles Johnson always wanted to be a cartoonist. Growing up in Evanston, Illinois, he drew cartoons for his high school, for a local magic company, and then for both his college newspaper and his local newspaper, the *Southern Illinoisian*. He took a correspondence course offered by novelist and longtime *Best Cartoons of the Year* editor Lawrence Lariar, and while in high school would visit him on Long Island during the summer, when he stayed with relatives in Brooklyn and looked for cartooning work in Manhattan. In January 1969, having grown increasingly political in his life and art, he attended a lecture by Amiri Baraka and "dragged home in the rain, seeing nothing on either side of me because my brain reeled with a hundred images for moving American comic art toward expressing the culture of people of color." He cut his classes and drew the eighty-nine cartoons for his book *Black Humor* in a single week. It was published by Johnson Publications, which knew the young cartoonist's work from his contributions to its own *Negro Digest*, *Players*, and other magazines.

In 1970 he told the *Chicago Tribune*, "Every man, I imagine, must entertain some cherished dream to which he devotes a great deal of his energies. After stumbling onto the untapped market of racial humor reflected in the cartoons, mine has been to develop this area to its fullest." From 1968 to 1973 Johnson published hundreds of cartoons, drew a handful of scripts for Charlton Comics, and hosted a how-to-draw television program called *Charlie's Pad*

in 1971. Another book, *Half-Past Nation Time*, followed in 1972 and was focused on the aftermath of the civil rights movement. Though he has continued publishing cartoons in the decades since, his primary focus shifted to prose in the mid-1970s after he studied with the writer John Gardner.

Johnson's prose works include the novels *Oxherding Tale* and *Middle Passage*, three collection of short stories, and numerous books of nonfiction, *The Way of the Writer* among them. With his daughter Elisheba, he has coauthored and illustrated a young adult series, *Bending Time: The Adventures of Emery Jones, Boy Science Wonder*. Johnson holds a PhD in philosophy, is a 1998 MacArthur Fellow and the 2002 recipient of an American Academy of Arts and Letters Award for Literature, and is a professor emeritus at the University of Washington.

Pages 99–115: selections from *Black Humor*,
Johnson Publishing Company, Inc., 1970 (pages
99, 104, 105, 106, 108, 109, 110, 111, and 112
redrawn by the the artist at his request, 2020).
Pages 116–121: cartoons from various Black
magazines, 1970–1971.
Photography by Nathan Keay, © MCA Chicago.

Well, have we been a credit to our race today?

I'm wearing a corsage so you'll know me.

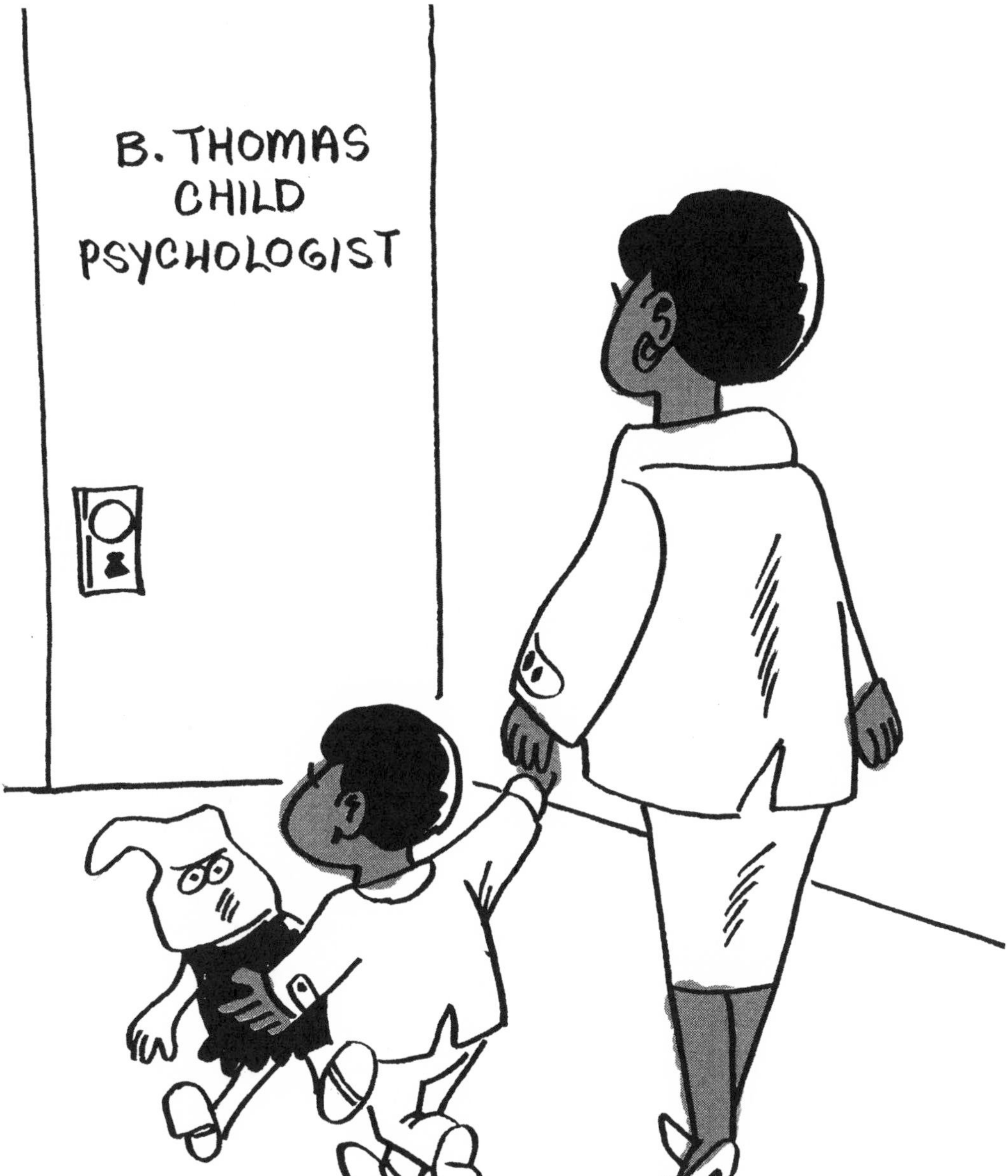
B. THOMAS
CHILD
PSYCHOLOGIST

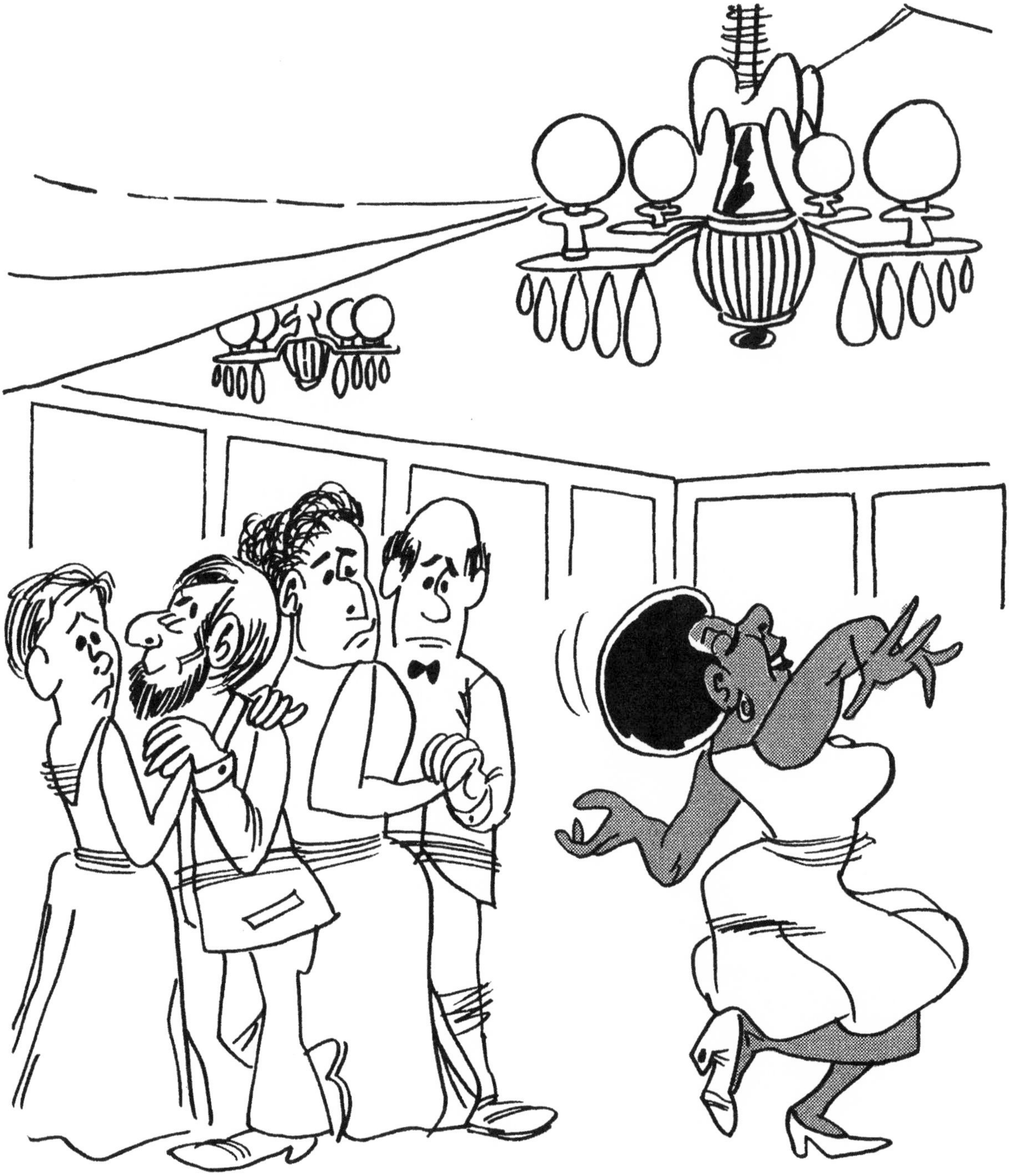

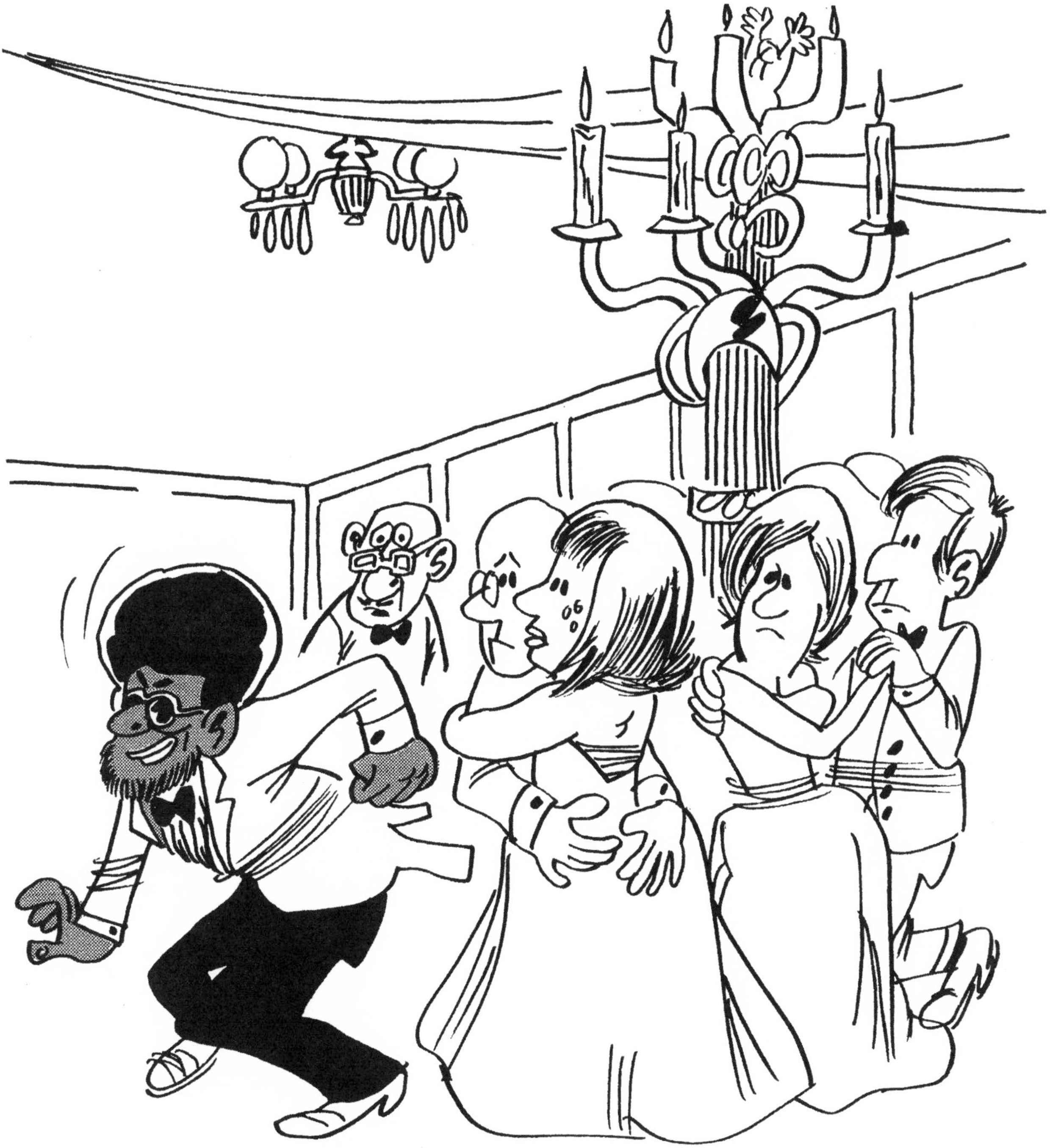

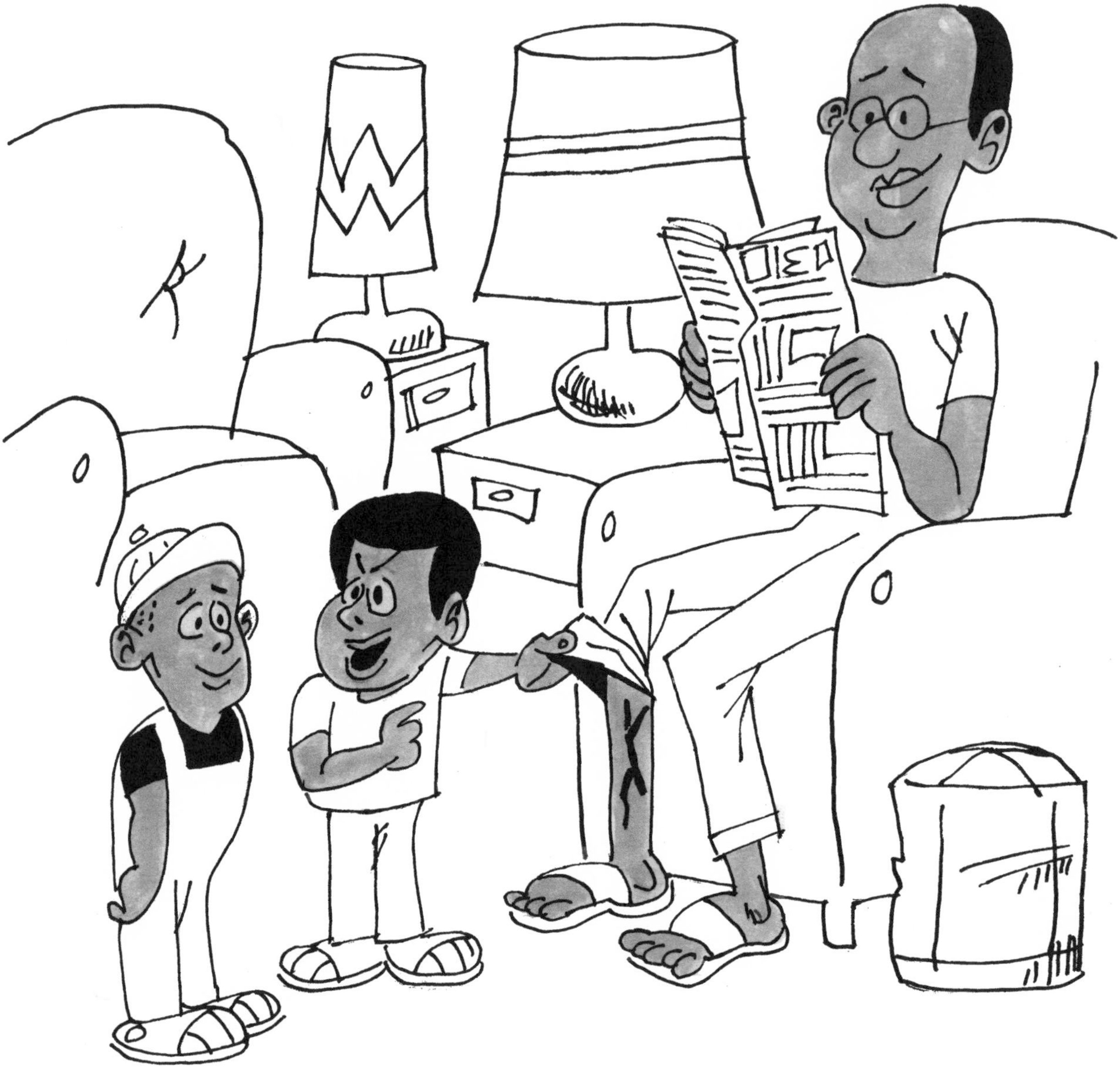

Watts.

Do you have a date for tomorrow's riot?

He bought them all so he could set them free.

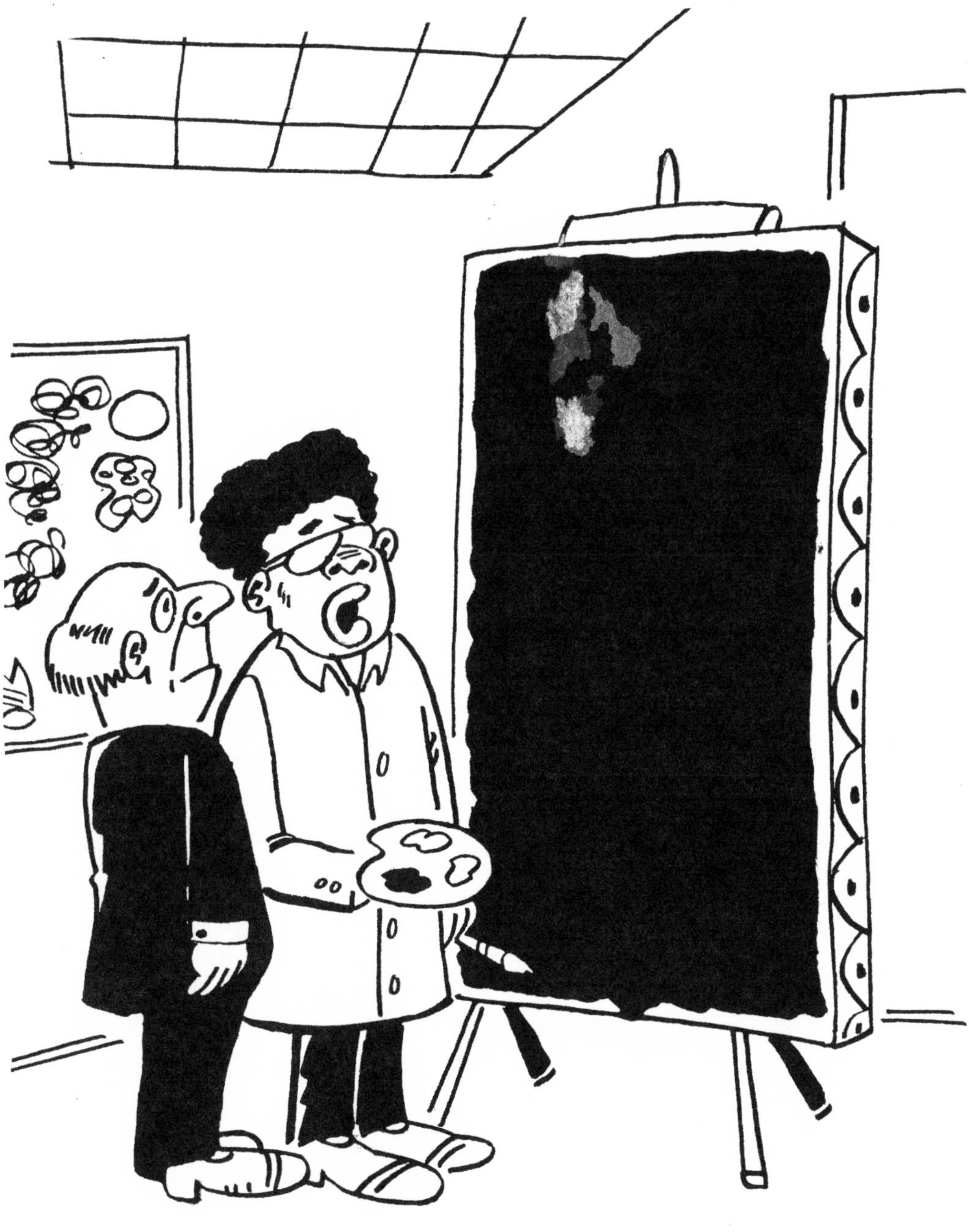

It's life as I see it.

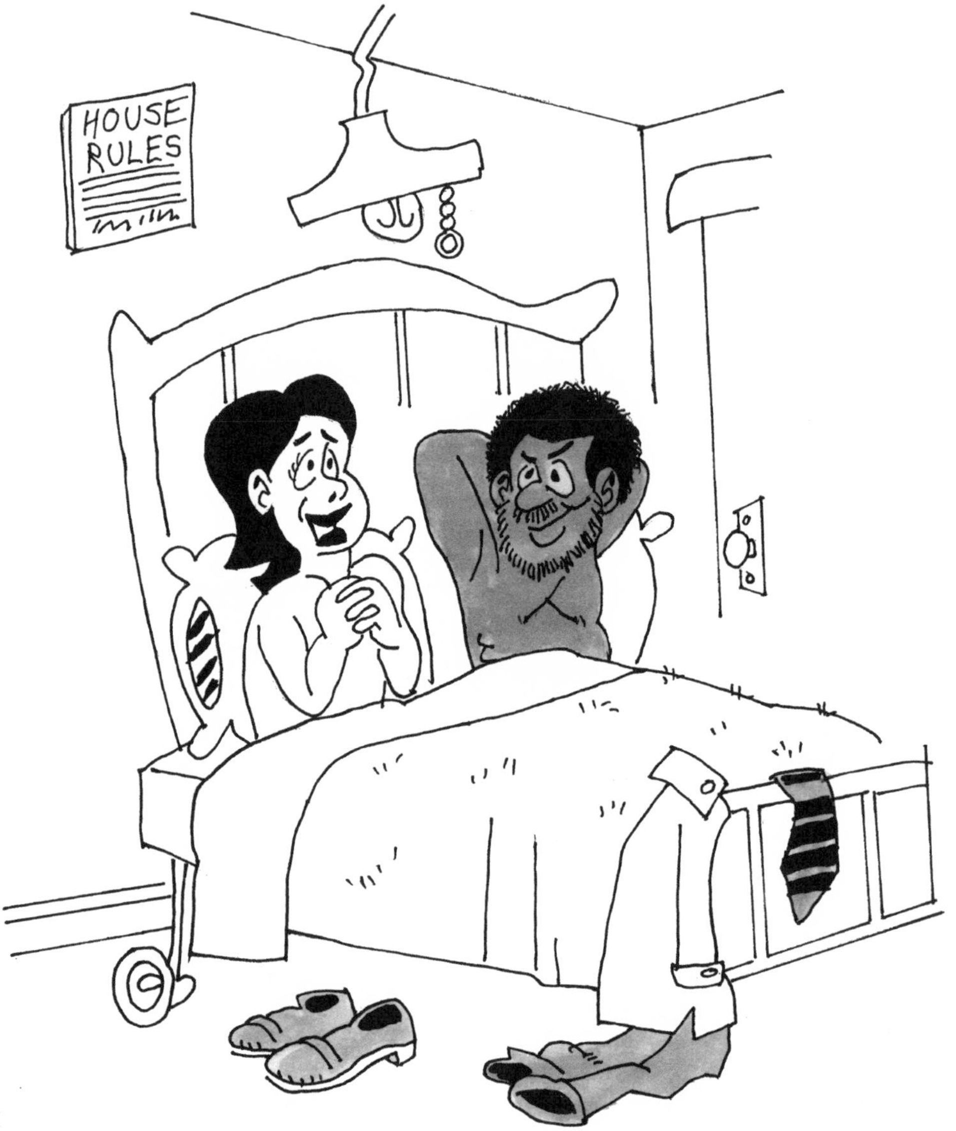
HOUSE
RULES

Now have I done my share?

There's a couple here I'm dying for you to meet.

The answer is 7,856,902,549, boy.

Brace yourself, mother is visiting again.

And here's my first panther.

It's the reds who are causing all these problems.

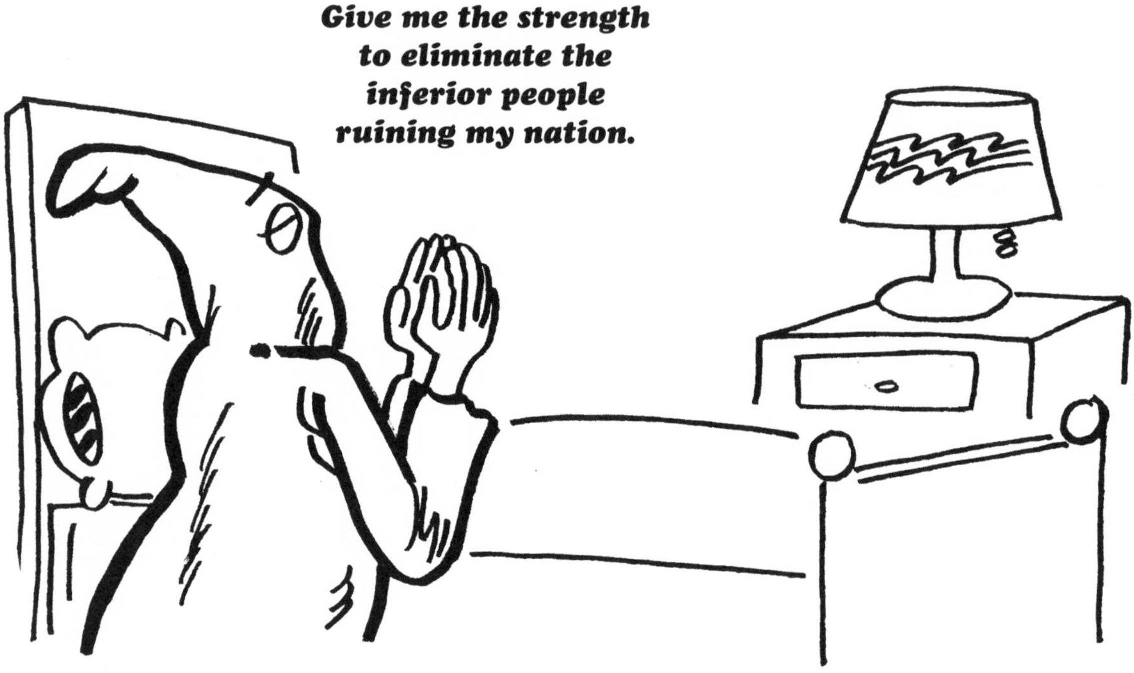
Give me the strength to eliminate the inferior people ruining my nation.

Sho 'nuff boss!

Dad? He's busy changing races right now.

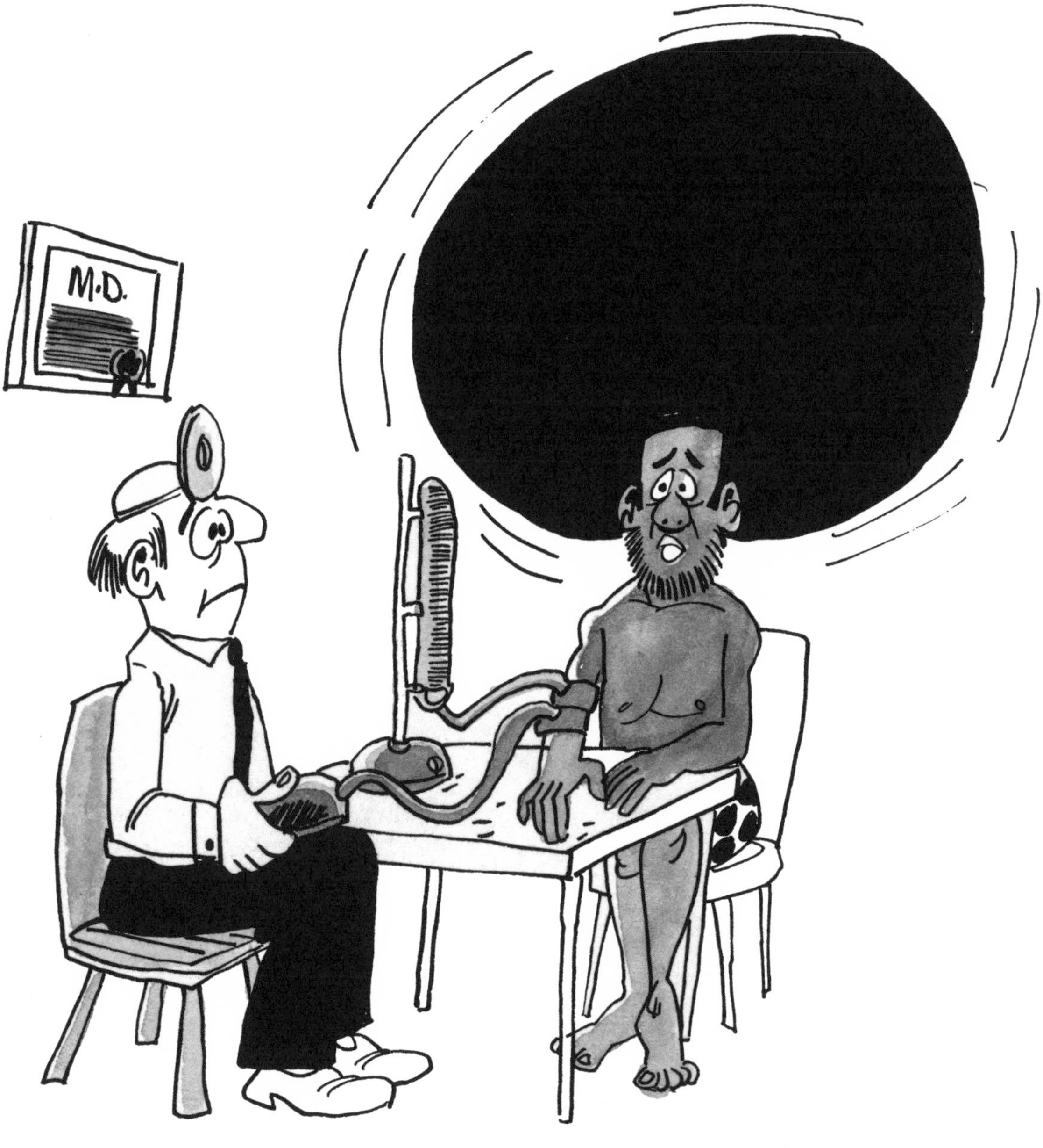
M.D.

**Let's put it this way, if you were a ghetto
I'd have you apply for urban renewal.**

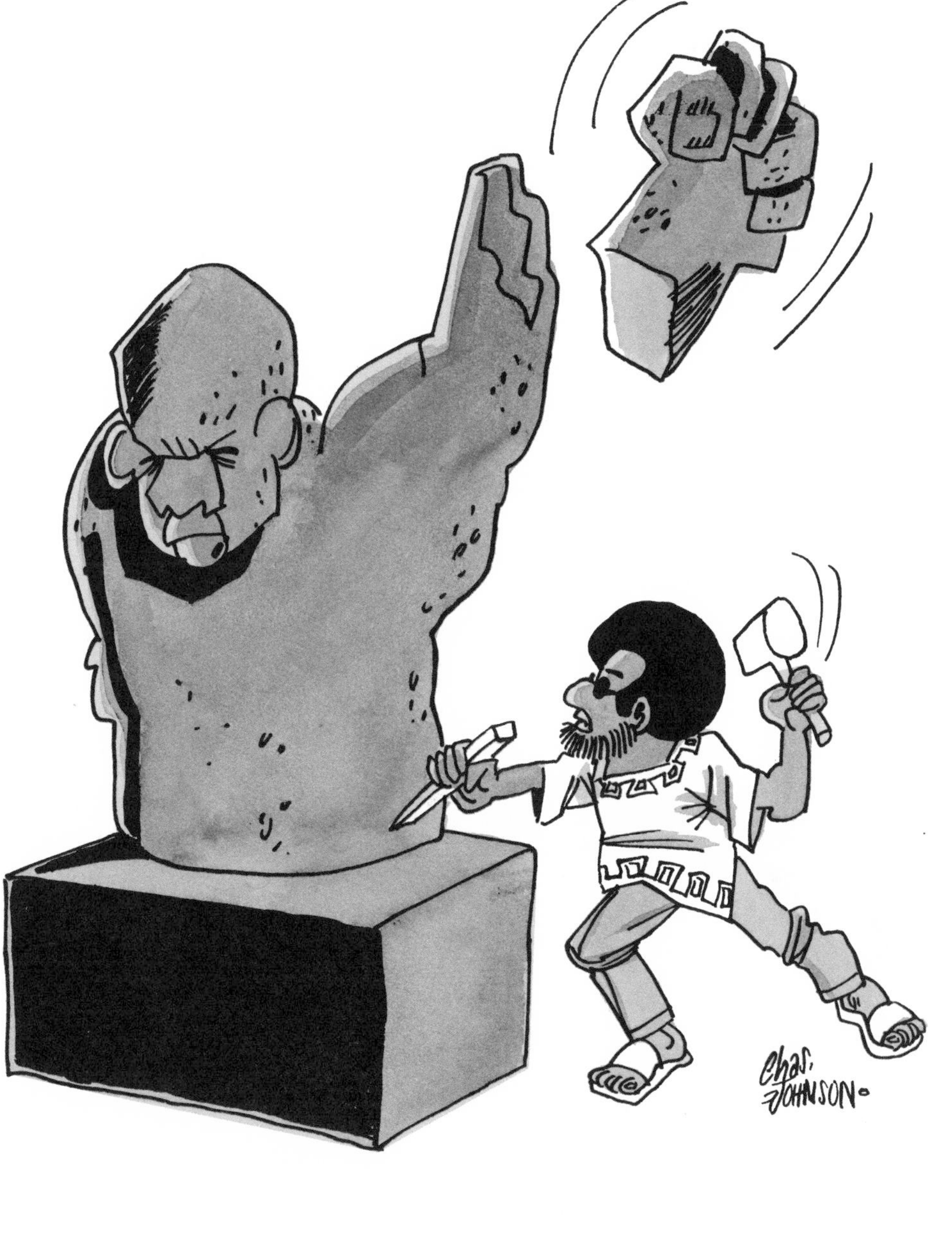
Chas. Johnson

Maybe it's a reminder for you to return his lawn mower.

Why can't you be constructive? If you end discrimination, what do you replace it with?

YAOUNDÉ OLU
b.1945

Photograph by Jonas Dovydenas, June 10, 1977. Chicago Ethnic Arts Project collection, Library of Congress.

Yaoundé Olu grew up science-and art-obsessed in Chicago. She was born in Chicago's Englewood community, later moved to the North Lawndale community on the West Side of Chicago, and then returned to Englewood, where she spent her high school and undergraduate years. She attended Chicago Teachers College, later renamed Chicago State University, earned a BS in Education, and began teaching in Chicago public schools in 1966. She later earned an MA from Governors State University in University Park, Illinois, and a PhD from the Union Institute in Cincinnati, Ohio. Teaching and education, alongside art and music, have been central to her life.

In 1968 she founded Osun, an alternative art gallery in the South Shore neighborhood of Chicago, an area she and others were trying to transform into a colony of artists. Until it closed in the early 1980s, Osun hosted a vibrant, diverse group of visual artists, dancers, musicians, writers, and poets. During that time, Olu was developing her own artwork rooted in her study of physics, time, and futurities. She was a visual-arts delegate to FESTAC, the Second World Festival of Black and African Arts and Culture in Lagos, Nigeria, in 1977.

In the late 1960s she began making narrative comics, inspired by her lifelong love of the form and the work of Robert Crumb, Jay Lynch, and other underground cartoonists of the time. During the 1970s she drew comics for *The Chicago Defender*, *Papers* (which she copublished with Turtel Onli), and numerous other alternative newspapers. Her comics play out all of her artistic and community interests in concise, formally astute strips. They range from the observational to the speculative to the satiric, with visuals created to suit the themes. Olu's approach to drawing is as experimental as her narratives. And, as with Osun, Olu pursued independent entrepreneurship, publishing and distributing her own minicomics and zines. Since 1980 she has been an editorial cartoonist for the Chicago and Gary *Crusader* newspapers, and has won four Wilbur L. Holloway's Best Editorial Cartoon Awards given by the National Newspaper Publishers Association. She maintains a studio in the Bridgeport Art Center in Chicago and continues to publish comics.

The Making of Money, exhibited at the South Side Community Art Center and sold as a broadside, 1982.

Calci and Oxy Adams, self-published comic book, 1982.

Jerri Kirl, published in *Black Lines*, *The Literary Xpress*, and the *Chicago Crusader*, 1983.

Uncle Sammy Jones: Life in America, self-published comic book, 1982.

Slinky Ledbetter & Comp'ny vs. the Gravity Gang, published in *Papers* no. 1, 1980.

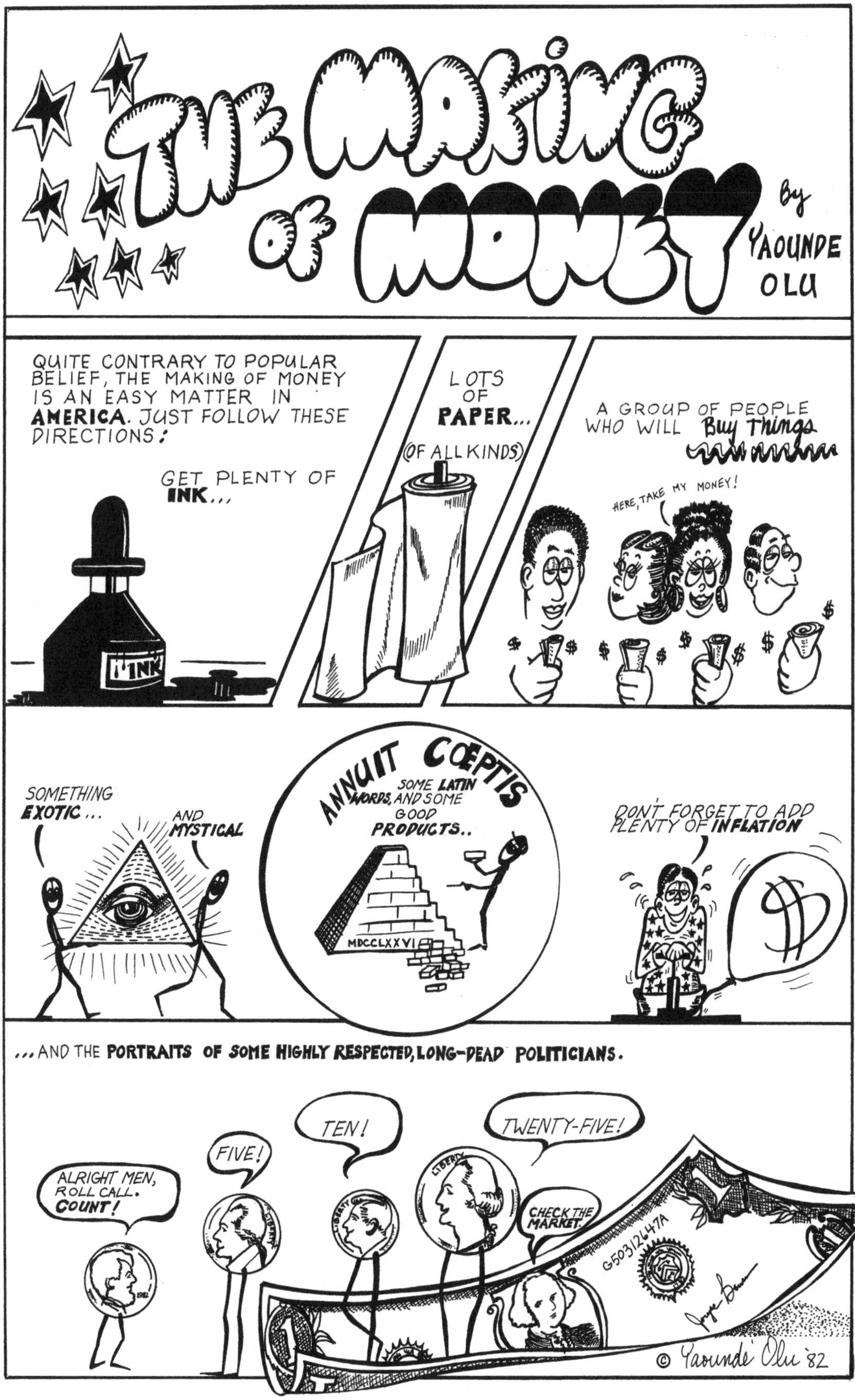
THE MAKING OF MONEY
By YAOUNDE OLU
QUITE CONTRARY TO POPULAR BELIEF, THE MAKING OF MONEY IS AN EASY MATTER IN AMERICA. JUST FOLLOW THESE DIRECTIONS:
GET PLENTY OF INK...
INK
LOTS OF PAPER...
(OF ALL KINDS)
A GROUP OF PEOPLE WHO WILL Buy Things
HERE, TAKE MY MONEY!
SOMETHING EXOTIC...
AND MYSTICAL
ANNUIT COEPTIS
SOME LATIN WORDS, AND SOME GOOD PRODUCTS..
MDCCLXXVI
DON'T FORGET TO ADD PLENTY OF INFLATION
...AND THE PORTRAITS OF SOME HIGHLY RESPECTED, LONG-DEAD POLITICIANS.
ALRIGHT MEN, ROLL CALL. COUNT!
FIVE!
TEN!
TWENTY-FIVE!
CHECK THE MARKET.
G50312647A
© Yaoundé Olu '82

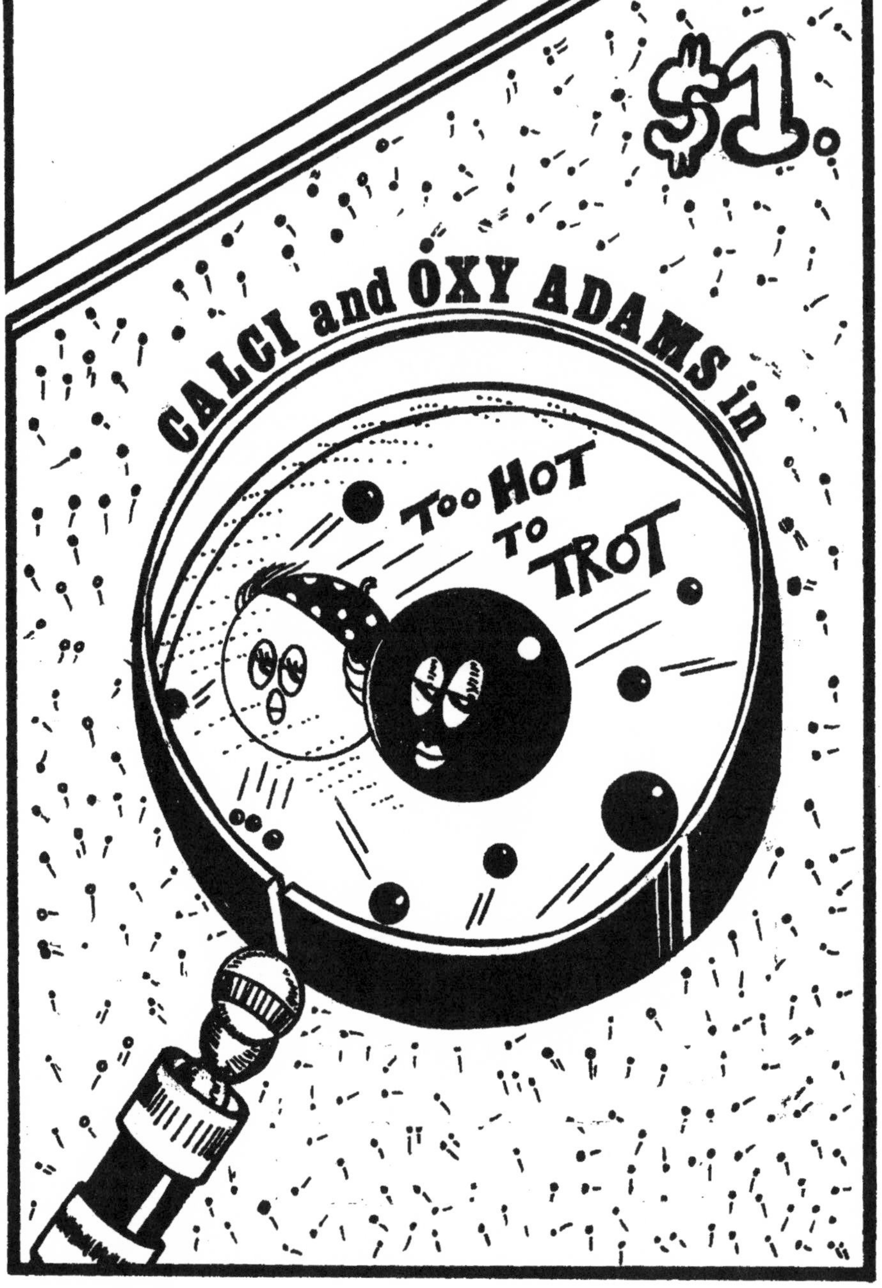
$1.
CALCI and OXY ADAMS in
TOO HOT TO TROT

DEEP IN THE EXHAUST OF AN IDLING LIMESTONE CAR...
ATOMIC LOVE UNFOLDS
CALCI...
...AND OXY ADAMS
RUSH IN HEAD-LONG ABANDON
TOWARD LIME GROVES
...AND EACH OTHER
UNKNOWINGLY...
FROM OPPOSING LIME-STONE GALAXIES.
WOW!

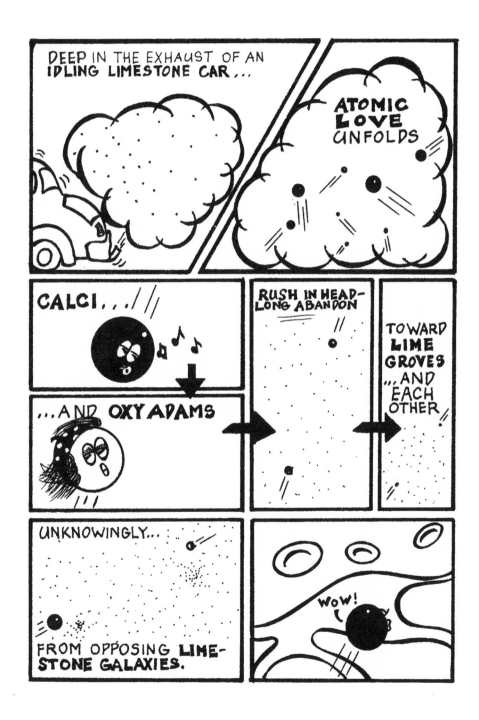

I, DON'T KNOW WHERE I'M GOIN' BUT, I'LL BE GLAD WHEN I GET THERE!
HEY, WHAT'S UP?
ATOMIC LOVE
CAN'T WAIT!
CaO

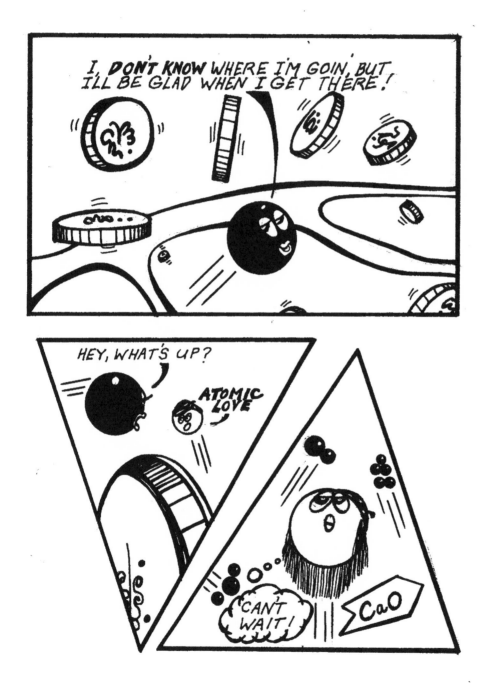

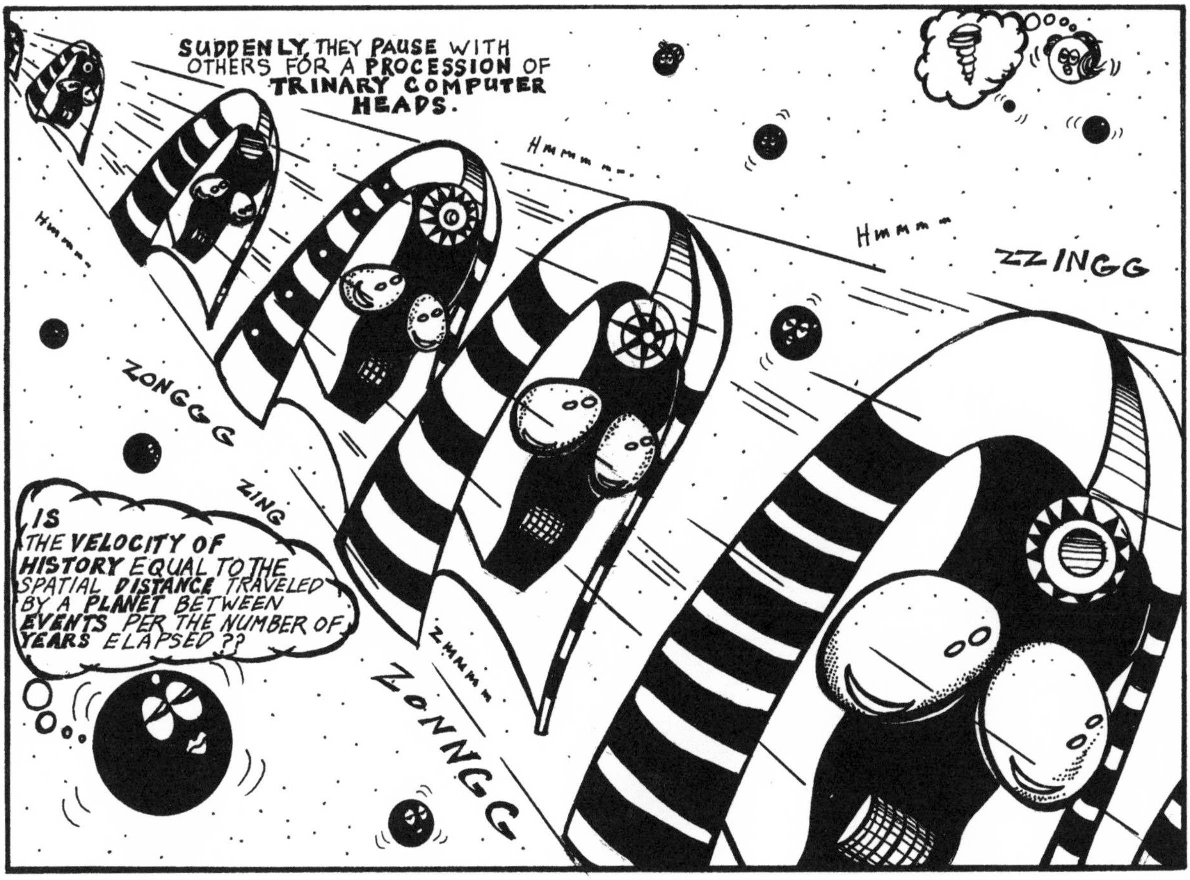
SUDDENLY, THEY PAUSE WITH OTHERS FOR A PROCESSION OF TRINARY COMPUTER HEADS.
Hmmm...
Hmmmm
ZZINGG
Hmmmm...
ZONGGG
ZING
IS THE VELOCITY OF HISTORY EQUAL TO THE SPATIAL DISTANCE TRAVELED BY A PLANET BETWEEN EVENTS PER THE NUMBER OF YEARS ELAPSED??
ZMMMM
ZONNGG

OXY CONTEMPLATES SYMBOLISM, BUT CONTINUES ONWARD BECAUSE...
3
4

SOMEHOW SHE KNOWS
THAT IN LIME GROVES
SHE'LL FIND A SOLUTION
FOR HEIR POLLUTION

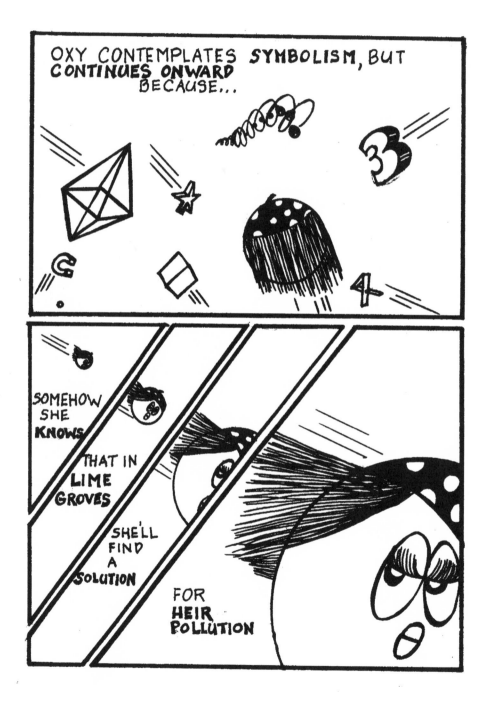

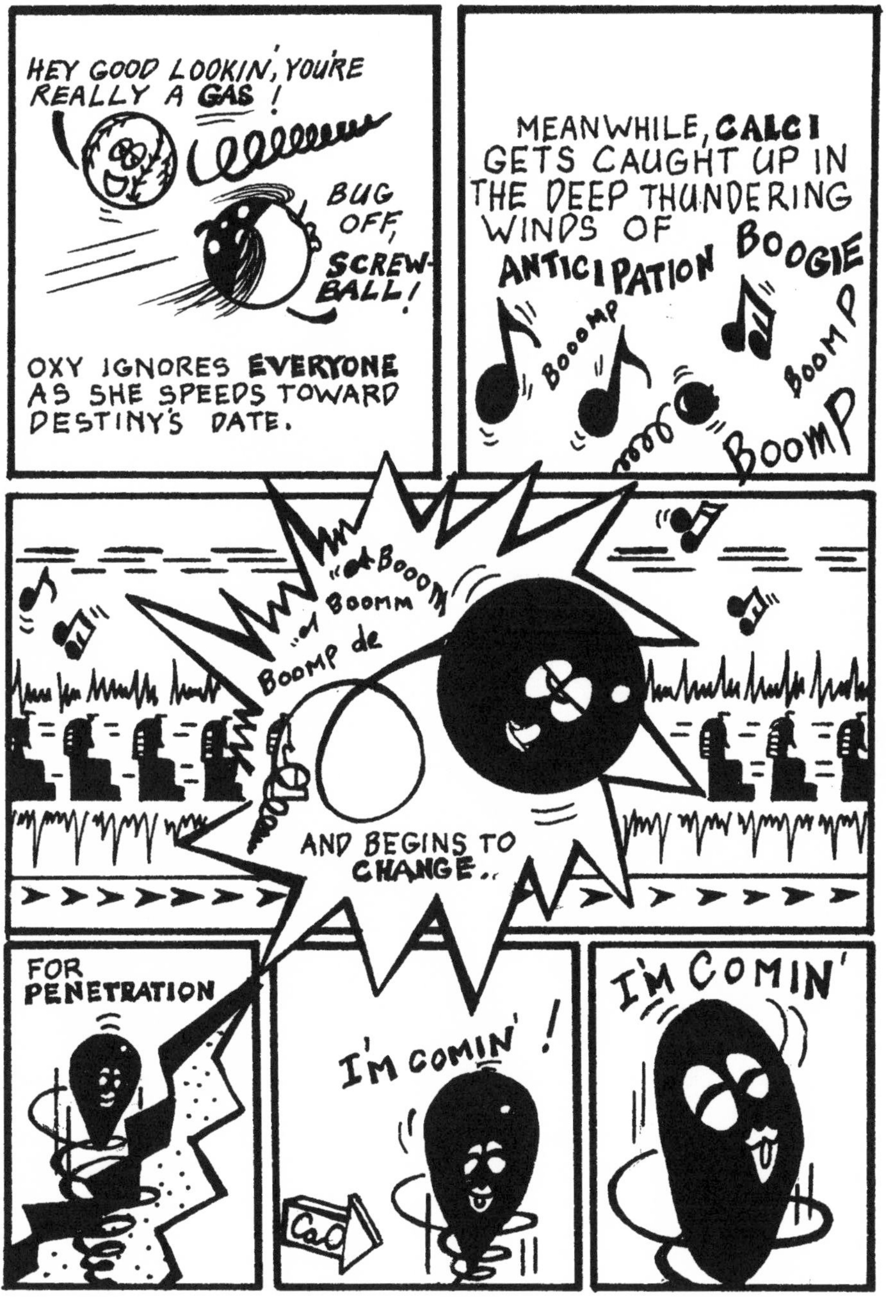
HEY GOOD LOOKIN', YOU'RE REALLY A GAS!
BUG OFF, SCREW-BALL!
OXY IGNORES EVERYONE AS SHE SPEEDS TOWARD DESTINY'S DATE.
MEANWHILE, CALCI GETS CAUGHT UP IN THE DEEP THUNDERING WINDS OF ANTICIPATION BOOGIE
BOOOMP
BOOMP
BOOMP
BOOMP de
BOOMM
AND BEGINS TO CHANGE..
FOR PENETRATION
I'M COMIN'!
CaO
I'M COMIN'

I'M COMIN'
OOOWHEEE
PLOOOOSH
NEW-CLEAR FUSION (ATOMIC LOVE)
...IN THE LIMELIGHT
Ca.O

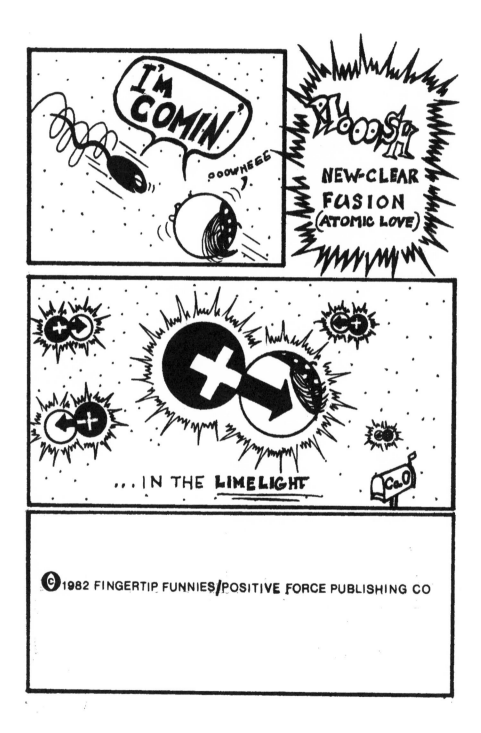

JERRI KIRL

BY YAOUNDE OLU

JERRI KIRL

BY YAOUNDE OLU

JERRI KIRL

BY YAOUNDE OLU

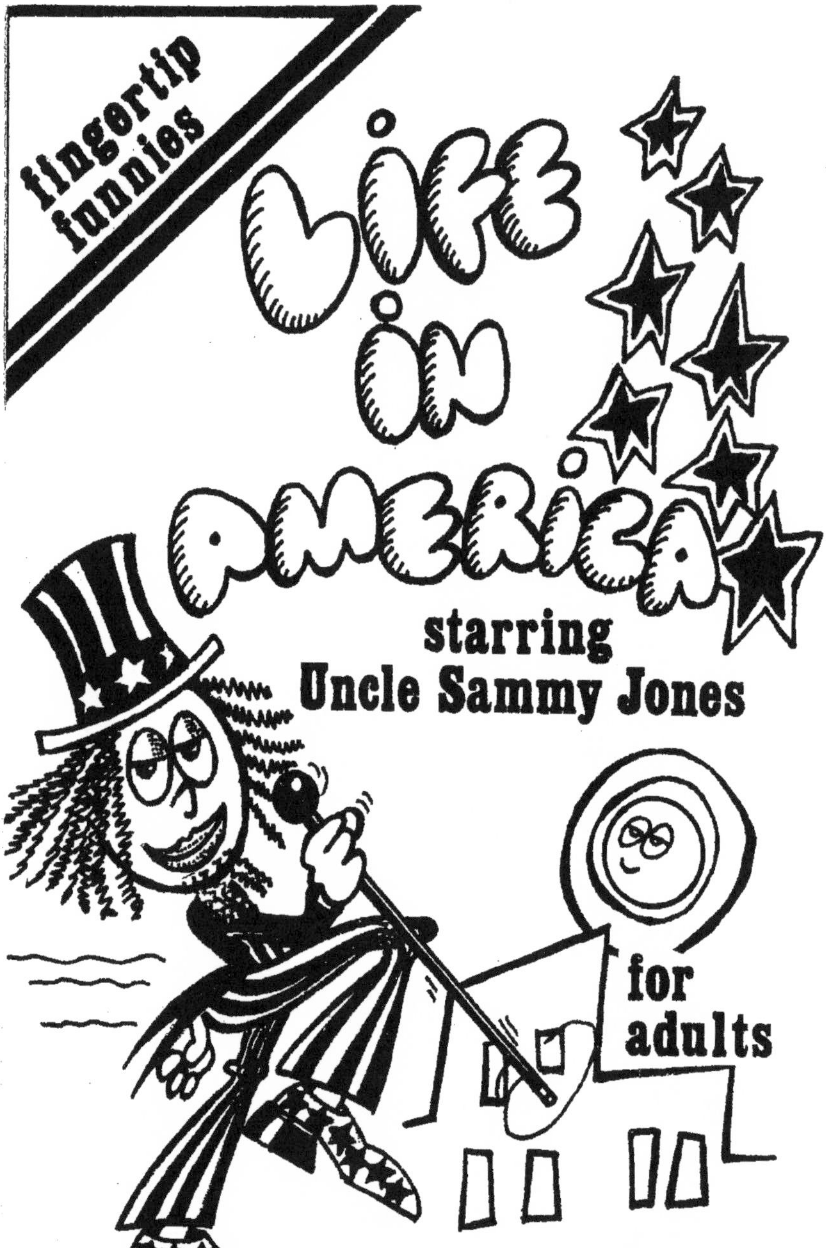
fingertip funnies
LIFE IN AMERICA
starring
Uncle Sammy Jones
for adults
by Yaounde Olu

HI GANG, WELCOME TO AMERICA!
BRUSH BRUSH BRUSH YOUR BREATH
SPEND SPEND
BUY BUY
$
TV
THE
PUBLIC

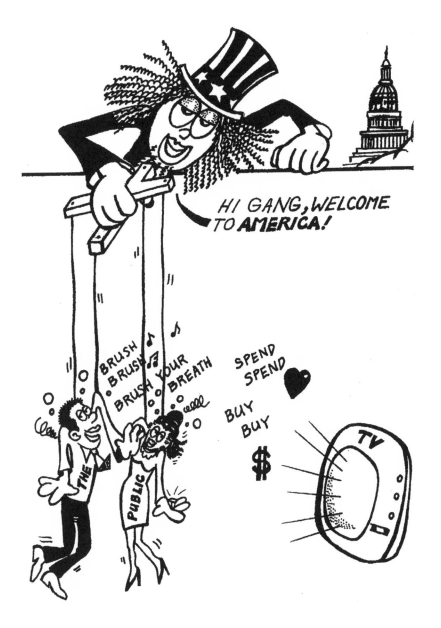

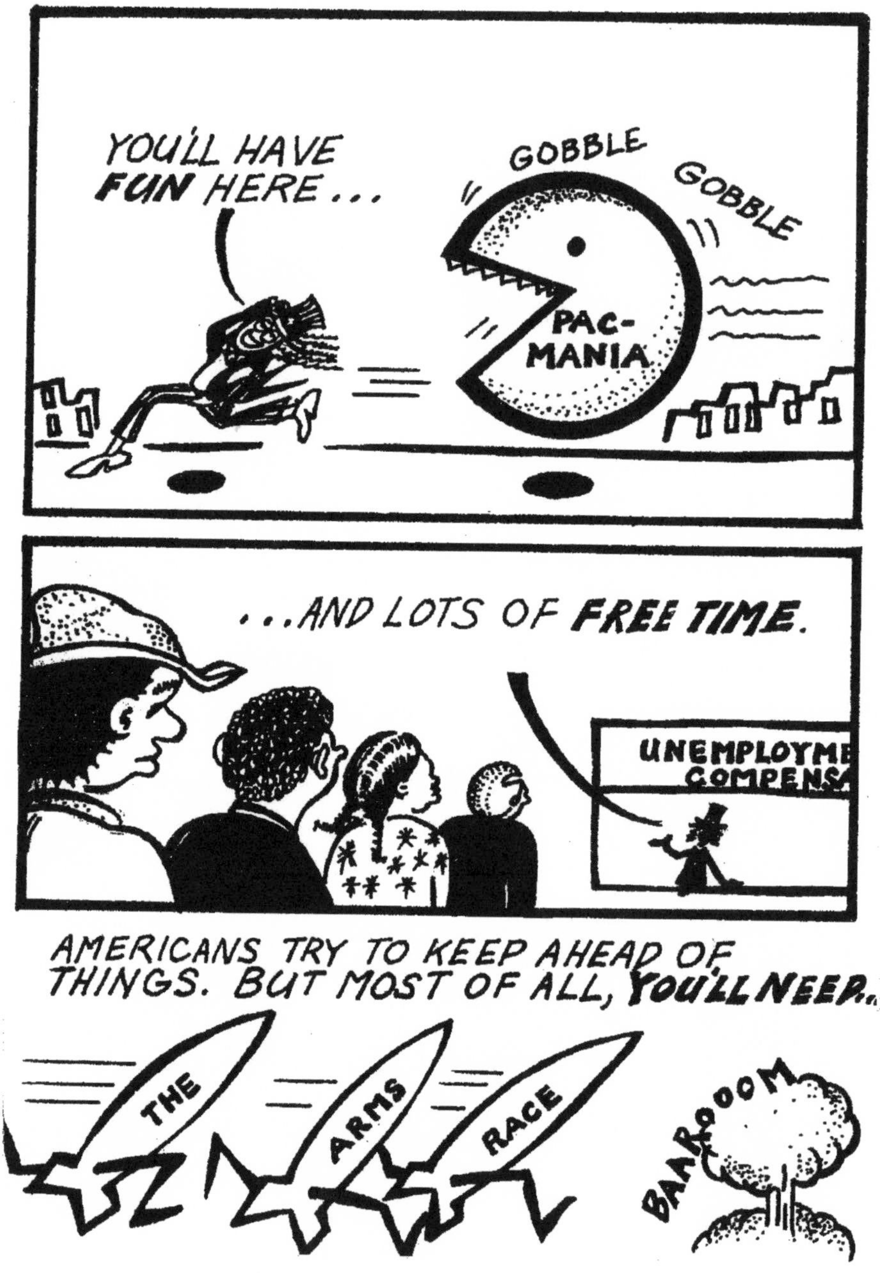
YOU'LL HAVE FUN HERE...
GOBBLE
GOBBLE
PAC-MANIA
...AND LOTS OF FREE TIME.
UNEMPLOYME
COMPENSA
AMERICANS TRY TO KEEP AHEAD OF THINGS. BUT MOST OF ALL, YOU'LL NEED..
THE
ARMS
RACE
BAAROOOM

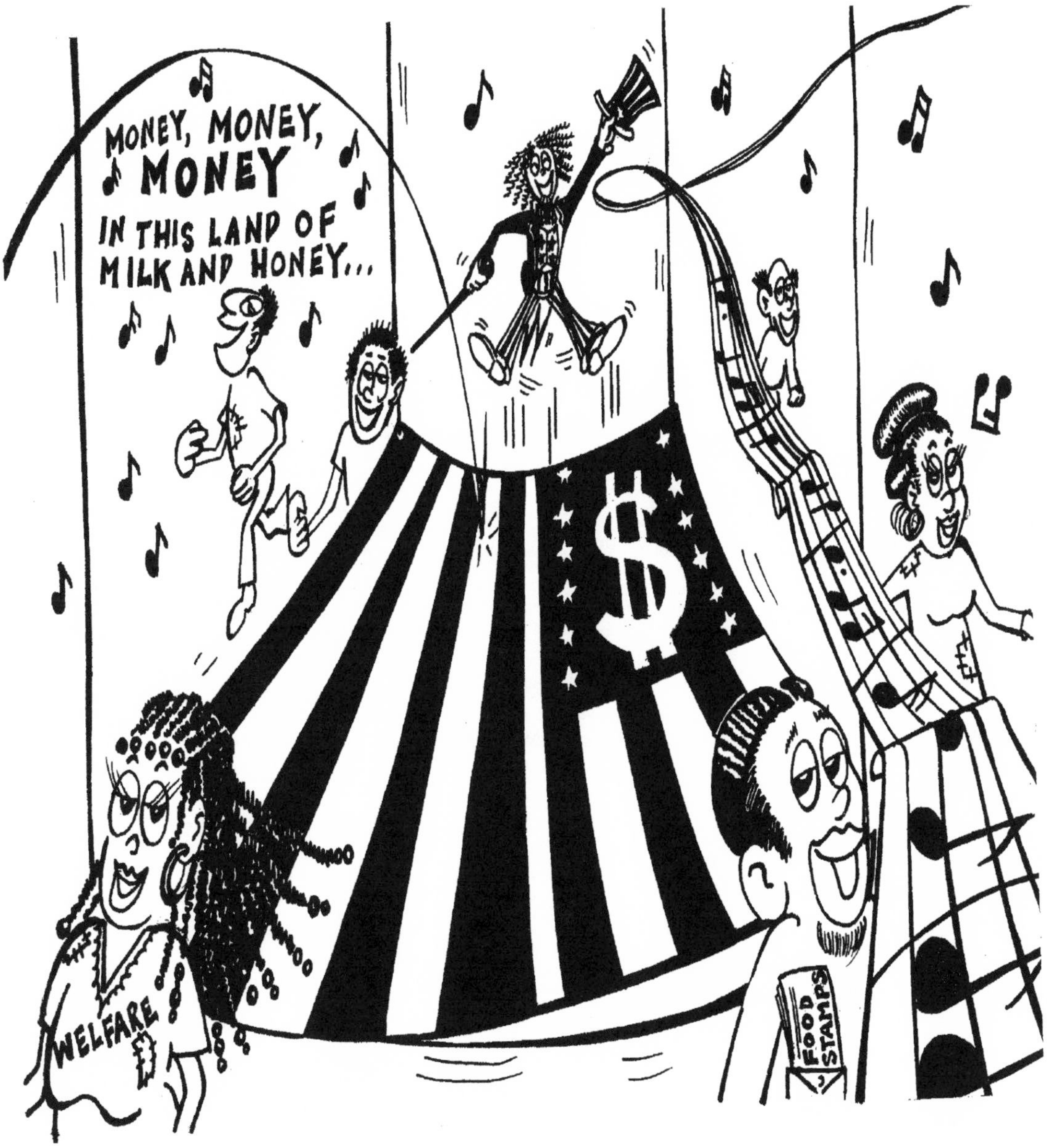
MONEY, MONEY,
MONEY
IN THIS LAND OF
MILK AND HONEY...
$
WELFARE
FOOD
STAMPS

SLINKY LEDBETTER & COMP'NY VS THE GRAVITY GANG
BY YAOUNDE OLU

* TRADIN' POWER

HAVING LEFT MAE ETTA IN A STATE OF **IRREVOCABLE PROSPERITY**, SLINKY AND COMPNY HEAD NORTH.

MEANWHILE, BACK HOME IN THE CONSTELLATION OF BENZENE, **A.I.M.** ASSOCIATES DISCUSS THEIR PRIZED COLLEAGUES

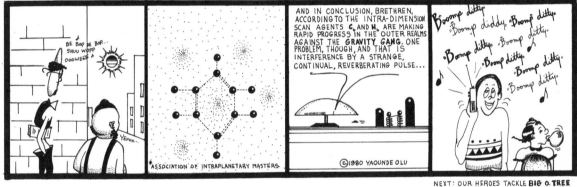

NEXT: OUR HEROES TACKLE **BIG O. TREE**

139

SLINKY AND COMP'NY COMMENCE
TO RAP ABOUT THE KNOWER'S ARC...

SLINKY AND COMP'NY COMMENCE
TO RAP ABOUT THE KNOWER'S ARC...

THE NEXT MORNING...

SIGHTSEEING IN THE BIG CITY...

SLINKY LEDBETTER, DISTINGUISHED PROFESSOR OF UNIPHYSICS,* DISCUSSES THE SOCIABILITY OF WATER.

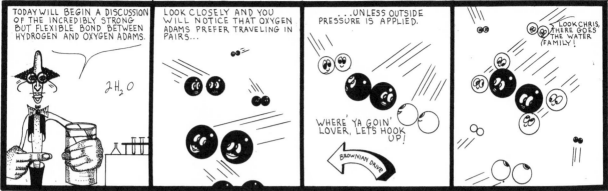

* BRIDGE BETWEEN PHYSICS AND METAPHYSICS

NEXT: HIGH DRAMA IN A LOW GLASS.

SLINKY CONTINUES HIS DISCUSSION ON THE SOCIABILITY OF WATER.

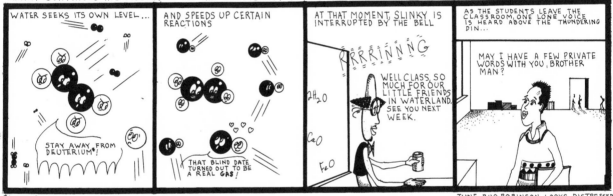

*"HEAVY" WATER

JUNE BUG ROBINSON LOOKS DISTRESSED COULD IT BE THE GRAVITY GANG???

IN A DANK, DUSTY, SMOKY ROOM, **AL K. HALL**, EXECUTIVE SECRETARY OF THE GRAVITY GANG, DISCUSSES STRATEGY.

TURTEL ONLI
b. 1952

Photographer unknown, circa 1970s. Courtesy of Turtel Onli.

Turtel Onli was raised by his grandfather, the late Reverend Samuel David Phillips, a Pentecostal pastor and visionary artist, in the South Side of Chicago. His uncles were members of the infamous gang the Egyptian Cobras, and his first job as an artist was designing a gang insignia. Lessons with his grandfather kept him engaged with art, and his uncles' example inspired him to form an "art gang": the Black Arts Guild (BAG), which he directed from 1970 until 1978. Onli attended the School of the Art Institute of Chicago from 1972 to 1978 and drew record covers and illustrations for magazines such as *Playboy* and *The Paris Metro*. In 1976 he discovered *Heavy Metal* magazine and its French predecessor, *Metal Hurlant*.

A trip to Paris and an encounter with the cartoonist Jean Giraud (Moebius) inspired him to create a magazine of his own. When he returned to Chicago he began publishing *Papers* with Yaoundé Olu. He also created *NOG, Protector of the Pyramids*, which ran in *The Chicago Defender* from July through September 1979. Those strips, along with some additions, formed the core of the *NOG* comic book, which Onli self-published in 1981. "I wanted to make sci-fi that's based on black culture, and I made it Nubian," he recalls. "Let's not talk about Egypt, cause we always want to take Egypt out of Africa, and put it in the Mideast, so let's put it in Africa, black Africa, and better yet, let's give them a planet. And so now it's a Nubian worldview, under attack. Within the comics, I used the French 'Pyramides' in homage to Moebius and my emergence on the European publishing scene." In 1982 Onli returned to the anthology format with *Future Funk*, an alternative Black newspaper that combined fashion reporting, comics, and illustrations. He printed 25,000 copies, which were distributed to clubs, schools, and arcades. Though it had only a five-month run, *Future Funk* has proven prescient in its wild combination of genres and media. In 1993 Onli launched the Black Age of Comics, a publishing initiative and series of comic book conventions in Chicago. An art therapist and art instructor, Onli also taught in the Chicago public school system for twenty-two years. He continues to make comics and paintings in his South Side studio.

NOG, Protector of the Pyramids, Onli Studios, 1981.

THIS IS MOST IMPORTANT BECAUSE THE CHILD OF THIS UNION WILL BECOME THE FIRST **MUTANT** BORN **GUARDIAN** OF THE **PYRAMIDES**.

ALONG THE BLUE NILE GROWING **UNDER** HER **AFFECTIONATE** DISCIPLINE HE DEVELOPES INTO THE FIRST **CHAMPION** OF THE **NUBIAN** SPACE-WAY KNOWN THROUGH LEGEND AS **NOG**.

THE PEOPLE OF NUBA ARE MOST **FORTUNATE** BECAUSE IN NOG THEY ALSO HAVE THE PROTECTOR OF THE PYRAMIDES. THIS ENABLES THE **NUBIANS'** THE PRIVLEDGES AND BASIC **FREEDOMS** OF COLLECTIVE HARMONY.

THEY EXPLORE AND STUDY THE UNKNOWN MYSTERIES OF TIME, SPACE, AND MATTER. ENTERING INTO THE MONASTIC LIBRARIES OF THE PYRAMIDES THEIR NEW FOUND DATA FOR THE **BENEFIT** OF NUBIAS' YET UNKNOWN **GENERATIONS.**
BUT NOW SENSES OF ADAPTIVE **PERCEPTIONS ARE** ABLE TO PICK UP PSYCHIC SIGNALS FROM HIS SPIRITUAL-SELF. IT IS THE CALL OF **EMERGENCY** DEMANDING THAT NOG ABANDON HIS COSMIC EX-PLORATIONS AND RETURN TO **DEFEND** THE **PYRAMIDES.**

2

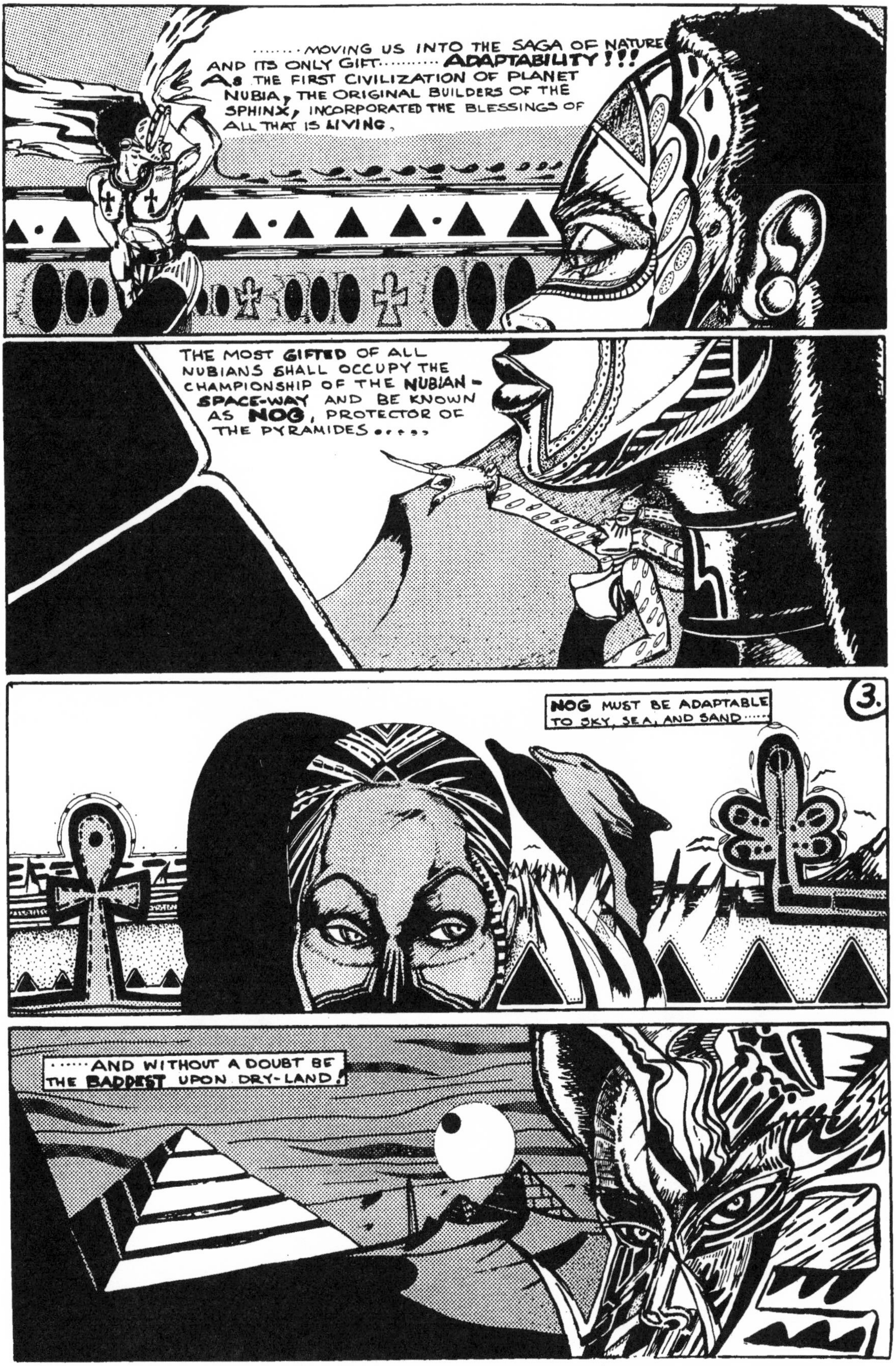
.......MOVING US INTO THE SAGA OF NATURE AND ITS ONLY GIFT.......... ADAPTABILITY!!! AS THE FIRST CIVILIZATION OF PLANET NUBIA, THE ORIGINAL BUILDERS OF THE SPHINX, INCORPORATED THE BLESSINGS OF ALL THAT IS LIVING.
THE MOST GIFTED OF ALL NUBIANS SHALL OCCUPY THE CHAMPIONSHIP OF THE NUBIAN-SPACE-WAY AND BE KNOWN AS NOG, PROTECTOR OF THE PYRAMIDES.....
NOG MUST BE ADAPTABLE TO SKY, SEA, AND SAND.....
3.
.....AND WITHOUT A DOUBT BE THE BADDEST UPON DRY-LAND!

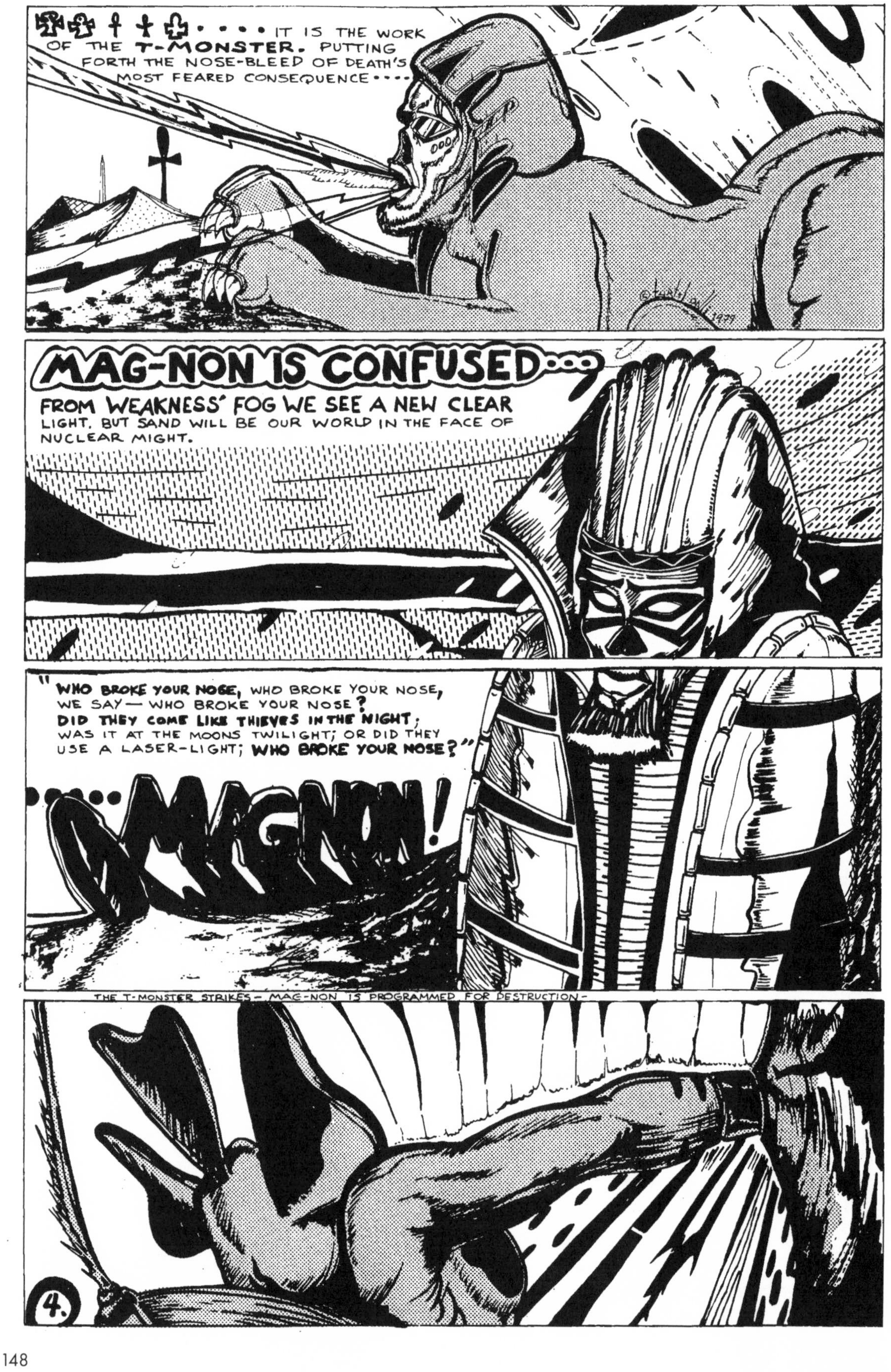

IT IS THE WORK OF THE T-MONSTER. PUTTING FORTH THE NOSE-BLEED OF DEATH'S MOST FEARED CONSEQUENCE....
MAG-NON IS CONFUSED...
FROM WEAKNESS' FOG WE SEE A NEW CLEAR LIGHT, BUT SAND WILL BE OUR WORLD IN THE FACE OF NUCLEAR MIGHT.
"WHO BROKE YOUR NOSE, WHO BROKE YOUR NOSE, WE SAY— WHO BROKE YOUR NOSE? DID THEY COME LIKE THIEVES IN THE NIGHT; WAS IT AT THE MOONS TWILIGHT; OR DID THEY USE A LASER-LIGHT; WHO BROKE YOUR NOSE?"
.....MAGNON!
THE T-MONSTER STRIKES— MAG-NON IS PROGRAMMED FOR DESTRUCTION—
4.

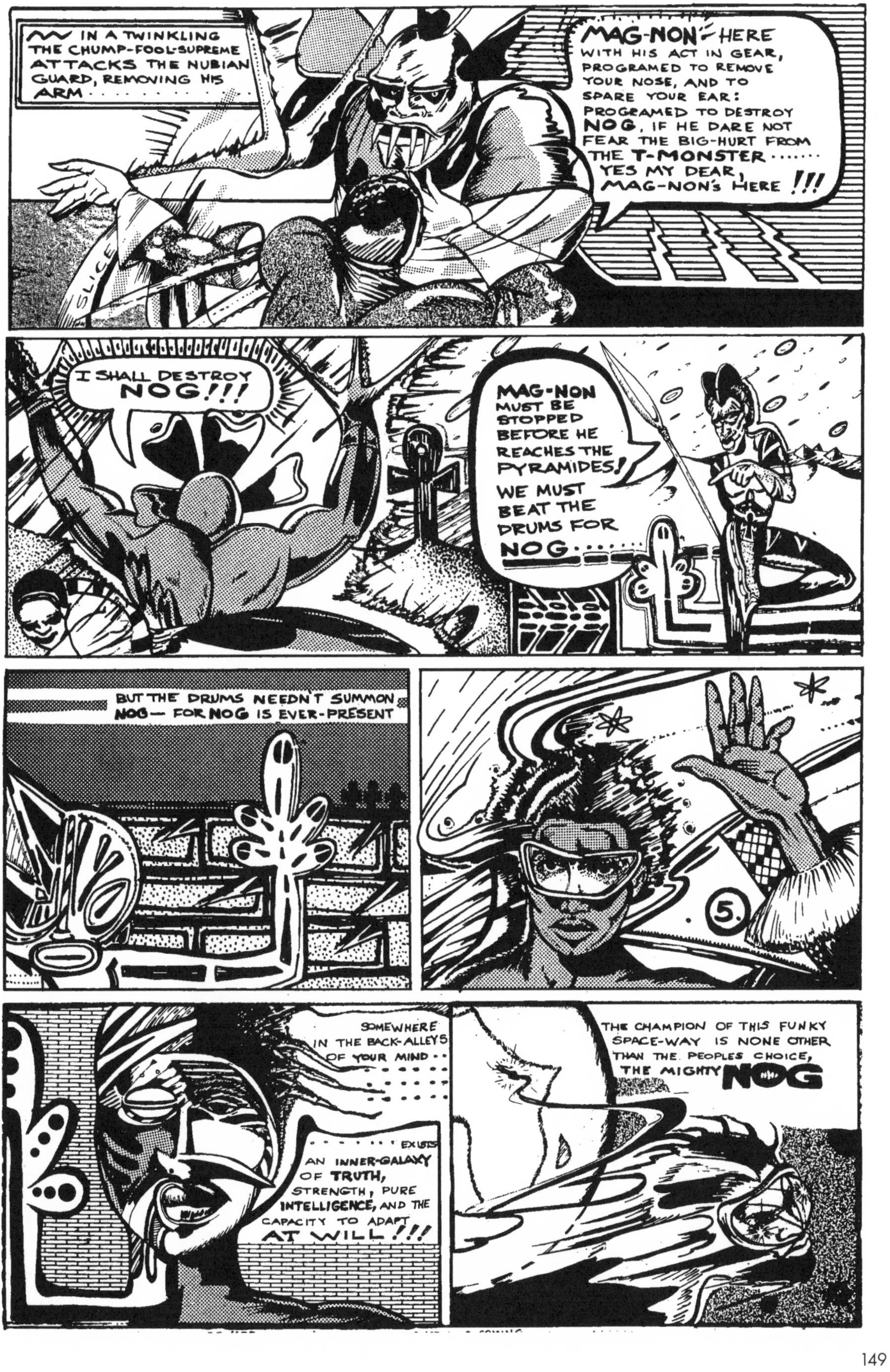
IN A TWINKLING THE CHUMP-FOOL-SUPREME ATTACKS THE NUBIAN GUARD, REMOVING HIS ARM.........
MAG-NON - HERE WITH HIS ACT IN GEAR, PROGRAMED TO REMOVE YOUR NOSE, AND TO SPARE YOUR EAR: PROGRAMED TO DESTROY NOG, IF HE DARE NOT FEAR THE BIG-HURT FROM THE T-MONSTER....... YES MY DEAR, MAG-NON'S HERE !!!
SLICE
I SHALL DESTROY NOG!!!
MAG-NON MUST BE STOPPED BEFORE HE REACHES THE PYRAMIDES! WE MUST BEAT THE DRUMS FOR NOG.......
BUT THE DRUMS NEEDN'T SUMMON NOG— FOR NOG IS EVER-PRESENT
5.
SOMEWHERE IN THE BACK-ALLEYS OF YOUR MIND.........
........EXISTS AN INNER-GALAXY OF TRUTH, STRENGTH, PURE INTELLIGENCE, AND THE CAPACITY TO ADAPT AT WILL!!!
THE CHAMPION OF THIS FUNKY SPACE-WAY IS NONE OTHER THAN THE PEOPLES CHOICE, THE MIGHTY NOG

IMMEDIATELY **NOG CONVERTS** INTO A
TRAVELING SPECTRUM OF ORGANIC ENERGY.
HIS IS THE ABILITY TO TRAVEL ACROSS TIME
AND SPACE PURELY ON THE WAVELENGTHS OF
COSMIC THOUGHT ALONE. ALL TO • • • • • •

6.

…SAVE NUBIA !!!

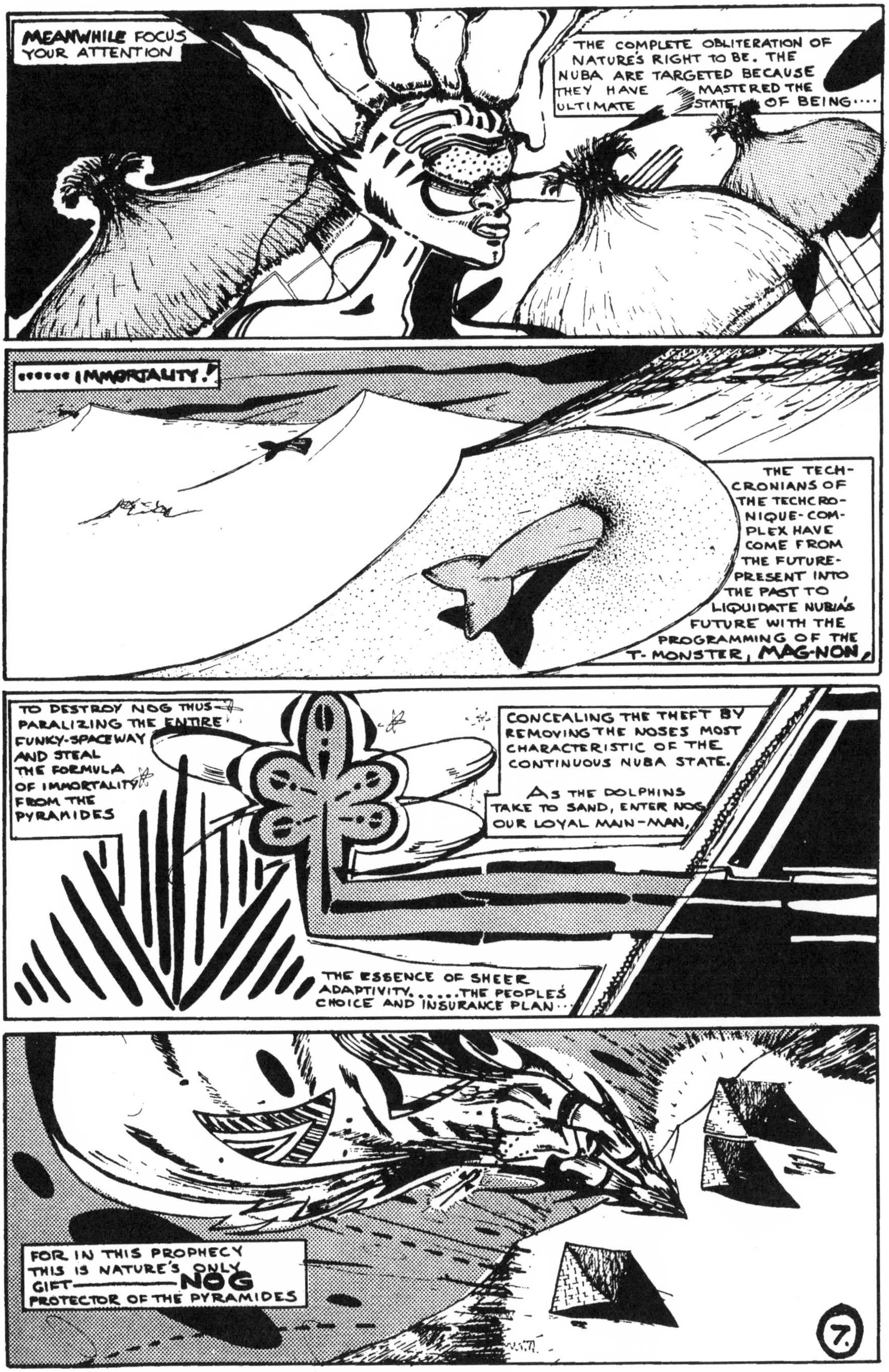
MEANWHILE FOCUS YOUR ATTENTION
THE COMPLETE OBLITERATION OF NATURE'S RIGHT TO BE. THE NUBA ARE TARGETED BECAUSE THEY HAVE MASTERED THE ULTIMATE STATE OF BEING....
......IMMORTALITY!
THE TECH-CRONIANS OF THE TECHCRO-NIQUE-COM-PLEX HAVE COME FROM THE FUTURE-PRESENT INTO THE PAST TO LIQUIDATE NUBIA'S FUTURE WITH THE PROGRAMMING OF THE T-MONSTER, MAG-NON,
TO DESTROY NOG THUS PARALIZING THE ENTIRE FUNKY-SPACEWAY AND STEAL THE FORMULA OF IMMORTALITY FROM THE PYRAMIDES
CONCEALING THE THEFT BY REMOVING THE NOSES MOST CHARACTERISTIC OF THE CONTINUOUS NUBA STATE.
AS THE DOLPHINS TAKE TO SAND, ENTER NOG OUR LOYAL MAIN-MAN,
THE ESSENCE OF SHEER ADAPTIVITY......THE PEOPLE'S CHOICE AND INSURANCE PLAN...
FOR IN THIS PROPHECY THIS IS NATURE'S ONLY GIFT——NOG PROTECTOR OF THE PYRAMIDES
7.

LITTLE DOES THE T-MONSTER REALIZE THAT MERELY HIS PRESENCE CAUSES A RIPPLE IN THE FUNKY SPACE — WAY RETURNING.

NATURES GIFT TO NUBIA AT TWICE THE SPEED OF THOUGHT..

...NOG IS AS HE IS, TRUTH, STRENGTH AND INTELLIGENCE, NOG DOES AS HE DOES — ADAPT AT WILL, BECAUSE ALL THAT'S CORRECT KNOWS NOG, BECAUSE NOG KNOWS ALL THAT'S CORRECT....... HE IS NOG THE PROTECTOR OF THE PYRAMIDES!

CHAMPION OF THIS FUNKY SPACE-WAY IS NONE OTHER THAN NOG — WHO IS RACING TOWARD THE PYRAMIDES TO STOP MAG-NON, THE T-MONSTER, CHUMP-FOOL SUPREME ——

WITH EYES AGLARE IN HORROR FOR THE ACT HE IS PROGRAMMED TO ACTUATE, THE T-MONSTER STRIKES

MAG-NON'S HERE.....

SAVAGELY LIKE A TRUE CHUMP-FOOL SUPREME......

AND RIPS-OFF THE NOSE OF A NEARBY NUBIAN STATUE.

RIP

THE T-MONSTERS ATTACK SENDS THE FUNKY SPACE-WAY INTO A STATE OF TRAUMA. ACCORDING TO NUBIAN DESTINY, MAG-NON MUST COME AND HE MUST DESTROY NOG IN ORDER TO STEAL FROM THE PYRAMIDES

8.

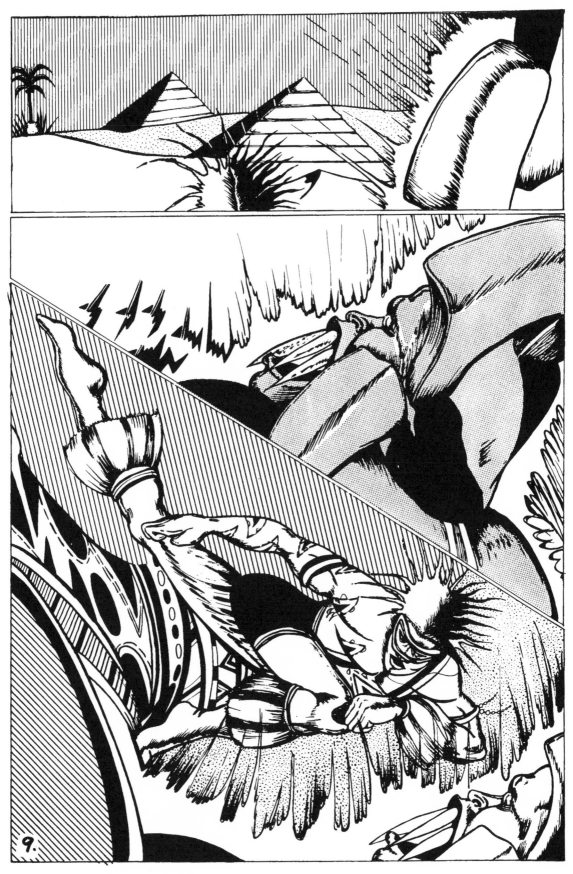

9.

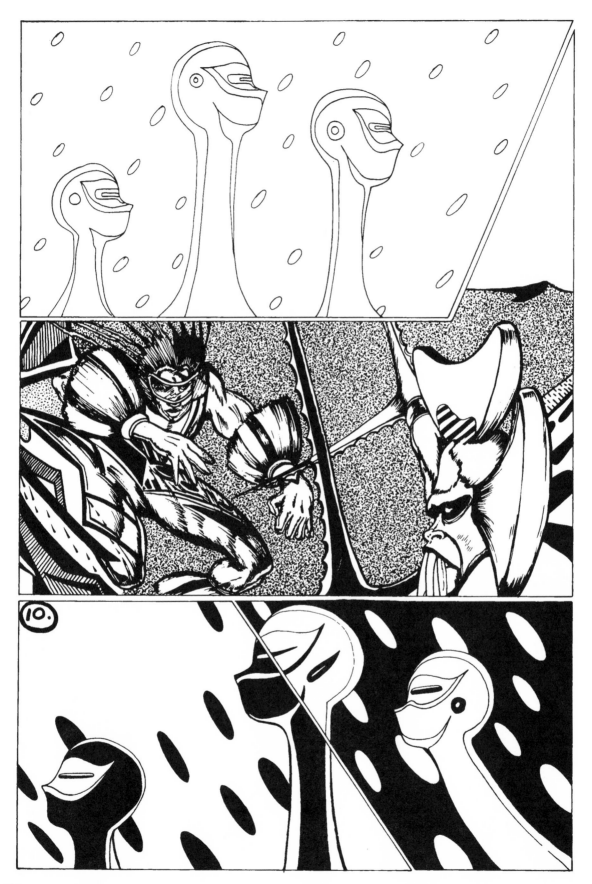

154

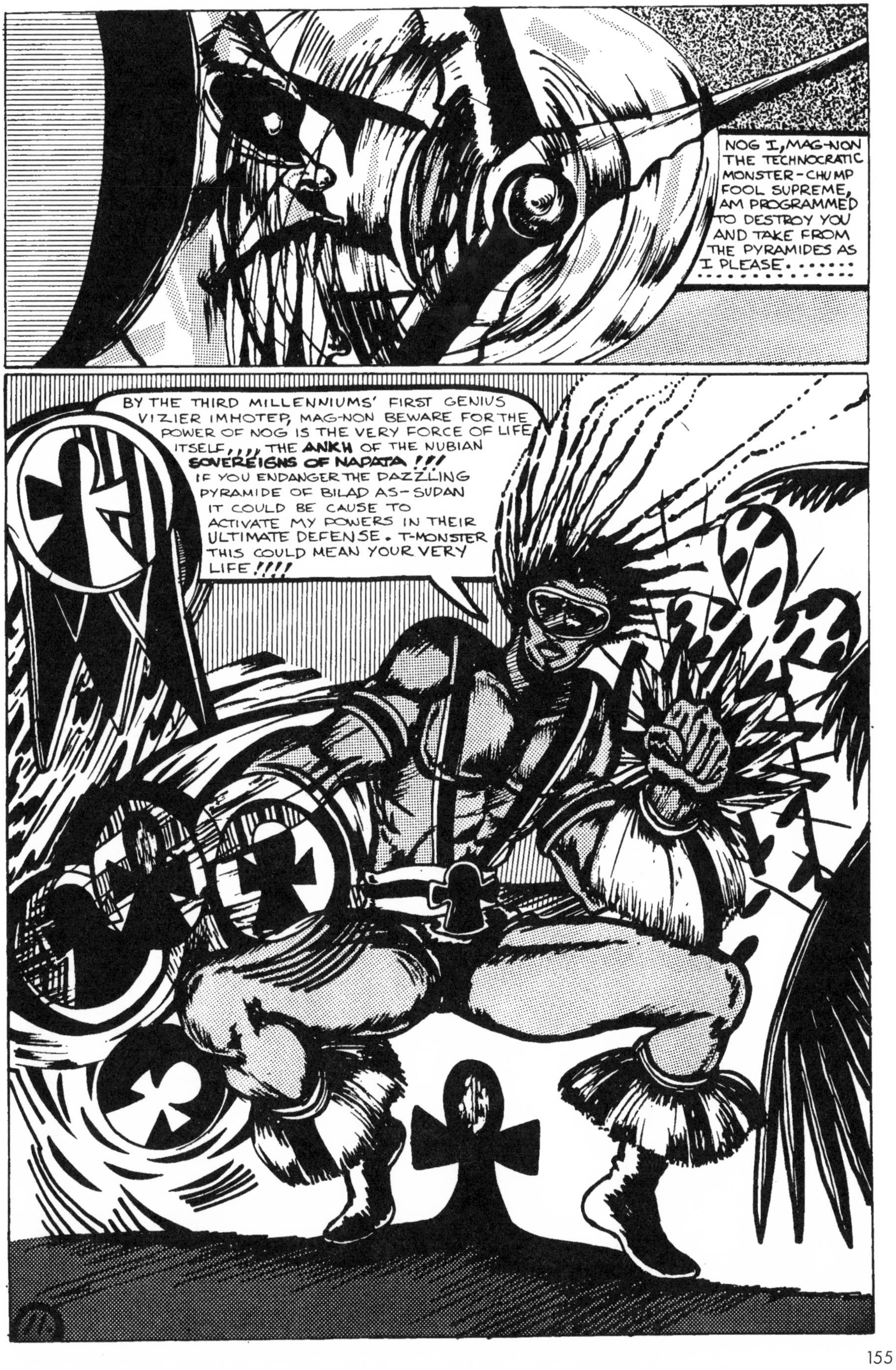
NOG I, MAG-NON THE TECHNOCRATIC MONSTER-CHUMP FOOL SUPREME, AM PROGRAMMED TO DESTROY YOU AND TAKE FROM THE PYRAMIDES AS I PLEASE.......
BY THE THIRD MILLENNIUMS' FIRST GENIUS VIZIER IMHOTEP, MAG-NON BEWARE FOR THE POWER OF NOG IS THE VERY FORCE OF LIFE ITSELF,,,,, THE ANKH OF THE NUBIAN SOVEREIGNS OF NAPATA!!! IF YOU ENDANGER THE DAZZLING PYRAMIDE OF BILAD AS-SUDAN IT COULD BE CAUSE TO ACTIVATE MY POWERS IN THEIR ULTIMATE DEFENSE. T-MONSTER THIS COULD MEAN YOUR VERY LIFE!!!!
11

NOG MUST STOP MAG-NON BEFORE HE REACHES THE PYRAMIDES. WHY ??? BECAUSE SHOULD THE T-MONSTER ENTER THE PYRAMIDES HE IS CERTAIN TO VIOLATE THEIR STORAGE VAULTS AND LIBRARIES. THE COMPLETE WORKS OF WRITTEN NUBIAN INTELLIGENCE WILL BE DESTROYED WITH MAG-NON STEALING FOR HIMSELF THE KNOWLEDGE OF UNIVERSAL IMMORTALITY.

THIS WOULD BE A DISASTER OF THE MOST INCREDIBLE TYPE BECAUSE IT WOULD SURELY LEAVE THE NUBA DEVASTATED FOR 2,000 YEARS AND THE TECHNOCRATIQUE-COMPLEX WITH THE POWER TO ENSLAVE THE GALAXIES THROUGH THE ABRASIVE MANIPULATION OF TIME, SPACE, AND NATURE. IT IS IMPERATIVE........ NOG MUST NOT FAIL !!

12.

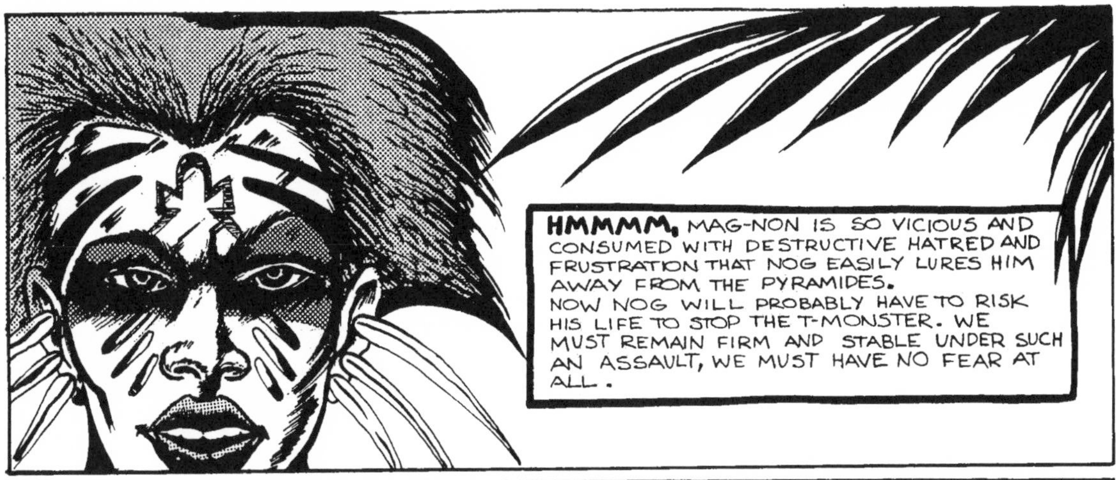
HMMMM. MAG-NON IS SO VICIOUS AND CONSUMED WITH DESTRUCTIVE HATRED AND FRUSTRATION THAT NOG EASILY LURES HIM AWAY FROM THE PYRAMIDES.
NOW NOG WILL PROBABLY HAVE TO RISK HIS LIFE TO STOP THE T-MONSTER. WE MUST REMAIN FIRM AND STABLE UNDER SUCH AN ASSAULT, WE MUST HAVE NO FEAR AT ALL.

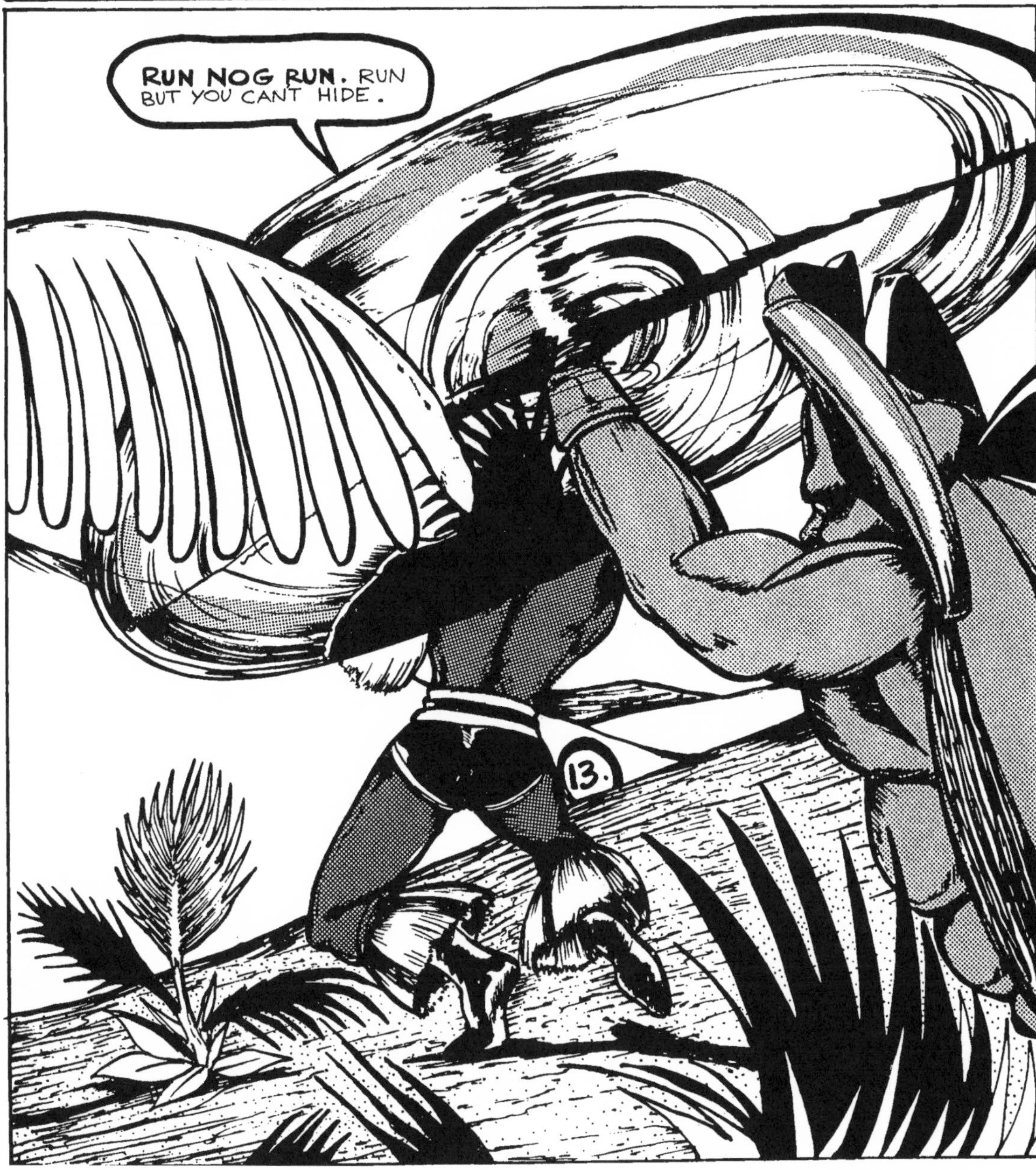
RUN NOG RUN. RUN BUT YOU CAN'T HIDE.
13.

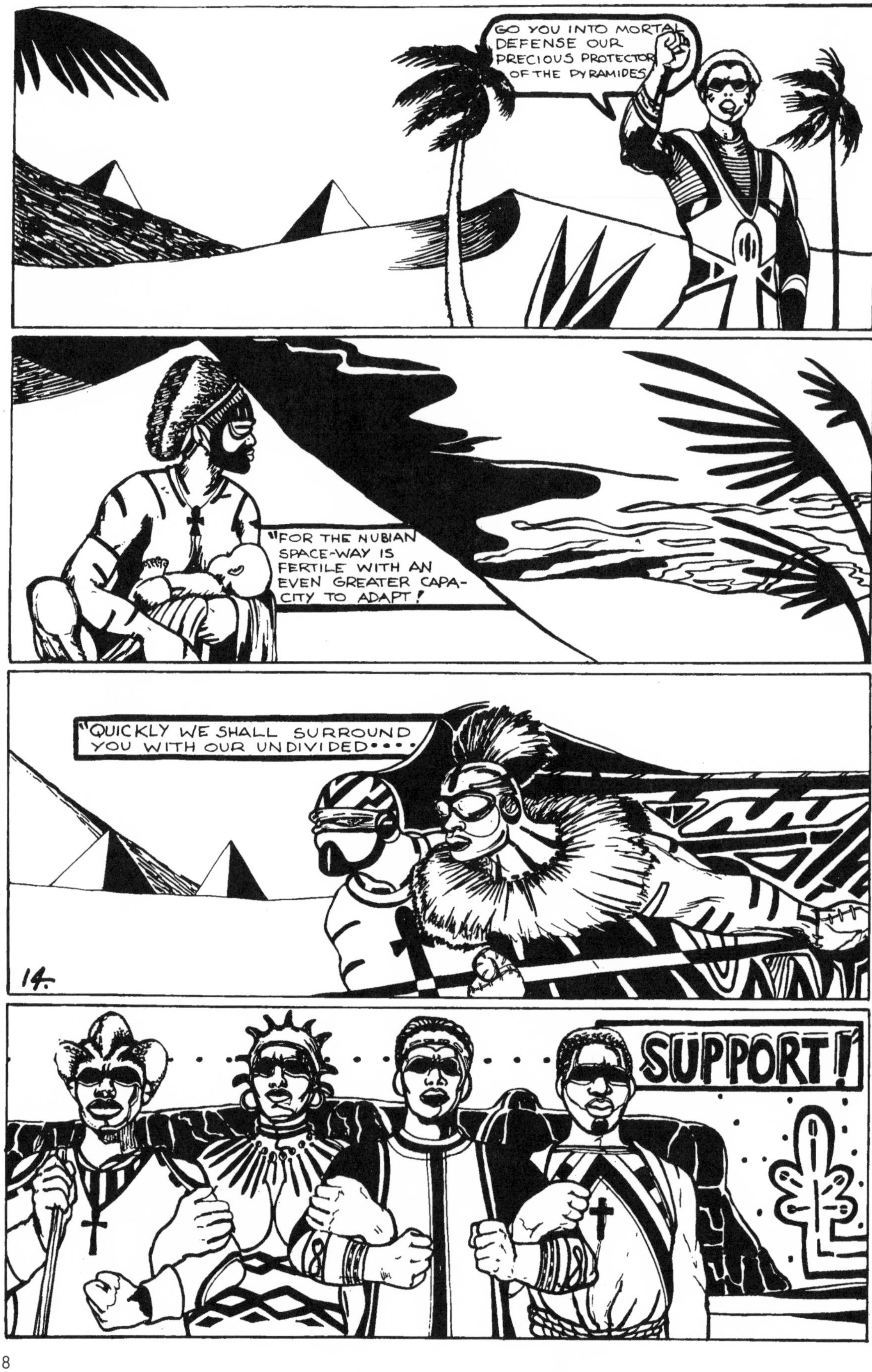
GO YOU INTO MORTAL DEFENSE OUR PRECIOUS PROTECTOR OF THE PYRAMIDES
"FOR THE NUBIAN SPACE-WAY IS FERTILE WITH AN EVEN GREATER CAPA-CITY TO ADAPT!
"QUICKLY WE SHALL SURROUND YOU WITH OUR UNDIVIDED••••
14.
••••SUPPORT!

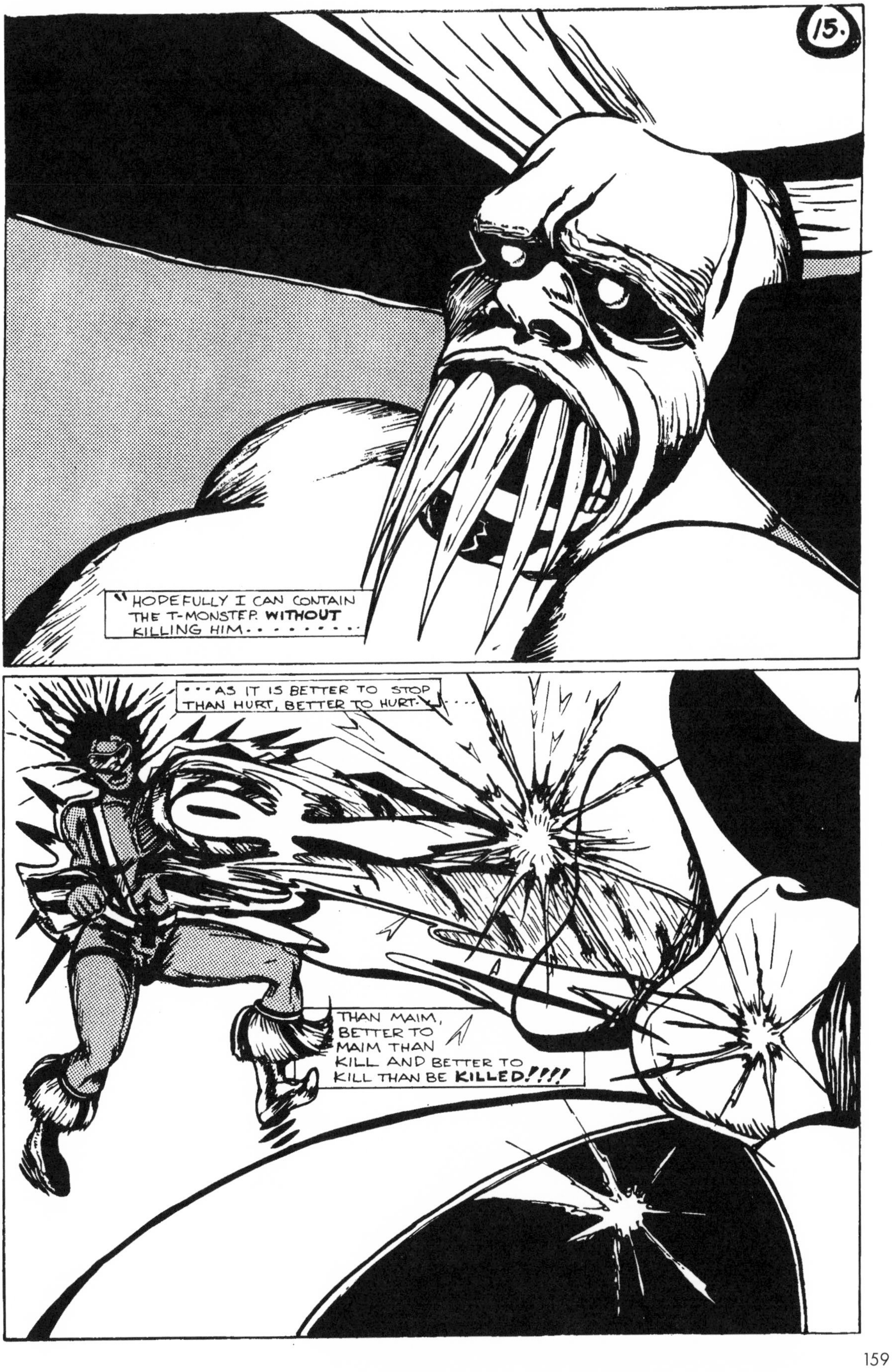
15.
"HOPEFULLY I CAN CONTAIN THE T-MONSTER WITHOUT KILLING HIM.........
...AS IT IS BETTER TO STOP THAN HURT, BETTER TO HURT...
THAN MAIM, BETTER TO MAIM THAN KILL AND BETTER TO KILL THAN BE KILLED!!!!

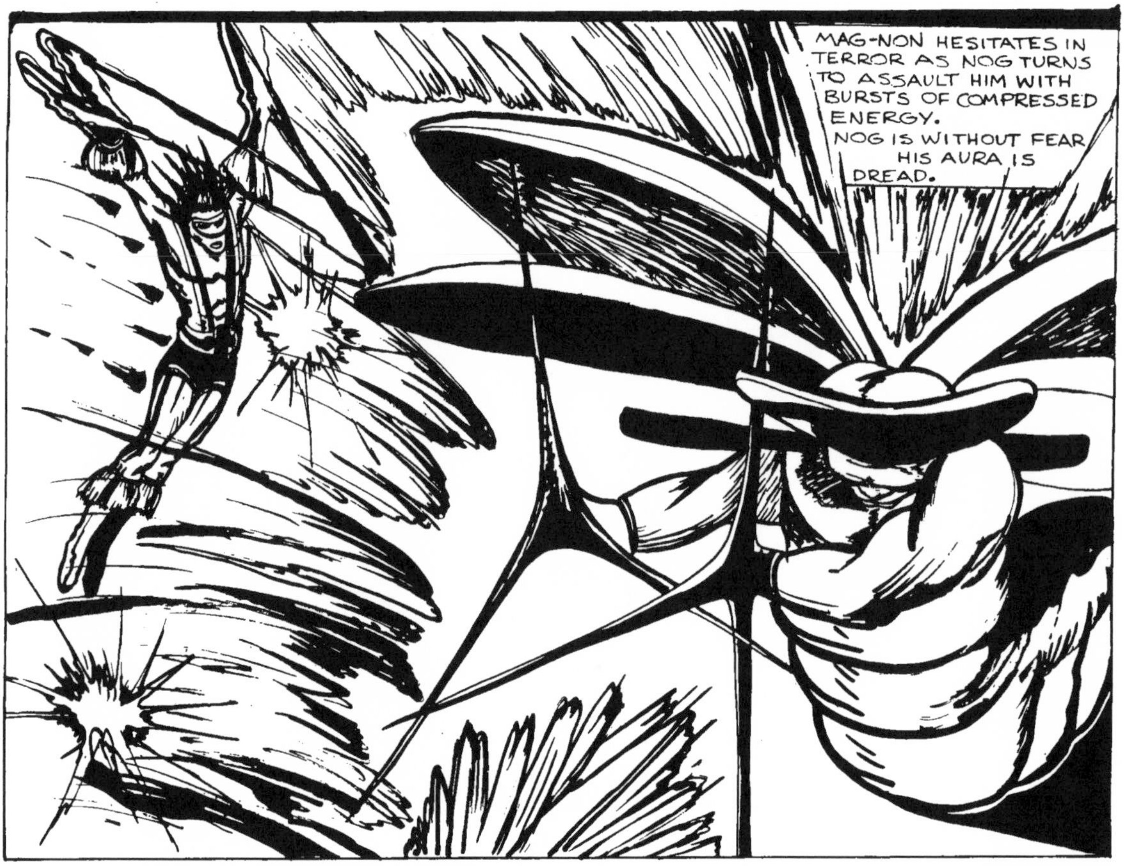
MAG-NON HESITATES IN TERROR AS NOG TURNS TO ASSAULT HIM WITH BURSTS OF COMPRESSED ENERGY.
NOG IS WITHOUT FEAR HIS AURA IS DREAD.

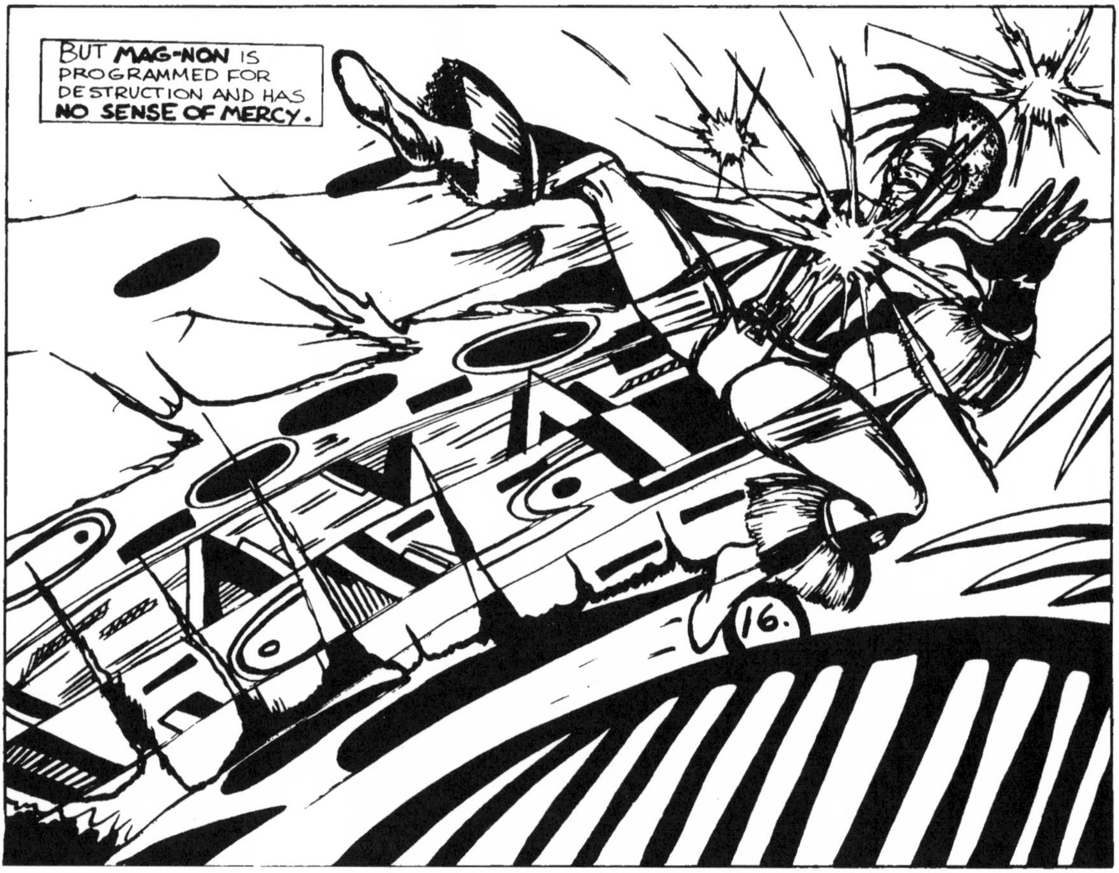
BUT MAG-NON IS PROGRAMMED FOR DESTRUCTION AND HAS NO SENSE OF MERCY.
16.

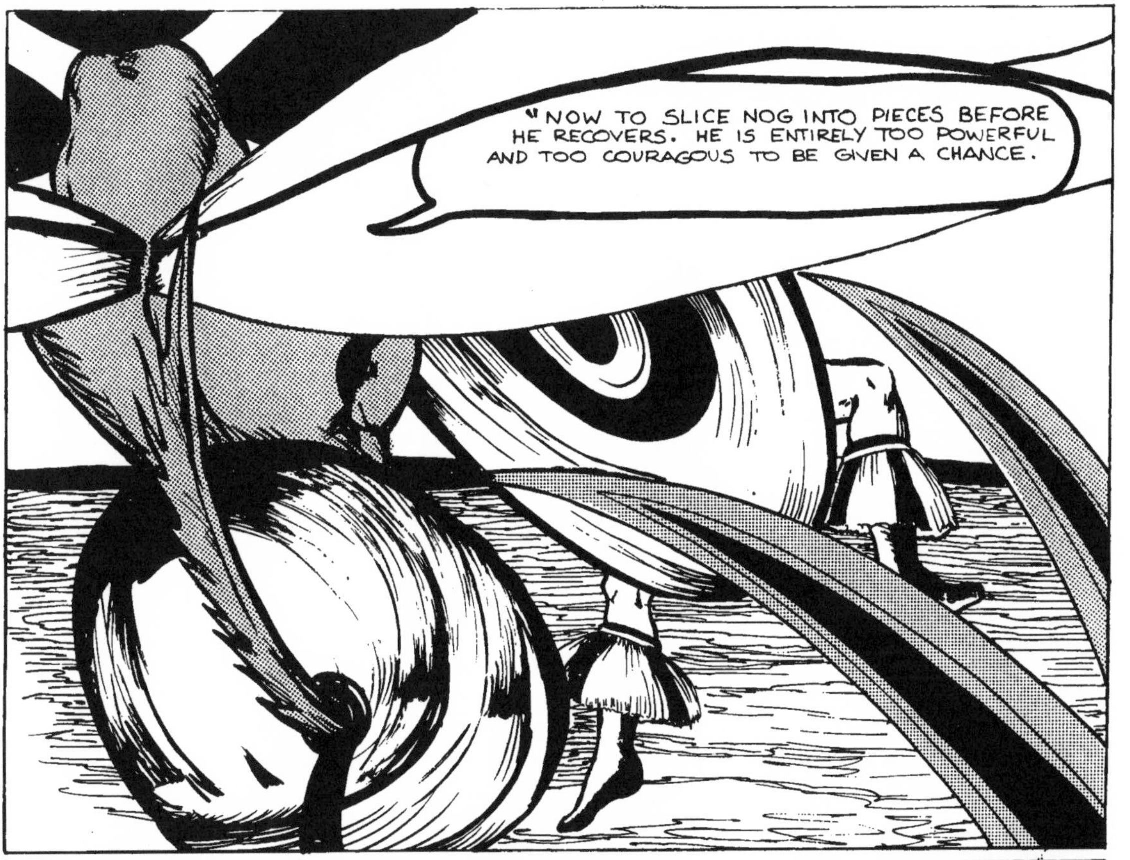
"NOW TO SLICE NOG INTO PIECES BEFORE HE RECOVERS. HE IS ENTIRELY TOO POWERFUL AND TOO COURAGOUS TO BE GIVEN A CHANCE.

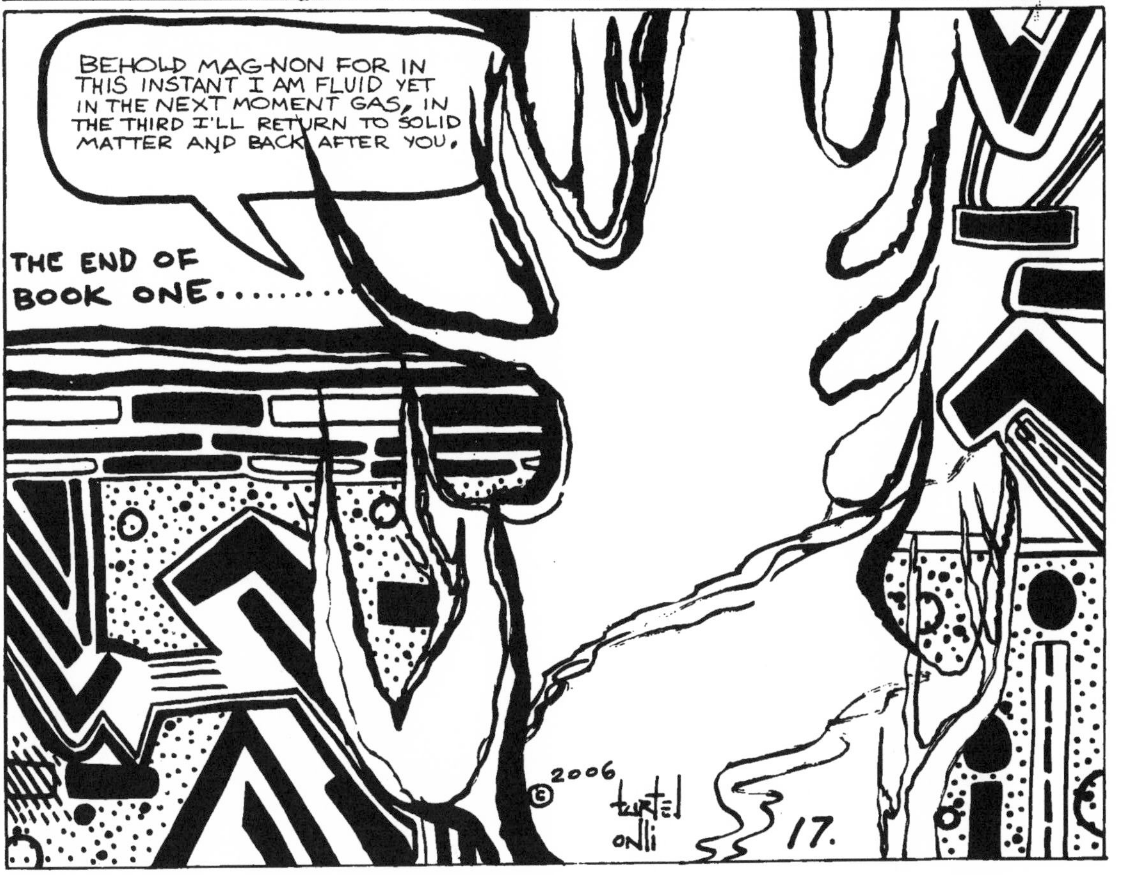
BEHOLD MAG-NON FOR IN THIS INSTANT I AM FLUID YET IN THE NEXT MOMENT GAS, IN THE THIRD I'LL RETURN TO SOLID MATTER AND BACK AFTER YOU.
THE END OF BOOK ONE........
© 2006 turtel onli
17.

JACKIE ORMES
1911–1985

Photographer unknown, 1950s. Photograph courtesy of Judie Miles and the University of Michigan Press.

Zelda Jackson Ormes, a Pennsylvania native, published her first cartoons in her high school yearbook, and became an assistant proofreader at the *Pittsburgh Courier* as soon as she graduated. In Pittsburgh she chased down sports-writing assignments, immersed herself in the city's vibrant jazz scene, and met and married Earl Ormes in the early 1930s. The two had a child, Jacqueline, who died of cancer at just three and a half. Ormes rarely spoke of her loss, but it may have been the spark for her professional art career. From 1937 to 1938 she drew herself a new life in the pages of the *Courier* through the comic strip saga of nightclub star Torchy Brown. In 1942 Jackie and Earl Ormes settled in the Bronzeville neighborhood of Chicago and became an active part of that era and neighborhood's Chicago Black Renaissance.

She began publishing again in 1945 in the *Defender*, first with a politically tinged society column and then a panel cartoon, *Candy*. *Patti-Jo 'n' Ginger* debuted that year in the *Courier* and its fourteen national editions; it was an immediate sensation from coast to coast for the next two decades. *Patti-Jo 'n' Ginger*, like Morrie Turner's later *Dinky Fellas*, used a child's perceptions to understand the world. Ginger, Patti-Jo's high school– or college-aged companion, is stylish but nearly always mute. For Ormes, this meant a chance not only to envision a new daughter but to offer a perspective on the experiences of middle-class Black Americans as subjects equal to any that white culture produced. She was not shy about criticizing union-busting, racism, and fascism. The Ormes combination of high style, wit, and political critique made her beloved by her readers, as well as fashion and merchandise companies, but also earned her a 287-page FBI dossier.

In 1950 the Smith-Mann syndicate offered to revive and widely circulate *Torchy Brown*, so Ormes produced a smart, empathetic adventure comic that dealt with social, political, and even environmental issues. Throughout her life, Ormes appeared in the pages of the *Defender* as a public figure—working for civil rights and arts funding, and organizing fashion shows for the Black community. By the late 1950s rheumatoid arthritis made it impossible for her to draw, so she devoted the rest of her life to business and activism, fundraising and organizing for the cultural life of Black people in Chicago.

Patty-Jo 'n' Ginger, Pittsburgh Courier, 1947–1951. Courtesy of Tim Jackson.

"Shucks—let's go price atom bombs—they haven't outlawed THEM yet!"

"Gee—now I got worries! Sis says if he doesn't run down SOON his union'll be after me!"

"Sure—what's a few dollars? We're playing liberation army so I bought all they had and gave them their freedom!"

"What do we need with the li'l ol' exclamation point? . . . Is ANY-BODY ever surprised at ANYTHING anymore?"

"Course, COULD be he's not WASHABLE, Mrs. Jackson!"

"What'd I tell you? . . . UNDERGROUND works–jus' wait till the Un-American Committee hears about this!"

"Don't worry 'bout me if we 'run out of gas' in the park,
  sis . . . bikes never touch the stuff!"

"I wouldn't say WHO'S responsible, 'zactly–but you MIGHT consider chargin' the damages to the Army Air Corps."

"It's a letter to my congressman: I wanta get it straight from Washington—just WHICH IS the 'American Way' of Life, New York or Georgia???"

"Gee . . . I don't know 'em either . . . but they agreed to behave themselves if I gave them all the popcorn they could eat!"

"I always figured this thing was a world map from the **DARK AGES**, but the way Daddy talks about Truman's new foreign policy it must be shapin' up this way again!"

MORRIE TURNER
1923–2014

Photographer unknown, 1970s. Courtesy of African American Museum & Library at Oakland.

The youngest of four sons of a Pullman porter, Morris "Morrie" Turner was born December 11, 1923, and raised in Oakland, California. An artist from an early age, he drew a strip called *Rail Head* for the military newspaper *Stars and Stripes* while serving in the 477th Bombardment Group of the Tuskegee Airmen during World War II, and once spent a week in the brig at Fort Knox because he fell asleep with a copy of Richard Wright's *Black Boy* in his hands while on duty.

Working as a clerk for the Oakland Police Department, he found his first successes by selling cartoons to magazines such as Johnson Publication's *Negro Digest.* While trying to break into the comic strip world, Turner became friendly with *Peanuts* creator Charles Schulz, who encouraged him to create a feature comic strip that could offer a vision of Black childhood equivalent to the one Schulz had put forth for white children in his own work.

In response, Turner took inspiration from his childhood friends to create the all-Black cast of *Dinky Fellas*, which launched in *The Chicago Defender* in 1964. In its announcement of the strip, the *Defender*, already a home for Turner's gag cartoons, noted that he was a "brilliant cartoonist" and that *Dinky Fellas* would be "a daily humorous commentary on some funny and lighter aspects of America's bi-racial situation." *Dinky Fellas* lasted just a year before it added more and ethnically diverse kids, was renamed *Wee Pals*, and was syndicated in five newspapers. After the assassination of Martin Luther King Jr. in 1968, newspapers were suddenly eager for Black voices that had been conspicuously absent, and *Wee Pals* was picked up by scores of papers. The strip spawned a brief television series in 1972–1973 as well as numerous book collections, and made Turner into a spokesman in cartoon form. He also continued drawing race-focused panel cartoons for the Black press throughout the 1970s. *Wee Pals* remained popular and inspirational until it ended with its creator's death in 2014.

Dinky Fellas, The Chicago Defender, 1964–1965.

Dinky Fellas

DINKY FELLAS, America's first and only Negro daily comic strip starts to-day in the Chicago Daily DEFENDER, America's largest Negro daily. Enjoy "Dinky Fellas" drawn by the talented Morrie Turner each and every day from Monday to Friday in your Daily DEFENDER, the only newspaper in Chicago that swings . . . . . every day.

July 25, 1964

Dinky Fellas

July 27, 1964

Dinky Fellas

August 1, 1964

Dinky Fellas

August 18, 1964

Dinky Fellas

August 24, 1964

Dinky Fellas

August 25, 1964

DINKY FELLAS

September 2, 1964

DINKY FELLAS

September 5, 1964

DINKY FELLAS

September 15, 1964

October 27, 1964

October 29, 1964

November 9, 1964

November 11, 1964

November 12, 1964

November 23, 1964

December 16, 1964

December 22, 1964

December 23, 1964

December 29, 1964

January 4, 1965

January 26, 1965

February 3, 1965

February 17, 1965

March 18, 1965

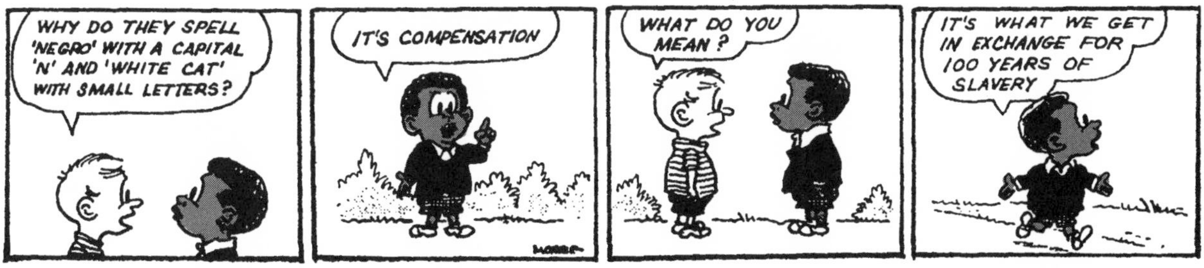
WHY DO THEY SPELL 'NEGRO' WITH A CAPITAL 'N' AND 'WHITE CAT' WITH SMALL LETTERS?
IT'S COMPENSATION
WHAT DO YOU MEAN ?
IT'S WHAT WE GET IN EXCHANGE FOR 100 YEARS OF SLAVERY

March 31, 1965

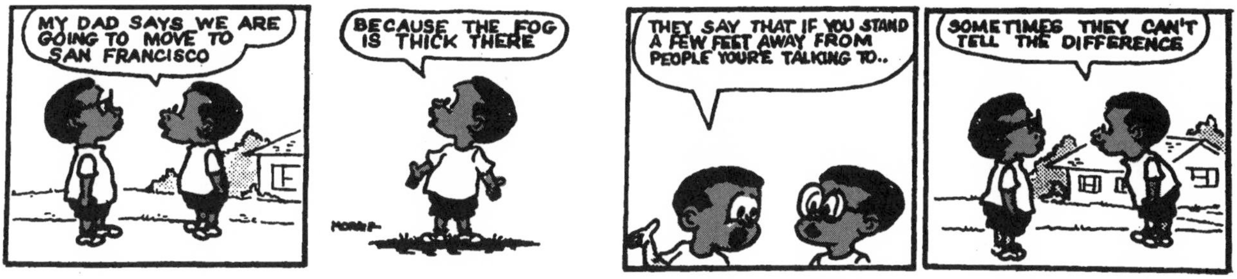
MY DAD SAYS WE ARE GOING TO MOVE TO SAN FRANCISCO
BECAUSE THE FOG IS THICK THERE
THEY SAY THAT IF YOU STAND A FEW FEET AWAY FROM PEOPLE YOU'RE TALKING TO..
SOMETIMES THEY CAN'T TELL THE DIFFERENCE

June 8, 1965

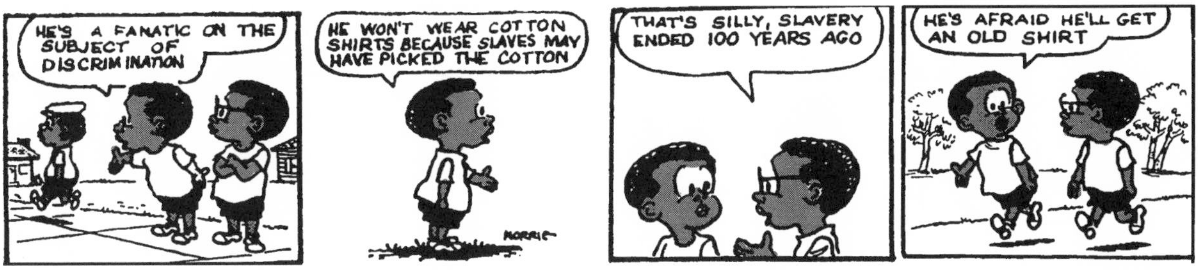
HE'S A FANATIC ON THE SUBJECT OF DISCRIMINATION
HE WON'T WEAR COTTON SHIRTS BECAUSE SLAVES MAY HAVE PICKED THE COTTON
THAT'S SILLY, SLAVERY ENDED 100 YEARS AGO
HE'S AFRAID HE'LL GET AN OLD SHIRT

June 17, 1965

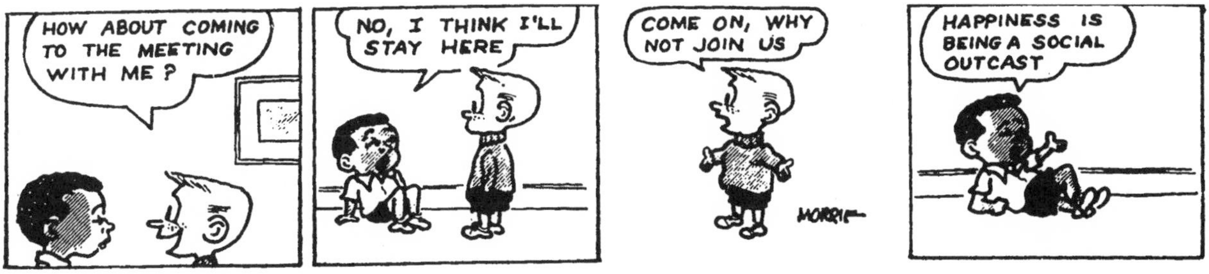
HOW ABOUT COMING TO THE MEETING WITH ME ?
NO, I THINK I'LL STAY HERE
COME ON, WHY NOT JOIN US
HAPPINESS IS BEING A SOCIAL OUTCAST

August 3, 1965

August 30, 1965

September 8, 1965

September 16, 1965

October 6, 1965

October 20, 1965

November 1, 1965

November 3, 1965

November 13, 1965

November 16, 1965

November 24, 1965

December 4, 1965

December 6, 1965

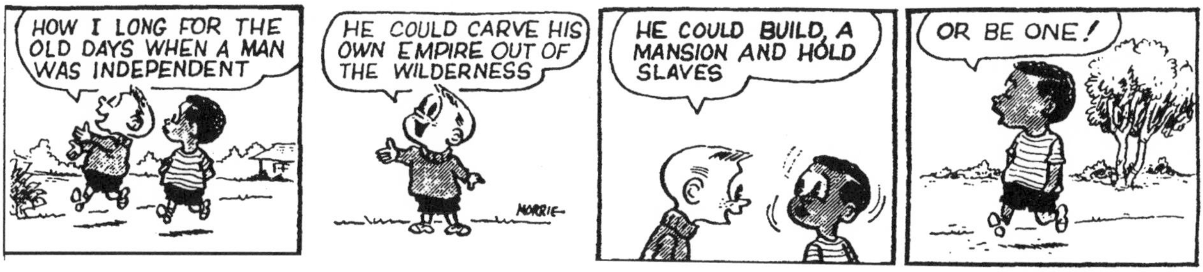
HOW I LONG FOR THE OLD DAYS WHEN A MAN WAS INDEPENDENT
HE COULD CARVE HIS OWN EMPIRE OUT OF THE WILDERNESS
MORRIE
HE COULD BUILD A MANSION AND HOLD SLAVES
OR BE ONE!

December 8, 1965

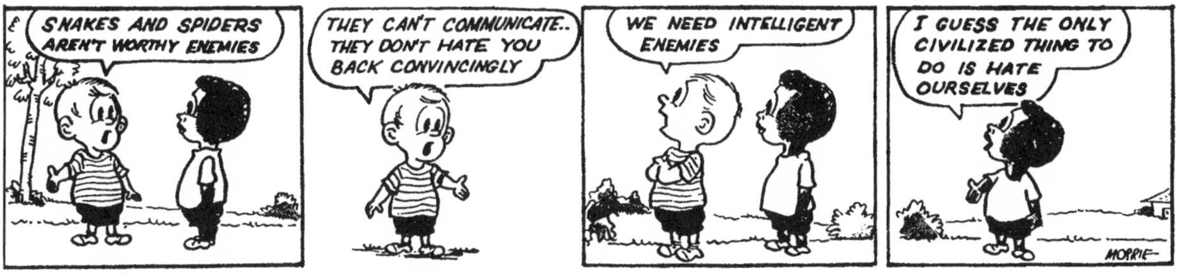
SNAKES AND SPIDERS AREN'T WORTHY ENEMIES
THEY CAN'T COMMUNICATE.. THEY DON'T HATE YOU BACK CONVINCINGLY
WE NEED INTELLIGENT ENEMIES
I GUESS THE ONLY CIVILIZED THING TO DO IS HATE OURSELVES
MORRIE

December 13, 1965

AFTERWORD
RONALD WIMBERLY

Morrie Turner's *Dinky Fellas* on a page from the April 29, 1965 edition of *The Chicago Defender*.

In the summer of 2020, I was asked to make a single-page journal cartoon for *The New York Times*. My task was to craft a cartoon that described my daily practice while also assigning a part of that practice to the reader. After a couple of unsuccessful, apolitical shots at cracking the piece, the editor goaded me into exploring the candid feelings I'd expressed in our email correspondence. What resulted was a cartoon about how I felt witnessing the recent George Floyd uprisings, and how the pictures of burning police vehicles provoked a deep emotional response in me. I asked the reader to examine what looking outward provoked in them.

Ultimately *The New York Times* decided not to run the cartoon on the grounds that it "editorialized violence." The central image of a burning police car was too much. The *Times* had a double standard. While editorializing property damage was verboten, editorializing systemic, racist violence against Black people often got a pass. This is, after all, the same newspaper that ran Tom Cotton's "Send in the Troops" editorial earlier that summer, and that ran Donald Trump's notorious Central Park Five ad in 1989.

After looking over the cartoons presented in this anthology, I wondered if, were it still around today, The *Chicago Defender* would have refused to publish my cartoon. I thought about the impact of the Free Black Press (publications prioritizing Black voices) on the lineage of Black cartooning; the importance of a place for cartoonists to grow and produce works and aesthetics that otherwise might have been suppressed by the latent, unquestioned white supremacy of integrated institutions.

While Black people were still in bondage in the United States, John Russwurm and Samuel Cornish founded *Freedom's Journal* in New York on March 16, 1827, to platform Black voices outside of the context and editorial power of the white press. Soon other

Black papers were born, circulating Black voices, depictions of Black life, and the call to abolish slavery throughout the country. Within four years Nat Turner led a slave rebellion. Subsequently, all slave states except for Maryland, Kentucky, and Tennessee banned teaching the enslaved to read and write. Literate slaves could forge their own papers, and worse, literacy was a tool for organization. The Black Free Press survived the Civil War and the Thirteenth Amendment, but not integration, at least not for long, and not in any meaningful way. As the dream of an integrated society took hold of Black America, the integrated economy absorbed the talent and the market of the Black economy. Newspapers were not exempt. But somewhere between Frederick Douglass launching the *North Star* and Don King buying the *Call and Post*, the Free Black Press, this pillar of black culture, ran cartoons!

For Black folks of a certain age, the 1977 TV show *Roots*, adapted from Alex Haley's novel *Roots: The Saga of an American Family*, was an epiphanic moment. *Roots* follows a family line from West Africa, through the Middle Passage and the Antebellum period, to Emancipation. It was a jumping-off point for many people to question their lineage, to explore history and their place in it. It also sold a ton of dashikis.

What does lineage mean for an artist? Artists pass on fragments of their DNA in conversation with each other through time. It's a call and response as contemporary artists find new ways of seeing the context of their predecessors. The past expresses itself in contemporary work. Through epochs, artists talk about their time and place to each other and to their audience. There's great value in this conversation. It's how the language of expression evolves.

As for my lineage, I'm embarrassed to admit that I was only marginally familiar with many of the cartoons presented here. I'm a Black cartoonist, but manga hooked me on comics. Anime was my gateway drug. I was part of a vanguard that has normalized American consumption of Japanese visual culture. This bore out in my art practice. Kewpie-eyed Black characters manifested in the gutters of my schoolbooks. By the time my mom emailed me a link to the *Boondocks* comic to tell me that there was someone else like me, I'd already been at Pratt for two years, having the anime influence beaten out of my hands (it didn't stick). In 2001 I attended the *My Reality: Contemporary Art and the Culture of Japanese Animation* exhibition at the Brooklyn Museum. I picked up Takashi Murakami's *Superflat*, named for the art manifesto contained therein. In outlining his and a generation of Japanese contemporary artists' place in an aesthetic tradition, Murakami cites Nobuo Tsuji's seminal 1970 text, *Lineage of Eccentrics*. There, Tsuji traced an aesthetic heritage, connecting artists from antiquity to contemporary pop culture. When I read this work I felt like I had found family. I felt like even though I was far outside of this culture I was in conversation with this art, even though I couldn't speak the language of its producers. But reading Murakami's manifesto also made me feel a loss. What was my lineage here in my own country?

I grew up in the Eighties reading the *Washington Post*. I'd leaf past pages of "Reagan dismantling social welfare" and "Marion Barry smoking crack" to the bright colors in the center of the paper. There I'd find *Charlie Brown*, *Calvin and Hobbes*, *Prince Valiant*, *Beetle Bailey*, and *The Far Side*. I found copies of *Spiderman* or *Batman* next to *Archie* in the spinner racks of the 7-Eleven. I found no floppies created by and for Black readers from Black publishers on those racks or among my uncle's precious, hidden stack of superhero comics. And I never read *Dinky Fellas*, or *Bungleton Green and the Mystic Commandos*. These artists cartooned the breadth and complexity of Black life, Black humor, and a Black imagining of the future explicitly for the Black gaze. They developed unique aesthetics and broached subjects untouched by white cartoonists. Looking over the work presented here I see a dialectic between depictions of the imagined integrated Negro life and the paradoxes of the reality of integrated Black life. On one hand we have works like Grass Green's *Smoke Power* depicting an "end of history" type fantasy (as if the Voting Rights Act were white supremacy's fall of the Berlin Wall) of a bougie Black man's struggle against discrimination, not for the color of his skin, but for his smoking habit. On the other hand we have Jackie Ormes's cynical depiction of the minefield of integration through the lens of a naive little black child.

Without Black newspapers as a platform this lineage seems to have been mostly diffused, though outliers like Jerry Craft, Keith Knight, Bianca Xunise, and Aaron McGruder have since carried the torch outside of explicitly Black publications. This volume presents an important piece of the American cartoonist's roots: its Black lineage. It's a call to contemporary Black cartoonists who might respond and for others who might want to ear hustle. There's value in cartoonists seeing where they come from or even just seeing who preceded them. There's value for the audience to see where artists fit into the continuum of the medium's history. With a fuller picture of American cartooning, one can glean details (material or mythic) about the society that produced it.

Ronald Wimberly is a cartoonist, illustrator, and two-time Eisner Award nominee. His works include the graphic novel *The Prince of Cats*; *Black History in Its Own Words*, a book of quotations that he edited and illustrated; and *Sentences: The Life of MF Grimm*, a collaborative graphic memoir with the rapper MF Grimm. Wimberly has worked as an artist and designer for a number of comics titles by publishers like DC, Marvel, and Dark Horse Comics. He is also the editor of the art magazine *LAAB*. He lives in Brooklyn, New York.

SOURCES

Carper, Steve. "Bungleton Green in the 21st Century: The First Black Superhero." Flying Cars and Food Pills (https://www.flyingcarsandfoodpills.com/bungleton-green-in-the-21st-century), August 28, 2018.

Chang, Jeff. "Morrie Turner and the Kids." *The Believer*, no. 67, November 1, 2009.

Cofield, Ernestin. "Being Prepared is Secret to Success, Says Artist." *Chicago Defender*, August 8, 1963.

Corum, Laverne A., and Steven L. Jones. *Pen an' Wit*, vol. 1 (no. 1), 1988.

Cremins, Brian. "'A Space of Concentration': The Autobiographical Comics of Richard 'Grass' Green and Samuel R. Delany," in Eric D. Lamore, *Reading African American Autobiography: Twenty-First-Century Contexts and Criticism*. University of Wisconsin Press, 2016.

Foster, William H. "The Image of Blacks (African Americans) In Underground Comix: New Liberal Agenda or Same Racist Stereotypes?" *International Journal of Comic Art*, vol. 4 (no. 2), 2009.

Larry Fuller, Seitu Hayden, Tim Jackson, Charles Johnson, Yaoundé Olu, and Turtel Onli interviewed by Dan Nadel, 2020.

Goldstein, Nancy. *Jackie Ormes: The First African American Woman Cartoonist*. University of Michigan Press, 2008.

"Jay Jackson's Art Work Was Seasoning For Life." *The Chicago Defender*, June 5, 1954.

Johnson, Charles. "Foreword," in Frederik Strömberg, *Black Images in Comics: A Visual History*. Fantagraphics, 2003.

Jones, Steven L. "From 'Under Cork' to Overcoming: Black Images in the Comics." *Nemo* no. 28, 1988.

Kreider, Tim. "Blacker in Hindsight: *Black Humor* by Charles R. Johnson." TCJ.com, January 18th, 2010 (no longer online).

Luti, Lulama. "Cartoonists Claim Being Black is Drawback in Their Field." *Chicago Tribune*, July 16, 1995.

Michaeli, Ethan. *The Defender: How the Legendary Black Newspaper Changed America*. Houghton Mifflin Harcourt, 2016.

Mooney, Amy M. "Seeing 'As Others See Us': *The Chicago Defender* Cartoonist Jay Jackson as Cultural Critic," *MELUS*, vol. 39 (no. 2), Oxford University Press, 2014.

Norman, Tony. "Seitu Hayden: Stories About People, Just Regular People." *The Comics Journal*, no. 160, 1993.

Schelly, Bill. *Founders of Comic Fandom: Profiles of 90 Publishers, Dealers, Collectors, Writers, Artists and Other Luminaries of the 1950s and 1960s*. McFarland, 2010.

Spurgeon, Tom. "Pioneering Underground Cartoonist Grass Green Passes Away at Age 63." *The Comics Journal*, no. 247, 2002.

Strömberg, Frederik. *Black Images in the Comics: A Visual History*. Fantagraphics, 2003.

Zorach, Rebecca. "Turtel Onli," *Never The Same* (https://never-the-same.org/interviews/turtel-onli/), 2014.

Zorach, Rebecca. "Yaoundé Olu," *Never The Same* (https://never-the-same.org/interviews/yaounde-olu/), 2013.

ACKNOWLEDGMENTS

Thank you to the good people at the Museum of Contemporary Art Chicago: to Michael Darling, for bringing me to the museum and encouraging my research and this book, and to Kelsey Campbell-Dollaghan, Leah Froats, Emilie Putrich, Elyssa Lange, and Bonnie Rosenberg for their invaluable help seeing it through.

I thank all the artists and estates for entrusting me with this work, Charles Johnson for his essay and guidance, Ronald Wimberly for his afterword, and Kerry James Marshall for his cover design.

For conversation and support for this project I'm grateful to Kathy Belden, Ivan Brunetti, Jessica Campbell, Anya Davidson, Sean Dickerson, Kim Floyd, William H. Foster, Larry Fuller, Nancy Goldstein, Ira Harmon, Sammy Harkham, Steven L. Jones, Sarah Lazin, Ethan Michaeli, Elisa Nadel, Tim Samuelson, Chris Ware, James West, and Rebecca Zorach. For additional materials I thank Tim Jackson and Brian Baynes. Thank you to Norman Hathaway for his cover design assist and all-around wisdom.

A very emphatic thank you to Lucas Adams for giving this book a home and then nourishing it at NYRC. I am grateful as well to Gabriel Winslow-Yost and the rest of the NYR team.

Exhibition Sponsors for
Chicago Comics: 1960s to Now,
organized by the Museum of
Contemporary Art Chicago,
June 19–October 3, 2021.